Re-Play

By the same author:

Drama For Youth. London: Sir Isaac Pitman.

College Drama Space (editor). London: Institute of Education, London University.

Teaching Drama. London: Cassell.

The School Play. London: Cassell.

The Drama Studio. London: Sir Isaac Pitman.

Play, Drama & Thought: The Intellectual Background to Dramatic Education. London: Cassell; New York: Drama Book Specialists.

Teaching & The Arts: Arts Education in Australia, with Specific Reference to Drama Education in Victoria. Melbourne: Melbourne State College.

The Dramatic Curriculum. London, Ontario: University of Western Ontario; New York: Drama Book Specialists; London, England: Heinemann.

Drama in Therapy with Gertrud Schattner, editors). 2 volumes. New York: Drama Book Specialists.

Outline History of British Drama. Totawa, N.J.: Littlefield, Adams.

Secret Spirits: Performance and Possession of Canadian Indians on Vancouver Island. Downsview, Ontario: Canadian Theatre Review, York University.

Richard Courtney

Re-Play

Studies of Human Drama
in Education

Occasional Papers/21

OISE Press
The Ontario Institute for Studies in Education

"Re-play is re-cognition"
— Marshall McLuhan

"Negations are not opposites;
Contraries mutually exist"
— William Blake

The Ontario Institute for Studies in Education has three prime functions: to conduct programs of graduate study in education, to undertake research in education, and to assist in the implementation of the findings of educational studies. The Institute is a college chartered by an Act of the Ontario Legislature in 1965. It is affiliated with the University of Toronto for graduate studies purposes.

The publications program of the Institute has been established to make available information and materials arising from studies in education, to foster the spirit of critical inquiry, and to provide a forum for the exchange of ideas about education. The opinions expressed should be viewed as those of the contributors.

© Richard Courtney 1982
   252 Bloor Street West
   Toronto, Ontario
   M5S 1V6

All rights reserved. No part of this publication may be reproduced in any form without permission from the publisher, except for brief passages quoted for review purposes.

Canadian Cataloguing in Publication Data

Courtney, Richard
   Re-Play : studies of human drama in education

(Occasional papers ; 21)
Co-published by Ontario Institute for Studies in Education.
Bibliography: p.
Includes index.
ISBN 0-7744-0248-2

1. Learning, Psychology of. 2. Drama in education.
I. Ontario Institute for Studies in Education.
II. Title. III. Series: Occasional papers (Ontario Institute for Studies in Education) ; 21.

LB1051.C68   370.15   C82-095102-1

Canadian Cataloguing in Publication Data
ISBN 0-7744-0248-2   Printed in Canada
1 2 3 4 5 TO 68 58 48 38 28

Contents

Preface	vii
Introduction	1
1 Developmental Drama	5
2 Human Dynamics: Drama and Motivation	43
3 Drama and the Transfer of Learning	69
4 Drama and Instruction	86
5 Drama and the Different: Creativity and Giftedness	98
6 Expression: The Drama of English and Language Learning	108
7 Dramatherapy	126
8 Culture and Curriculum: A Dramatic Context	135
9 Axioms and Maxims: A Rationale for the Arts in Education	154
Appendix A: Drama and the Field of Curriculum	166
Appendix B: Drama and Research	192
Notes	199
References	204
Selected Index	221

Figures

1 Theory of Imagination	8
2 Theory of Learning	10
3 The Development of Media	11
4 Comparison of Developmental Stages	13
5 Method of Analysing the Dynamics of Cultural Drama	33
6 Cultural Development of Drama	39
7 The Developmental Patterns of Human Enactment	41
8 Typology of Giftedness	103
9 Levels of Curriculum Discourse	175

for
PETER

Preface

This book consists of a series of essays relating the human drama to education. Five have been previously published, though they have been entirely recast for this book. As each theme is treated independently, there is necessary overlap between them. I am grateful to the editors of following journals for permission to reprint them here: *Fine. Journal of the Fine Arts Council, Alberta Teachers' Federation*, Fall 1979 (Chapter 3); *Teaching Drama* (Scotland), Winter 1977/78 (Chapter 5); *The English Quarterly*, Spring 1978 (Chapter 6); *Dramatherapy*, Spring 1979 (Chapter 7); *Orbit*, February 1979 (Chapter 9).

Although I do not wish to implicate them in my arguments, I am most grateful to a number of colleagues and friends, as follows:

Dr. David Best (University College of Wales, Swansea) and Dr. Kenneth Leithwood (Ontario Institute for Studies in Education) for their detailed comments on Appendix 1; Dr. Garnet McDiarmid and Dr. F. Michael Connelly (The Ontario Institute for Studies in Education) for issues related to Appendix 2;

Dr. Sandra S. Shiner (Toronto) and Rev. E. J. Burton (Ashford, England) for issues related to Chapter 5;

Graham Scott (Drama Resource Centre, Melbourne) and Paul Stevenson (Mount Gravatt College, Queensland) for issues related to Chapter 4;

Dr. Robert W. Witkin (University of Exeter), Dr. David Hawkins (University of Colorado), Judith Koltai (Camosun College, British Columbia), and Dr. Chester D. Carlow (Ontario Institute for Studies in Education) for points related to Chapter 2;

Professor Carl Hare (University of Victoria), Professor V. E. Mitchell (University of Calgary), Rev. E.J. Burton (Ashford, England), Dr. Peter Prouse (University of New Mexico), Dr. Jack Morrison

(Washington, D.C.) and Professor G. Wilson Knight (Exeter) for discussions of concepts developed in Chapter 1;

Christine Turkewych Broda (Edmonton), Zina Rosso Barnieh (Calgary), Mwai Magondu (Kenya), Nina Consunji (the Philippines), Takako Shimizu (Japan), and Ksana Maraire (Zimbabwe) for discussions that have affected Chapter 8;

Nikki DiVito, who was the research officer for drama in the study cited in Chapter 4, together with Paul Park, Dean of the Faculty of Education, University of Western Ontario, who was the co-principal investigator;

the late Dr. H. Marshall McLuhan (University of Toronto) and Professor James Britton (London, England) for their comments on the draft for Chapter 6.

I also wish to thank Kathy Turner, Barbara Parish, Dianne M. Byrne, Ina Dumphie, Diana Postlethwaite, Mary Maxwell, Audrey Hille and Theadora van der Wiel, who typed the material at various stages; Diane Mew for her editorial assistance; and, as always, my wife Rosemary for the Selected Index and for overseeing the manuscript.

R.C.
Toronto, Ontario, and
Elephant Butte, New Mexico
1982

Acknowledgements

The author and publishers wish to thank the following for permission to reprint copyright material: Heinemann Educational Books Ltd., for extracts from *Learning through Drama* by Lynn McGregor, Maggie Tate and Ken Robinson (a Schools Council project); Methuen & Co. Ltd., for extracts by J. M. Heaton in *Phenomenology and Education*, edited by Bernard Curtis and Wolfe Mays; and the Ministry of Education, Ontario, for the citations from *Learning through the Arts: The Arts in Primary and Junior Education in Ontario — Roles and Relationships in the General Program of Studies (1980)*, by Richard Courtney and Paul Park, a research project funded under contract by the Ministry of Education, Ontario.

Introduction

"[The student] shall not so much repeat as act his lesson. . . . There is no better way of alluring the affection or tempting the appetite, otherwise you merely produce asses laden with books. By dint of the rod you fill their pockets full of learning for them to keep. To do the job properly, this learning should not only be billeted on them but wedded to them."
—Montaigne

The human drama pervades all that we do. It makes our life significant. It creates for us meaning, meaning that becomes wedded to us.

My purpose in writing this book is to contribute to the theory of drama education. This is not a "how to" book. Its theoretical nature requires no apology, but an explanation may be in order. Fifteen years ago there was very little theoretic work in this field. Virtually all books were directed to the classroom teacher and contained simple descriptions of what to do. When reasons were given for the value of the work, they were usually relegated to an introductory chapter containing simplistic statements. Since I wrote *Play, Drama and Thought* in 1968, however, the field has matured. There has been an increasing need for intellectual explorations. Senior educators and graduate students urgently require scholarly materials which they can use, take issue with, build upon, and from which they can extrapolate. They wage a continual battle of justification. This book is intended to offer them some support.

The book probes a number of ideas in the hope that others will continue the explorations. It is specifically *not* concerned with advocating one particular way of teaching drama and theatre. There are a myriad ways of approaching the field and each has its advantages and disadvantages. I happen to believe that spontaneous methods are more effective than those which are more formal and closed. But I hope that this belief will not obscure the fact that the deliberations which follow go beyond a comparison of methodologies and raise issues to an intellectual level.

The book has a secondary purpose. Drama is so central to the creation of meaning that I have deliberately related it, first to the arts as a whole, and second to the whole of education. The ideas explored here can be generalized in such a way — witness the many senior educators who have worked with me in doing so.

Senior educators, particularly those who are studying for M.A., M.Ed., Ed.D., and Ph.D. degrees, constantly request two types of material. I have already dealt with the first in *The Dramatic Curriculum* (1980): the design and implementation of drama programs. This book deals with some of the second: specific intellectual issues around which controversies rage.

Many of these questions have no easy answers. One thing that drama teaches is that there are a multiplicity of answers to the major issues of life. For example, almost all of the plays of Pirandello deal with the problem of reality and illusion, yet all are resolved differently. The solution proposed by *Enrico IV* is not the same as that in *Six Characters in Search of an Author*. Similarly in drama education, everything depends on the persons involved, and on the culture and context in which they exist. To the ubiquitous question, "In my classroom, what would you do if. . . ?" there is no immediate practical answer. I have not met those particular students, nor do I know the specific school or administration. What I can do, however, is to put forward a series of possibilities based on my previous experience. Like Pirandello in the theatre, I can put forward a series of possible futures. Thus educational theory is the examination of a series of dramatic fictions; and that is what this book is all about.

Yet that places the onus upon you, the reader. You must relate these fictions to your own practical situation. Moreover, you must resist the temptation to categorize me. If you pin a label on me, I shall attempt to wriggle away. At various times in the past I have been called a liberal, a radical, an existentialist, a pragmatist, a conservative — but the theoretical discussion in this book denies such pigeon-holes. Rather, it is an inquiry into the dramatic nature of life and education. It specifically looks at alternatives and, in that sense, is non-categorical.

Marshall McLuhan once wrote that my theory of imagination might be encapsulated as "re-play is re-cognition." This book explores this aphorism from a variety of perspectives but underlying each essay are two principles. First, *drama is the spontaneous human process of identification with, and impersonation of, others.* Each of us, uniquely, creates our own meaning and understanding of life by acting with role models. Second, *theatre is the art form of the dramatic process.* Theatre codifies in temporal form the dramatic life process and becomes, in fact, like "the tip of the iceberg."

We use dramatic re-play in life, general learning, education, human interaction, therapy—indeed, in virtually every aspect of existence. But perhaps the most remarkable use is in schools. The growth of spontaneous drama in education has been a twentieth-century phenomenon. In the Victorian village schoolhouse ruled over by my grandfather, drama entered only as theatre—as the rare school play—just as it had in the Renaissance grammar schools. From the beginning of this century, however, spontaneous dramatic action has been increasingly used. Today, with younger children, it is the basis of play—the child's natural way to learn. In elementary schools, it is used for specific learning: children learn both subjects matters and the basic skills (listening, speaking, reading, writing and number) by creating their own improvisations which, in addition, help them to adjust to existence. As most secondary schools are still subject-oriented, spontaneous drama can be used in three ways: as a subject it teaches students to confront existence symbolically and discover new meanings in their existence; as a method, it provides a feeling base for learning other subject-matters; and it can, more rarely but increasingly, infuse the total curriculum.

Outside the formal system, spontaneous drama is increasingly used in general education. It is the basis of "play therapy" with younger children while the wide range of methods within drama-therapy makes it effective with students and adults. As simulation, it is more and more used for adult skills: in work, industry, business training, and so on. It provides genuine re-creation. And, as more formal improvisation, it gives a basis for professional actor-training.

The reason spontaneous drama is increasingly used is that it is a most effective method of human learning. Re-play enables us to face life experiences at a symbolic level: to engage in problem-solving in a deep personal way. We "try out" possible futures and "act out" the problems of the past; as we learn, we adjust to time. Each actor is protected by re-play—after all, drama is not life—yet it is so meaningful to him that it reaches down into his inner self. In re-play, to confront existence dramatically is *direct* learning; yet there is also the *indirect* learning of the content of what is acted (the subject-matter of the drama). Always drama provides a double meaning: the actor is himself and yet also another; the objects used are actual and also symbolic; and all exist in both everyday life and the world of "as if."

The chapters of this book deal with different aspects of this process. Chapter 1 concerns the study of the developments of human enactment. It provides an intellectual underpinning for drama practice both in schools and universities, as well as a basis from which to examine specific issues. The next two chapters deal with learning: Chapter 2 with motivation and Chapter 3 with the transfer of learning. The next group of chapters deal with particular issues. Some of the problems of instruction are dealt with in Chapter 4. Chapter 5 considers creativity and giftedness, while Chapter 6 relates drama to English and language learning. Chapter 7 asks questions of dramatherapy. Chapter 8 relates the dramatic metaphor to culture with particular implications for education. Chapter 9 provides a rationale for the arts in education through a series of axioms and maxims.

These are followed by an Appendix which examines the nature of curriculum per se. This extended exegesis delves into the thorny issue of the theory of Curriculum from the dramatic perspective. A second Appendix examines research.

Chapter 1
Developmental Drama

> "Thus play I in one person many people."
> —*Shakespeare*, Richard II, V, 5:31

Developmental Drama is the *study* of developmental patterns in human enactment. Drama is an active bridge between our inner world and the environment. Thus the developments studied are both personal and cultural, and each is in interaction with the other. These studies overlap with other fields: with psychology and philosophy on a personal level, and with sociology and anthropology on a cultural level. Despite the use of these allied fields, however, the focus of study within Developmental Drama is always the *dramatic act*. From these theoretical considerations, implications can be drawn for specific practical fields.

Thus in this chapter, drama will be considered first as mediation. This will be followed by a study of the dynamics and the developmental stages of personal drama. Then cultural drama will be examined, again through its dynamics and its developmental stages.

Drama as Mediation

We all constantly use dramatic action. Whether as children's play, the use of roles in adolescence, or "putting ourselves in someone else's shoes" when we are adults, human enactment is continuous from birth to death. It can be overt, as when a child plays at being a bear and crawls around the floor growling; it can also be covert, as when we rehearse "in our heads" an interview that is to take place later in the day.

Dramatic action serves a clear purpose in life. It is the prime mediator between our inner selves and the environment. It is a medium whereby our inner self works with the outer world and creates meanings out of it. Drama is a bridge, a filter, between the two worlds.

When we engage in spontaneous dramatic action we, ourselves, become a *symbol*. When the child acts as her mother, or the teenager role-plays as one of the heroes of adolescence, or the adult "puts up a bold front" in a difficult situation, each of them is acting symbolically. The symbol is the actor himself—the person in dramatic action. This symbol has certain constituent parts, each of which is essential to our understanding of it: the total self in dramatic action includes the movements of his body and the sound of his voice; it also includes his face (or mask), his clothes (or costume) and what he is carrying (or his attributes). Hereafter we shall refer to this symbol as "the costumed player." It occurs whenever the human actor makes a *representation* of himself in the external world, and does so in a whole way (with his self) rather than in a partial manner. In drama, we re-present ourselves in the environment symbolically. Then our performance mediates between the self and the environment.

We do this in order to create meaning—to understand experience and reinterpret it in ways that are meaningful to us. "Re-play is re-cognition," as Marshall McLuhan says. Spontaneous dramatic action is a form of re-cognizing—a way of knowing. The knowledge we obtain through such action becomes highly significant to us. We have experienced it, been through it, relived it. Thus we *feel* it; it has emotional significance for us and will be remembered. In such a way, dramatic learning is highly effective, mingling cognition and feeling into a whole experience that deeply touches the self. Michael Polanyi says:

> [T]he art of knowing is seen to involve an intentional change of being: the pouring of ourselves into the subsidiary awareness of particulars, which in the performance of skills are instrumental to a skilful achievement, and which in the exercise of connoisseurship function as the elements of the observed comprehensive whole. The skilful performer is seen to be setting standards to himself and judging himself by them; the connoisseur is seen valuing comprehensive entities in terms of a standard set by him for their excellence. The elements of such a context, the hammer, the probe, the spoken word, all point beyond themselves and are endowed with meaning in this context; on the other hand a comprehensive context itself, like dance, mathematics, music, possesses intrinsic or existential meaning.
>
> The arts of doing and knowing, the evaluation and the understanding

of meanings, are thus seen to be only different aspects of the act of extending our person into the subsidiary awareness of particulars which compose a whole.[1]

"The act of extending our person" provides what Polanyi calls "personal knowledge" which is the basis of all meaning for us. "Our minds live in action." He says further:

> Truth becomes the rightness of an action. . . . Truth conceived as the rightness of an action allows for any degree of personal participation in knowing what is being known. . . . Authentic feeling and authentic experience jointly guide all intellectual achievements.[2]

Spontaneous dramatic action is, precisely, the act of extending our person as a bridge to the external world. The personal knowledge it provides is based upon the rightness of that authentic action.

Given that the meaning of dramatic action lies in the active relationship between the inner and the outer, the question arises: how do these two elements develop in life? We shall examine each separately.

The Dynamics of Personal Drama

Although dramatic action relates our personal world to the environment, it is the self that initiates it. The inner activates the exchange with the outer. The environment is important, but it does not "determine" us as some would have us believe. No matter how forceful its impact is upon us, and in some societies it can be highly repressive, human beings always have the ability to create meaning out of it. Human consciousness is always consciousness-of. Our inner self requires the environment to provide it with materials with which to work; yet it is the inner that initiates the exchange. It does so through a dramatic act—and it is this which relates the environment to the self.

Theory of Imagination

The nature of imagination is illustrated in Figure 1. From what we perceive, images and imaginings are created in the mind so that we can act with them.

What we see, hear, smell, taste and feel depends largely on our state of awareness and our ability to concentrate. From these percepts we create images: individual mental units which are based on (but are not the same as) percepts. Images grouped together becoming imaginings. Our emotions tend to "block" certain imagin-

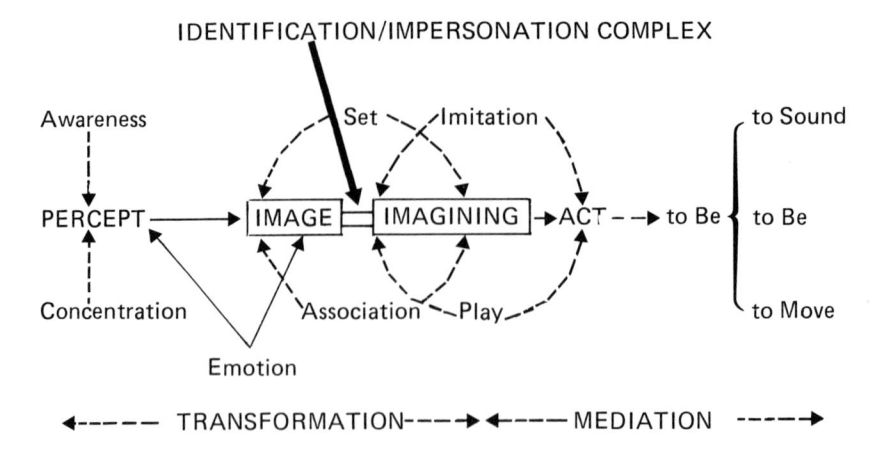

Figure 1: Theory of Imagination.

NOTE: This diagram is not linear. As every Act immediately becomes a Percept, the model works in a spiral fashion.

ings (whether through fear, or whatever) and to encourage others. Imaginings tend to flow through the mind in a variety of ways, of which the two most extreme are: sets, or usual and well-worn paths; and associations, where we tend to leap from one set of imaginings to another.

For imaginings to become externalized, we need to act with them. When we are very young this is to *Be*—"I am an airplane." Once this is achieved, the child can extend the action to *elements* of Being: *to Sound*—"I make the sound of an airplane"; and *to Move*—"I make the movements of an airplane."

The work of Piaget[3] has shown that when we are learning something new, imaginings become actions in a particular way. When we move from one mental pattern (schema) to another, we play with elements of the new schema for assimilation, and imitate elements of it for accommodation; when the two are synthesized, we have reached a new schema—we have learnt something new.

This process is subject to three dynamics:

Transformation;
Mediation; and
the Identification/Impersonation Complex.

These dynamics interrelate the elements of imagining and operate virtually simultaneously.

Transformation is what happens between the percept and the image; it alters what we perceive so that images can be formed of it. For example, if I see a table with four legs, but the fourth leg is obscured so that I can only see three, how do I think of that table when I recall it? Of course, I think of it as having four legs because "tables are like that." Mind transforms what we perceive by relating the perception to our previous experience.

Mediation, as we have seen, is the dynamic whereby our thoughts become action in the environment. Dramatic action is the primordial example of this, but other examples include language, painting, music and all other media.

The Identification/Impersonation Complex is the dramatic process of the mind. In the psychological literature this has been called the "as if" process. It is a dynamic, internal action whereby we consider a possibility "as if" we had already carried it out. Thus it relates to consequence and responsibility. The complex begins with the baby's identification with others and leads to "the primal act" whereby, at ten months old, he externalizes that identification in an act of impersonation.

Theory of Learning

If imaginative thought and action operate in such a way, what of learning? Learning occurs when there is a qualitative change in a person's understanding of experience. This change has two facets: apprehension, which is an innate grasping; and comprehension, which is a cognitive understanding.

Learning operates primarily in the area of mediation—that is, in the dynamic between imagining and action. By thinking about the environment and operating upon it, we change our perspective of the world around us. Although such learning is affected by perception, transformation, emotion and the like, it centres upon thought and action.

Learning theorists generally agree that there are two extremes in styles of learning: concept attainment and discovery. Concepts are ideas that group and classify experience. With older students, language can be indistinguishable from concepts, though this is not necessarily the case. Discovery, on the other hand, is the way we explore the novel. Concepts may result from this, but the actual exploration of something new is not in itself conceptual. Needless to say, concept attainment and discovery are not isolated from each other but represent two extremes in the styles of learning.

Figure 1 shows set and imitation at the top of the diagram while association and play are at the bottom. This is because set and imitation strongly affect concept attainment, while association and play have a direct bearing on discovery.

The natural method of human learning is illustrated in Figure 2. In everyday life, people learn in a particular sequence: from perception to thought and action and, finally, to thinking or talking about it. We perceive an action, or a process, or a thing. From this, imaginings are created which become actions—overtly when we are young, covertly when we are older. Subsequently, we can think or talk about it. This sequence is important for modern education. In the industrial societies of the Western world, the normal teaching process used is the lecture method. In these classrooms, the teacher talks about, and expects the students to think about, what is to be learned; thereafter, the students are expected to act (write about, or paint a picture) in relation to the material. But, as we have just seen, this is the reverse of what is required in a natural method of learning. Although we use language as one very important way of organizing a representation of the world, it is not the only one. Prior to the acquisition of language we have already organized a great many other representations—albeit more emotional and less cognitive than the linguistic. These earlier representations are dramatic, and they are the context from which the linguistic emerges.

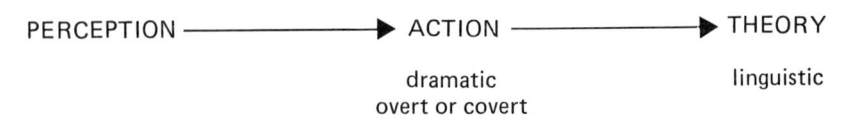

PERCEPTION ⟶ ACTION ⟶ THEORY
                                 dramatic   linguistic
                              overt or covert

Figure 2: Theory of Learning.

It follows that teachers need a different approach to the students' learning process than is normally used in schools. For really effective learning, the student should *watch* it, *do* it, and only then think or talk *about* it. The *doing* part should be overtly acted by the young child. With maturation, the actions can be increasingly covert and linguistic.

Theory of Media

We have seen that the symbol of "the costumed player" becomes, when we are very young, the act *to Be*. Looked at from a different perspective, this dramatic action is a medium—a way we mediate (make sense of) the world. Media develop in a *functional* way, by a process which E. H. Gombrich calls "substitution." The human mind has the capacity to substitute for a whole *an element* of that whole. As we have seen, *Being* can become *Sounding* or *Moving*. This occurs through substitution.

All human media emerge through the substitutional process. As each emerges, it becomes a more discriminating bridge between the self and the environment. From *Sounding* emerges the medium of Music—love of sound for its own sake. This love of sound develops into words when particular sounds become associated with certain meanings (things, people, actions). Words are codified music, so that "naming" becomes a medium. Words and music eventually develop into the medium of language.

From generalized *Movement* emerges Dance—the love of movement for its own sake. Shortly dance grows into an understanding of three dimensions ("frozen dance"). This leads to the medium of two dimensions—it is often forgotten that two dimensions cannot be comprehended without a basis in three dimensions.

From *Being* ("the primal act") emerges child's play. This develops in two styles: personal and projected play.[4] Personal play is drama as such: the whole self symbolizes what is imagined. Projected play occurs when the child projects his imaginings out onto objects—a stick becomes an airplane. From projected play emerges play with dolls and toys. Eventually, play develops into improvisation and role play; finally, in adulthood, theatre emerges (see Figure 3).

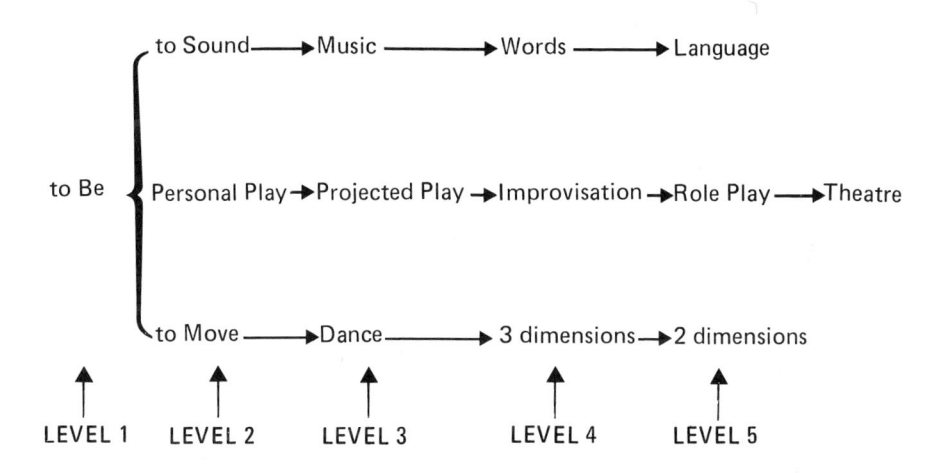

```
            to Sound ──▶ Music ──────▶ Words ──────▶ Language

to Be  {    Personal Play ▶ Projected Play ▶ Improvisation ▶ Role Play ──▶ Theatre

            to Move ─────▶ Dance ────▶ 3 dimensions ▶ 2 dimensions

  ↑           ↑              ↑              ↑              ↑
LEVEL 1    LEVEL 2        LEVEL 3        LEVEL 4        LEVEL 5
```

Figure 3: The Development of Media

Learning is the ability to use the skills of the media. It occurs, first, for expressive purposes and thereafter for critical purposes, so that the student can increasingly express his meanings to others. (For the effect of this theory of media on language, see pp. 108-25.)

Developmental Stages of Personal Drama

The concept of developmental stages has been used by many psychologists to describe the similarities and differences in the maturation of human beings. However, only Peter Slade has previously put forward a theory of developmental stages in dramatic terms. In order to provide an adequate frame of reference, therefore, the developmental theories of Piaget, Erikson, Kohlberg and Hoffman will be used.[5] This is illustrated in Figure 4.

In using the stages of developmental drama, however, the reader must take great care. First, these age stages are only approximate. The dramatic behavior described in each stage must be regarded not as highly specific but as a general guide. Second, the dramatic behavior described only applies to English-speaking children in industrialized countries; there may be substantial differences in other cultures. ("He" includes "she" throughout.)

The Identification Stage (0-10 months)

When the mother is the source of all goodness (food, love, comfort) the baby empathizes and identifies with her, which gives him an ego strength. His sensory apparatus is acute. When born his skin is highly sensitive, but steadily his most powerful tool for learning becomes his mouth. Identification centres upon feeding time and, in the subsequent ten minutes, loving games provide strong reciprocal experiences. The sucking and mouthing of fingers and fists develop into an attachment for a piece of self cloth or toy (a "cuddle," or "security blanket") which becomes "a mediate object".[6] Through this he begins to learn how to manipulate things in the world. This becomes overt when he so trusts his mother that he can give it to her—and then gurgles with delight when she returns it. Initially when the baby coughs and the mother imitates him, he can smile; later he will imitate her cough.

Between 3 and 6 months, he repeats sounds and movements and plays with them. He can "sing" with his parent and delight in games of crescendo. After 6 months he is crawling and develops a personal circle of power around his body. He can anticipate climax, make others his audience, have clear purposes, engage in repetition, explore objects, and create sound games and gestural language.

The Impersonatory Stage (10 months-7 years): "The Child as Actor"

THE PRIMAL ACT (10 months approximately)

At about 10 months old, there is a sudden change. He acts "as if"

AGE	DRAMA	COGNITIVE (Piaget)	AFFECTIVE (Erikson)	MORAL (Kohlberg)	EMPATHIC (Hoffman)
0–10 mo.	IDENTIFICATION	Sensory-Motor	Trust/Mistrust	Egocentric	Diffused Empathy
10 mo.–7 yrs	IMPERSONATION (the Actor)				
	10 m. The Primal Act	Sensory-Motor	Trust/Mistrust	Egocentric	Empathic Distress
	1–2 yr. Symbolic Play	Sensory-Motor	Trust/Mistrust	Egocentric	Role-taking
	2–3 yr. Sequential Play	Preconceptual	Trust/Mistrust	Egocentric	Role-taking
	3–4 yr. Exploratory Play	Preconceptual	Autonomy/Shame, Doubt	Egocentric	Role-taking
	4–5 yr. Expansive Play	Intuitive	Autonomy/Shame, Doubt	Egocentric	Role-taking
	5–7 yr. Flexible Play	Intuitive	Initiative/Guilt	Egocentric	Sense of Identity
7–12 yrs	GROUP DRAMA (the Planner)	Concrete	Industry/Inferiority	Individualism	Complex Roles Empathic Sympathy
12–18 yrs	ROLES (the Communicator)				
	12–15 yr. Role "appearance"	Formal	Identity/Role Confusion	Interpersonal	Empathic Sympathy
	15–18 yr. Role "truth"	Formal	Intimacy/Isolation	Social System	Empathic Sympathy

Figure 4: Comparison of Developmental Stages (from Courtney *The Dramatic Curriculum*).

he is his mother. Then he feels he can control the environment because what he thinks becomes what he does. Founded on previous empathy, identification and imitation, this occurs in all cultures: for example, it is recognized by American Indians and others who have the first "naming" ceremony of the child about this time. Once achieved, this step becomes generalized to all other types of activity.

SYMBOLIC PLAY (1-2 years)

Projected play and substitution are begun, but the child cannot distinguish the real from the acted. Yet he begins to understand that he can delay his actions. Action and movement have more meaning than speech, and his mental processes are a mixture of analogy, animism, omnipotence of thought, the irrational and the illogical. He is mischievous, insists on "me" and "mine," makes exits and entrances, and loves being chased.

SEQUENTIAL PLAY (2-3 years)

He demonstrates strategies and completes sequences of action although his attention span is short. He makes running commentaries on his drama, and sentences develop. He uses basic time concepts ("in a minute") and can distinguish between himself as actor and others as audience. He can now defer his imitation and can change roles. He develops and expands narratives, and can join in group games.

EXPLORATORY PLAY (3-4 years)

He constantly explores (asks "Why?"), loves puzzles, and investigates length, weight, number and size. He creates music, pretence environments and rules for play. He can take turns and share. He tells exaggerated stories. Sentences develop and rudimentary grammar appears. He plays matching games (with boxes, buttons, etc.) as well as "follow my leader." He plays groups of characters, has pretence emotions, acknowledges spatial differences, participates in narratives and runs from "monsters." Although identifying with both parents, he tends to model himself more on the parent of the same sex, exaggerating and caricaturing their actions. From about 3 years old he constantly uses "I" to identify himself but will accept synonyms like "boy" or "girl."

EXPANSIVE PLAY (4-5 years)

His growth is now expanded through widening experiences and

abilities. He develops imaginative roles, uses different voices, and slowly distinguishes the symbol from reality. He has secrets and surprises, friends and enemies, and seeks peer approval. He engages in gymnastics, creates free movement to music, and plays both "creeping" and relay races. He pretends to tell the time. He plays games of order ("Ring around a Rosy") and develops dramatic rituals of possession and sequence. Conscious of the roles of others, he has a greater range of models; yet h·s play is still egocentric and he focuses upon one aspect while appearing oblivious to others. He anticipates the future and relies on his own judgment. Sentences expand, grammar develops and he invents narrative.

FLEXIBLE PLAY (5-7 years)

He now builds flexibly on his previous growths, coordinating what he has achieved. He imitates his own play and, because he gets about more, dramatizes a wide range of experiences. He plays any number of roles and begins to understand complex social situations. Social roles are begun in caricature but he still has some difficulty in distinguishing fantasy from reality. He develops realistic themes with episodic plots, and imitates actual situations to accommodate to new experience. Still working by analogy and animism, he learns time beat, "left and right," and the "appropriate" play for girls, boys and babies. He loves chasing and running games, and demonstrates a knowledge of relationships: taller/shorter, bigger/smaller, etc. He needs adult recognition for his play creations. Language becomes more important and perceptual discrimination increases. He begins to empathize well with his peers, reacts well to others (as people or characters), and communicates well with them in speech. His drama shows a concern for the wholeness of his body: dramatized surgery is strongly felt. He invents dramatic ways to overcome threats: through magic, skill, force or ways not normally permitted by adults (such as trickery). Fears and more generalized anxieties are constantly expressed in his drama, while themes of flight, being chased, attacked and bitten, witches and resurrection are common.

The Group Drama Stage (7-12 years): "The Child as Planner"

The major change is toward group drama—a genuine social activity where ideas and actions are shared. Natural play shapes have previously been in large circles. These now break up so that, in due course, the natural shapes are small circles. Then, about 10 years old, play takes a horseshoe shape often backing onto a wall.

Games of dominance ("King of the Castle") emerge and from large group improvisations, or pair and solo dramas, leaders arise. Exaggerated roles are played, and there is a genuine feeling for the roles of others.

He now plans his activity and experiments with form: long endings or abrupt finishes, subjects that are realistic or fantastic, and small moments when he needs to show his work to his peers (the beginnings of theatre). For all his concentration upon planning, he is still primarily a player and his spontaneity develops through action.

He can distinguish between media—say, between creating in drama and creating in paint. He classifies people and characterization is understood by type; he tends to act people in two dimensions. Yet the role he is playing can change with the action (paralleling transformation in scientific thinking) although the character's motivation remains arbitrary and categorical. Until about 9 years, he has to play out ideas physically in order for them to take up meaningful dimensions. He needs countless handling and playing experiences for the foundation of concepts.

Role-playing is vital for the development of morality at this stage: the more drama experiences he has, the more this experience will help moral development. Reciprocal role-taking does not normally occur before 12 years old.

Spontaneous drama is important for inference—what a child concludes about another person. Through role-taking and modelling, the child makes many inferences (not always with accuracy) about the emotional states of others and increases his awareness of the expression of emotion in others (such as in facial expression, body language, etc.).

The strong identification with the group can result in cumulative plots with their own inner rules. The child develops a sense of fairness in board and card games which spills over into the drama. The communication level between children (in roles, or as themselves) improves considerably.

Dramatic themes often reflect concern with working hard (home and family, recreation and school) but imaginative activity with exaggerated plots can also occur. Through drama, the child develops notions of "what he is like inside," together with who is like him and who is not; in this way he makes a conscious choice of friends. Personal esteem and morality appear related to warm and supportive atmospheres provided by parents and teachers. Spontaneous dance and speech (including gibberish) can erupt with excitement. He plays with puppets and puppet theatres, mechanical toys and dolls, and has collections, crazes and hobbies.

The Role Stage (12–18 years): "The Student as Communicator"

An adolescent's maturation hinges upon his concept of roles: on his progress from role "appearance" to role "truth."

ROLE "APPEARANCE" (12–15 years)

The physical and psychological changes of adolescence are a commonplace, but in early adolescence the student is concerned with role "appearance." Drama at this stage is concerned with hypothesis: "If I hypothesize my role as *this*, then my actions are so-and-so; but if my role is *that*, then my actions become such-and-such. But who, then, is the real me?" This is related to cause-and-effect: "If I play my role *that* way, does it produce (cause) particular actions?" Thus dramatic activity underpins, personally and emotionally, the cognitive aspects of thought. This particularly occurs in improvisation. The adolescent considers the possible factors in the dramatic situation (plot, characters, performers, space, structure, etc.) and a set of hypotheses ("If we do it this way, then . . ."); then he draws logical conclusions ("The play will be like this . . .") whereby he judges the truth or falsity of propositions according to logic. Thus drama provides the *felt* basis for rational thought.

His drama makes him more aware of personal alternatives: he can imagine an ideal self separate from his present real self, and he improvises with both as well as with future social and occupational roles. He alternates the real with the possible; facets of symbols are tested against reality in the many possibilities of personality and identity. Becoming aware of the inconsistencies of adult behavior, he can express them in improvisation.

His emotional judgments can often be in error. The final improvisation may not turn out as he expected; the planned comedy may become a tragedy and vice versa. His drama constantly explores social possibilities, including vocations. He also explores social relationships and friendships, testing out the qualities of character in terms of what is most desirable. He struggles with morality in his dramas; he tries out moral decisions of his own, or the inconsistencies observed in adults.

Language begins to replace the physical symbolism in drama. Creative writing can become fluent. The student can invent his own language and private codes.

There is a curious beginning to a theatre sense. At times he will wish to "show" and at other times not. These changes can come quickly and it is not performance per se that he is seeking but role communication. The large group drama dwindles and the small one (particularly pair drama) appears. Dramatic structure is explored and end-shapes emerge: in natural play, students use one end of a space, any audience being on one side; also a platform is often used. Although communication develops strongly, and there is still much planning, the improviser is still primarily a player exploring each through the immediacy of dramatic action.

ROLE "TRUTH" (15-18 years)

With maturation, the stable student recognizes that his personality is multidimensional: that although he has many "masks" he also has a permanent and continuing self (or "face"). When he achieves this recognition, he can perform equally well in spontaneous improvisation or theatre, though the latter is the prerogative of the few rather than the many. He can see his future-oriented role as only one of many valid views. In Western industrial cultures, this stage can be considerably delayed. This development is an advanced form of abstraction; it helps to develop the ideal self.

These age stages of Developmental Drama should be closely related to the dynamics of personal drama. For example, the teacher who wishes to design a program for 9-year-old children should not only understand the normal dramatic developments of such children but also must be able to relate these to imagination and action, learning and the use of media. Even further, however, all these personal dramatic developments are set in a particular cultural context. We shall now examine the nature of such contexts.

The Dynamics of Cultural Drama

Although the self activates the exchange with the environment, it is the latter which provides the limits within which we work.

Our culture provides us with the materials with which we create meaning. Our ability to create meaning is not determined by our environment although it can be limited by it. For example, a stage designer in Manhattan may have the widest possible range of materials and fabrics to choose from; by comparison a stage designer in, say, Omsk may be much more limited in materials. However, their relative ability to create meaning can be judged by what they achieve out of their resources.

We create meaning dramatically within our culture, through the following dynamics:

Rites of intensification, specifically myths and rituals;
Rites of passage; and
Acculturation.

These will be dealt with separately although, in reality, there is much overlap between them.

Rites of Intensification

Rites of intensification are dramatic actions that hold the greatest significance for human life. They attempt to unify, with as much intensity as possible, human beings with the cosmos—with supernatural beings, or the spiritual life, or the gods, or God. They have two component elements: myths—the beliefs upon which the rites are based; and rituals—the actions which activate these myths.

MYTHS

In order to understand the significance of myths, it can be valuable to look at them historically from prehistory to the present day. In each case, they relate narratives about human beings and the Ultimate. Ancient myths of prehistory were religious stories of creation which served as models for the dramatic rituals that imitated them. Both were so intricately tied together that it is common to speak of them as ancient ritual-myths. Tribal man used the ritual to enact the ancient myths. Within them:

> religious man assumes a humanity that has a transhuman, transcendent model. He does not consider himself to be *truly man* except in so far as he imitates the gods, the culture heroes, or the mythical ancestors. This is as much as to say that religious man wishes to be *other* than he is on the plane of his profane experience.[7]

In trying to be other than his profane self, the human being ritualizes the models given by the myths.

We can look at this historically. Tribal people of the past told their myths about the events of creation (the fabled "beginnings") where supernatural beings brought everything into existence. These "beginnings" were thought to be more "real" than everyday life, and they provided models for living. Thus the paleolithic peoples of prehistory had their rituals imitating the "beginnings" just like contemporary tribal peoples today: American Indians on the Pacific Northwest Coast have ritual-myths about those who "dropped down" to create life on earth; in modern Polynesia, the cosmogenic myth is the archetypal model for all types of creation —the reign of a new king, a fresh crop, a sea voyage, and so on; and in Australia today, aboriginals go on "walkabout" to relive the events of "the Dreamtime" in a drama that is more "real" to them than everyday existence. Ancient and contemporary hunters have sacred places "revealed" to them. Amongst the Kamilaroi of Australia, "the bora ground represents Baiamai's (the Supreme Being's) first camp."[8] On the sacred bora ground they have two circles: one is 70 feet in diameter with a pole in the centre some 9 feet high that has emu's feathers at the top; in the smaller, two trees are fixed to the ground with their roots in the air within which two old men chant the traditions of the bora; and the two circles are joined by a path along which are clay models of Baiamai and other supernatural beings. In this sacred ground, initiation ceremonies occur that imitate Baiamai's gestures and acts. The place "is at once an image of the world (*imago mundi*) and a world sanctified by the presence of the Divine Being."[9]

In the city life of the first civilizations of Mesopotamia, India and Egypt, everyone had a trade speciality. As human life was in imitation of the "real," individual gods arose who had their own specialist concerns. Each city became an *imago mundi* and each house was a microcosm; the world of the gods was dramatized on earth. With the ancient tribal people, the central pillar of a dwelling had been dramatized as the cosmic axis (the *axis mundi*): a sacrificial tree with seven branches symbolized the seven spheres of heaven which unified heaven and earth. Before it was built, there was a sacrifice which was a dramatic imitation of the primordial sacrifice of a Divine Being when the world was created. In Sumer and Babylon, there was a similar sacrifice at the building of a temple (ziggurat)—a stepped pyramid in seven stages. These civilizations were based on the annual grain harvest. According to the myth, grain grew only in imitation of the rebirth (resurrection) of the god. Thus there were two dramatic rituals annually enacted: "the sacred marriage" of the god and goddess (performed by the king and a priestess) which took place at the top of the ziggurat; and the enacted death and resurrection of the god. In the city of Ur, "Shulgi (the king) dresses himself in a ritual *me*-garment, covers his head with a crown-like wig, and so impresses the goddess with his wonder-inspiring presence that she breaks spontaneously into passionate song."[10] And in Egypt, Mesopotamia and India there were ritual battles which dramatically represented the overcoming of chaos and the resurrection of life.

In due course, heroes—the children of gods and humans—emerged and became the basis of legends. So now there were two types of model for people to imitate: the gods of the myths and the heroes of the legends.

Writing was developed by the Phoenicians and, as a result, the myths of Homer and Hesiod came to be written down. However, the early Greek scientists could then study the myths as historical documents. As the myths did not stand up to the scientific scrutiny of historic time, the Ionians began to doubt their sacredness. Most of the "classic" Greek myths of which we know are not, in fact, descriptions of ancient religious experiences. Rather, they are rational and secular versions in literary form. Yet such forms also became models for the behavior of the Greeks and Romans.

The rites of intensification within the Judaeo-Christian traditions have a unique quality: they mix mythological and historic time.[11] Both traditions are based on the hope of re-entry into the original Paradise, but in different ways. In Judaism, God intervenes in history. The Temple at Jerusalem was an *imago mundi*. As it was the centre of the world, it sanctified both the cosmos and cosmic life. This unification was what constituted time. The twelve loaves of bread on the table of the Temple signified the twelve months of the year, while the candelabrum with seventy branches represented the zodiac division of the seven planets into tens. In other words, like the aboriginal dance space in Australia and the Babylonian ziggurat, the Temple of Jerusalem was built in dramatic imitation of the spiritual world.

Whereas in Judaism God intervenes in history, Christianity goes one step further. God is incarnated as a historic being. As a result, the life, crucifixion and resurrection of Christ unify both mythological and historic events. The greatest of all miracles is the Incarnation. All others are judged against this: any miracles prior to that event were made meaningless after his coming; all subsequent miracles must, according to the Roman Catholic Church, be vouchsafed by grace—that is, they are dependent on or in imitation of Christ. He is the model for all Christians. The religious experience of any Christian is based upon the imitation of Christ—a dramatic act.

The symbol of Christ's Cross has an ancient history. The tribal Tree of Life was not merely the *axis mundi*; it was also the mythological prototype for all miraculous plants and trees that brought the dead to life, healed the sick and restored youth. With a snake at its base and a bird at the top it took innumerable forms, including the totem pole of the American Indian. It was the Tree of Knowledge in Paradise—also with its serpent. It became the Cross of Christian iconography to which many meanings accrued. In one, the mother of the Emperor Constantine was said to look for the wood of the Cross that was supposed to bring the dead back to life.

In other versions, the wood of the Cross had seven notches in it like the cosmic trees of the ancient tribes.

As Europe developed, the dramatic quality of mythology was maintained. Medieval Christianity had to mingle with the tribal religions in order to capture the adherence of the common people. Gregory the Great deliberately assimilated pagan festivals with those of the Church so that dragon-slaying gods became St. George. Medieval Christianity, therefore, had a particular character: the religious experience and the symbolism of the old tribal religions were maintained but now based upon man's salvation through Christ; the nostalgia for Paradise, moreover, was not merely Christian but it also had the time-binding qualities of pagan creation myths.[12] Likewise, the ancient Celtic mythologies, such as the Arthurian legends and the search for the Holy Grail, mixed the traditions of Christianity and the tribal communities.

Despite the eventual secularization of kingship, Elizabeth I of England, Frederick II of Prussia, and Louis XIV of France ("The Sun King") were all thought of as model heroes who brought the hope of universal renewal. By extension, this becomes the model-making based on the "founders and leaders" of modern states: Abraham Lincoln, Simon Bolivar, Lenin and Jomo Kenyatta. Dramatic imitation is as much part of political mythology as it is of religion.

Yet dramatic mythologies have to be learned. The Judeo-Christian tradition looks forward to the final coming of a Messiah together with the renewal of a primordial "nature." This becomes a basis for child-rearing practices. We can see this in a major trait of European education from the late eighteenth century. For Rousseau, education was a return to primordial "nature." Lessing went even further: he postulated continual revelation which would culminate in a third age, combining the triumph of reason and the fulfilment of Christian revelation. This influenced the educational thought of such diverse figures as Hegel, Compte and Dewey. For Freud and those educationalists who followed him, psychological health is a "return to the past," to the primordial world of childhood, a kind of inner Paradise. What has evolved in the late twentieth century is that life history has become the paradigm of modern education. Unfortunately the mythology upon which it is based has become very diffuse, even fragmented. Students have a multiplicity of styles of hero—from adventure, war, sports, film and television. Institutions of learning must adjust to this, difficult though this may be. The basis of learning lies in the dramatization of significant models drawn from contemporary mythology and, as Eliade says: "This mythology is continually enriched with the growing years; we meet one after another, the exemplary figures thrown up by changes of fashion and we try to become like them."[13]

RITUALS

Rituals are dramatic actions performed in imitation of models. The act, by repetition, coincides with its archetype. Act and archetype fuse and time is abolished. The performer, through the heightened intensity of unified time, breaks through into the "real." He gives significant meaning to the inner and outer worlds through his dramatic acts.

In archaic societies, rituals were direct dramatic imitations of the myths. "We must do what the gods did in the beginning," say the ancient Indian scriptures. Thus all rituals were essentially religious acts. In modern industrial societies rituals can be indirect dramatizations of models. Many remain sacred: for example, the "beating of the bounds" of the English parish indirectly reflects the ancient pagan rites of passage that established tribal territory. Yet there are a host of profane rituals. One example is the ceremony that involves a performative utterance ("I declare this road open") and an enactment symbolic of the quality of the action (cutting a ribbon). Paleolithic peoples had no myth without a ritual, and vice versa. They enacted the lives of the original supernatural beings and what happened in the "beginnings." Thus the actor was translated back into mythical time which became "real" to him. This happens in contemporary tribal societies. The modern Coast Salish spirit dancer on Vancouver Island becomes fully possessed as he drives, through his intensity, into the life of his own spirit or supernatural being. Australian aboriginals still enact the mythological reality by creating or refreshing magical rock paintings (petroglyphs), chanting the myths and, particularly, performing what took place in "the Dreamtime." At a sacred place, each actor in a ceremony re-enacts (reincarnates) an ancestor while the chorus of old men "chant those verses of the traditional song which commemorate the original scene in the life of the ancestor which has been dramatized in the ceremony witnessed by them."[14]

In the ritual world, the human being *as actor* becomes something else—a supernatural being or god. Yet he continues to remain himself. It is the same with objects. A stone which is a sacred stone is two things: both its normal reality and a supernatural reality. Dramatization creates significant meaning, whether sacred or profane.

In the first civilizations of Mesopotamia, India and Egypt, agriculture was vital to existence. The seed grew into corn in the renewal of spring despite the "death" of winter: vegetation was seen to be resurrected. Thus the cosmos was considered to be renewed annually and the myth developed that the chief god was annually killed only to be resurrected again—as with Damuzzi in Sumer, Marduk in Babylon and Osiris/Horus in Egypt. Great New Year Festivals arose in which the king acted the role of the resurrected god as an exemplary model for the people. In such performances, the archetypal act was dramatized and time was abolished: the actor, although existing in the present, was thought to be performing in the mythological time that created life. In other words, dramatic re-creation brought about creation. In the Babylonian myth, the resurrected god, Marduk, fought the marine monster, Tiamat, dismembered his body to create the cosmos (sacrifice), and created man from the blood of the demon Kingu, Tiamat's chief ally (blood sacrifice). In the New Year Festival, the combat between Marduk and Tiamat was re-enacted by two groups of performers—a ceremonial performance that continued in history down to modern rural England, Newfoundland and the West Indies where the Mummers perform their St. George plays. New Year rituals reactualize the myths: they start time over again at the beginning.

But prior to creation there was chaos, just as prior to resurrection there was death. So Babylonians, Greeks, Romans, medieval rural folk and modern traditional peoples re-enact chaos—the extinction of fire, the return of the souls of the dead, social confusion and erotic orgies. The Roman Kalends and Saturnalia, the Celtic Yule and the Christian Twelve Days of Christmas all relaxed social rules and inverted social status.

Although there are considerable differences between the rituals of traditional peoples, in all cases, these rituals regenerate people by abolishing past time and reactualizing the birth of the cosmos and human kind. The models become actual.

The ritual myths became expanded in the ancient Near East. The priest-actors were slowly separated from the people who became "the congregation." Instead of everyone being part of the ritual myth, it came to be performed by a select group "on behalf" of the majority. This was the same group who developed the "inner secrets" of the ritual myth into the liturgy—a body of secret knowledge known only to the privileged few. Thus by the time we come to the rise of Attic drama in the fifth century B.C. with the creation of tragedy and comedy, we have reached ritual performmances enacted by a select group "on behalf" of the people (the "audience").

Just as the Judaeo-Christian sabbath was an act in imitation of God—"On the seventh day He rested"—so much of Christian ritual is a dramatic imitation based on the model of Jesus. Christ asked that this should occur: "For I have given you an example, that ye should do as I have done to you."[15] Within Church rituals, the Christian is required to become the contemporary of Christ.[16] Christ died for man, and man must live for Christ—"as if" he is Christ. In the words of St. Thomas Aquinas, *haec hominus est perfectio, simultudo Dei*. The liturgy is a re-enactment of the life and Passion of the Savior. The events of Holy Week are not just remembered, they really happen, then, before the eyes of the faithful. They are made present, re-presented. The same principle applies in many significant events of existence. Through the whole of human history, marriage rites have had divine models: the union of heaven and earth—the cosmic creation. "I am the heaven; thou the earth," repeat the Upanishads. The recitation of the cosmic myth was (and is) common amongst many peoples on the occasion of a marriage. In rural Britain, Europe, China and elsewhere, young couples copulated in the fields in dramatic imitation of "the sacred marriage" of the god of heaven and the Earth Mother. This re-creation was intended to promote cosmic, agricultural and human fertility. "Ploughing" was a synonym for sexual unity and in that sense was used by Shakespeare of Cleopatra:

> Royal wench!
> She made great Caesar lay his sword to bed:
> He ploughed her, and she cropped.

"Ploughing" was used in the same sense in rural England until recently. We should also know that "rehearse" derives from "to harrow over again"—that is, to level the earth once more after ploughing in preparation for seeding.

The drama of rituals concentrates time—gives time a heightened intensity and thus creates meaning. There are modern rituals which are residues and remnants of earlier ritual myths: bullfights, athletic contests, games, racing, the laying of ceremonial stones, and the like. These still concentrate time by unifying the present act with that of the "beginnings." But there are other modern rituals which are based on secular media. The essential quality of theatre and its contemporary substitutes (film and television) is that they provide a heightened intensity to ordinary life. They, too, become models and people tend to imitate the behavior and fashions of media heroes. In doing so, they are attempting to fuse the reality of the model with their own reality—a profane act, it is true, but one that can provide as much intensity and meaning as sacred acts within industrial societies.

The ritualist relates his inner thought to the external world. By performing the ritual, he attempts to re-create the elements of the environment into a significant pattern that brings about a new level of meaning—one that is intense and significant. It is dramatic in that it is based on the processes of empathy, identification and impersonation, either overtly or covertly. It has two levels of meaning: the actor and his action exist on the plane of everyday life (he does it in the here and now); and the actor and his action exist on a symbolic level (he does it within a ritualized plane that is intense and significant).

In today's industrial societies, therefore, we can distinguish between:

1 / a ritual that is an operative act which has become formalized; this is a formula which marks out what is done, such as sticking a pin in an effigy, or modelling oneself on a pop star in order to impress others;

2 / a ceremony whose elaborateness heightens the occasion and gives it aesthetic expression, such as cutting a ribbon to open a road or building;

3 / the sacraments where matter and form are equally indispensable for the efficacy of the act.

In each case, the dramatic quality of the action stems from the logic of operative action rather than the heightening function of the ceremonial within which it is set. Yet, at the same time, rituals encapsulate the norms of the culture within an emotional matrix.

There are many modern myths to ritualize. Real and imaginary heroes and heroines still play an important part in human life whether they come from history, tales of adventure, films or television. In fact, mythological images are to be found almost everywhere, even if they are fragmented and disguised.

Rites of Passage

Tribal and agricultural cultures have specific dramatic acts which mark the social change of an individual from one state in a society to another: at birth, the transition to adulthood (initiation), marriage and death. These are known as rites of passage.[17] Although theoretically different from rites of intensification, in one sense rites of passage are merely particular instances of the larger rites.[18] All rites of passage have three major phases: the preliminal, the liminal and the postliminal. The first detaches an individual from the group to which he belongs; it is a symbolic "death" in that it is a separation from the old. In the liminal phase the individual is between groups; it is a symbolic hiatus, an ambiguous situation which, when applying to a culture as a whole, becomes an intercalary period—that which is outside normal time so that the normal restrictions of society do not apply (as the original Twelve Days of Christmas were outside calendar time). The postliminal phase consummates the passage of the individual to the new group; symbolically it is a rebirth or aggregation.

Historically, the most significant of the rites of passage were acts of initiation.

INITIATION

Initiation rites have developed and changed over human history. In the tribal societies of prehistory it is probable that shamans (priests) conducted initiation rituals that made men out of boys and women out of girls—puberty rites. Those who had passed through the rituals were then in two groups, the men and the women, who in due course conducted the ceremonies themselves. In time, they used the initiation rites not only for puberty but also for a great many other rites of passage. Thus different "secret societies" arose; in each case, a small group of a single sex that identified with their particular totem, spirit or god acted out its mythological background to the initiate. Eventually traditional cultures performed three types of initiation ceremonies: puberty rites; initiation into secret societies; and initiation to obtain higher religious status.

Puberty rites are obligatory to all members of such cultures. Within them, the adolescent is re-created. The "separation" element divorces him from childhood, dramatized as a death, and the "aggregation" is dramatized as a resurrection. For example, amongst the Yahgan, the southernmost tribe in America, the boys go through separation rites and, blindfolded, are attacked by two performers in masks representing spirits. They are then ordered to unmask the actors whom they recognize as older men from the tribe. Two older women, bleeding from the nose, rush outside and cry to the onlookers that all the men have been killed by evil spirits. Later, the men appear and dance before everyone to demonstrate that they are alive and that the evil spirits are dead. Still later, there is much singing and dancing, the recitation of the myths, and the masked impersonation of many spirits including animals and birds.[19] All tribal cultures gave the highest priority to initiation.[20] In all instances, the ritual consisted of a body of dramatic rites and oral teachings. The ritual purpose was to give an individual a decisive social and religious status—to change him into *another*. In other words, initiation was the quintessential dramatic act.

Unlike puberty rites, initiations into secret societies and to obtain higher religious status are not obligatory. They are usually performed for individuals and small groups, and are often characterized by ecstasy. Those of secret societies are almost always confined to one sex, usually the males. They are very jealous of their secrets which may include cruel ordeals and the predominance of the cult of the ancestors, often personified by masks. For example, initiation into some African secret societies (such as the Ngoye among the Kuta) includes being beaten and hung from a horizontal beam with the body rubbed in an ointment that produces a terrible itching. Such ordeals symbolize the initiate's "death" at the hands of the spirits which will "kill" his old name so that he may be given another. Amongst the *hamatsa* (Cannibal) society of the Southern Kwakiutl on Vancouver Island, the initiate is captured and presumed dead; he spends months in the forest learning the secrets of the society (the myth of the Cannibal spirit and his great masked birds); when he returns he is thought to be reborn and his ceremonial dance begins with him possessed by the spirit. Slowly and by the alternate impersonation of the great masked birds, he becomes "normal."

PRIESTS

Religious personages in all cultures have to undergo initiation into the priesthood. The difference between the initiations of shamans and Catholic priests, for example, is simply one of degree.

Shamans (also called doctors, magicians, sorcerers) were the first religious figures of *homo sapiens*. They have existed for at least 25,000 years. Siberia and Central Asia is "the classic complex" of shamanism, from which they spread over the whole globe. Today, shamans can be found in all tribal cultures. In modern industrial societies, however, their traditions have become mere rural customs—like the Abbots' Bromley Horn Dance in England, a remnant of the old religion of Europe.

Amongst contemporary traditional tribes, the shaman is a dancing, possessed and ecstatic performer. He engages in animal impersonation and transformation, the control of the weather, trance states, bird-like flight of the soul to "the other reality," mastery of fire, rebirth from bones, knowledge of the world of the spirits and the dead, the magic arts of curing, and the guardianship of the equilibrium of the community. He can perform for any of these purposes. When he does so, the shaman thinks in dramatic metaphors. His dance and theatrical presentation is a metaphorical statement. The same applies to his art—the famous rock carvings (petroglyphs). Each presents an ambigious, paradoxical, poetic and magical statement. But this is specifically not abstract: it is always a representation of the myths and rituals of the culture. Thus the shaman is an exemplary model for the rest of the community. When he performs his rituals he is acting dramatically—he is performing "as if" he is a supernatural spirit. Through him, the audience can enter the spirit life. In a sense, therefore, the shamanic performance is the theatre of tribal cultures.

Although shamanic initiations are similar to those of the secret societies, they emphasize the personal experience of the initiate. Shamans receive two kinds of instruction: "The first is ecstatic (e.g. dreams, visions, trances); the second is traditional (e.g. shamanic techniques, names and functions of spirits, mythology and geneology of the clan, secret language)".[21] As bones are the essential element of life for hunting and gathering peoples, the shaman's initation includes the ability to see himself as a skeleton. In Siberia, the mythical ancestors tear away his flesh and the shaman has to learn the secret names for all the bones. While this occurs in dramatic action in Siberia and elsewhere, amongst the Inuit it is done in the mind alone. Once initiated, the shaman's behavior changes: the profane man has been "killed" and a new sacred personality has been born. Initiation is called a "curing": he has been cured of the profane life and has been resurrected to a new, superhuman condition.

With the rise of civilization in the Near East, the shamans who had been in touch with the supernatural spirits slowly grew into priests who were in touch with the gods. In time, the king became the chief priest; he was assisted by minor priests who interceded with the gods on behalf of the community. It was these priests who led the way to the actors of the Athenian theatre of the fifth century B.C., the Japanese *Noh* plays (the subject of which is often shamanic characters and spirits), and the Indian Kathakali theatre where the priest-actors still undergo initiation. Not only do many priests in modern religions undertake initiation but, in the Mass, the Catholic priest directly intercedes between God and the congregation.

GENERALIZATION OF RITES OF PASSAGE

Rites of passage are not limited to the initiations of adolescents, secret societies and priests. These happen to be three important forms of a style of dramatic action that is generalized to the total life of any culture.

The life of any individual is a series of passages from one status to another within a society. Birth, social puberty, marriage, fatherhood and motherhood, advancement to a higher class, occupational specialization, death—these are some of the important events in a society. Often there are ceremonies whose essential purpose is to enable the individual to pass from one social position to another. In traditional cultures, the passages are always enveloped in ceremonies which are seen as implicit in existence. Thus childhood rites might include the cutting of the umbilical cord, sprinkling and baths, naming, the first haircut, the first meal with the family, the first tooth—each event being accompanied by a ceremonial.

Rites of passage also became generalized to space. Early peoples have boundaries defined only by natural features—a sacred rock, tree, river or lake—or by specific objects, like a stake or gate, that have been consecrated. Strangers who cross such boundaries have committed sacrilege unless the correct sacred rite of passage has been enacted. This was common in ancient Rome while later expressions of this phenomenon include milestones, walls and statues; city gates which were still being built until quite recent time; and the boundary posts still used in today's rural communities. These rites were generalized to houses: particular rites of passage had to be enacted to cross a threshold, or to go through the door of someone else's house. The most spectacular modern example is the gods that decorate the doorposts of a Chinese house. Even in rural England within living memory, it was essential when a stranger crossed a threshold for him to say, "Bless all in this house!"—a remnant of an ancient rite. In the great events of a person's life hosts of smaller rites were gathered together around the change in status. This particularly applied to weddings. Cultures as diverse as that of the Ukraine and the Indians on the Pacific Northwest Coast complicated the event with a great many different small enactments. Although there are vast differences in the wedding rites of these two cultures, they have common patterns: dramatizations of fertility, of the relation of food to fecundity, and so forth.

Acculturation

Neither rites of intensification nor of passage remain the same over time. All cultures are in the process of change, some more than others. An important aspect of culture change is the effect of one culture upon another—or acculturation.

It was Thor Heyerdahl who, with voyages of rafts such as the *Kon-Tiki*, brought vividly to life the great sea voyages of ancient peoples. More recently, archaeological discoveries have shown that the peoples of the ancient Near East were in the Americas centuries before Columbus. Acculturation has been taking place over the whole of human history.

Nor has it ceased in modern times. The multicultural societies emerging in the great cities of the world continue the process. Students in classrooms everywhere are subject to acculturation.

Studies in acculturation have mainly been with the subordinate culture—those people who have been dominated by another. Yet acculturation concerns not only the influence of a dominant culture upon a conquered group but also the reverse. In modern multicultural societies it concerns the mutual effect of the home culture and the immigrants.

When culture contact occurs between peoples, cultural exchange takes place. Enactments vary, depending upon the degree of acculturation. During this process, a dominated culture passes through specific stages:

1/Steady state: the system operates without intolerable strain.
2/Stress: a period of increased individual stress takes place when the mechanisms for stress reduction become less effective.
3/Cultural distortion: amongst American Indians and Australian aboriginals, for example, such distortions can result in alchoholism and apathy.
4/Revitalization: attempts are made to regenerate a subordinate culture.
5/The establishment of a new cultural system that is viable, or the final destruction of the culture as an entity.

During these stages of development, dramatic ceremonials vary considerably between culture and culture.

REVITALIZATION

The most famous revitalization rituals were the "cargo cults" of the Pacific and the Ghost Dance of the North American Indian. Amongst the cargo cults, the Vailala Madness of Papua was a belief that the dead would return in boats carrying cargoes of wealth goods including guns that would drive the whites away. The central ritual was a mortuary feast for the dead.[22] Similar cults occured on various Pacific islands in the twentieth century, particularly after the Second World War.

The Ghost Dance first appeared amongst the Paviotsos of Nevada in 1870 and quickly spread the belief that the dead were returning and the whites would be driven out. The Sioux developed the idea that "the ghost shirt" (a special garment worn by dancers in the ritual) had supernatural properties and was inpenetrable to the bullets of the whites. Once this was seen to be an ineffective belief, the Ghost Dance died out.[23]

CULTURAL RESIDUES

Even though a culture has been destroyed, its remnants remain as a sub-culture within the dominant society. This was particularly the case with the old religions of Western Europe which became absorbed by Christianity and industralization. In rural England and Europe, Christmas "guizers" still go wassailing and offer liquid libations to the spirits of trees in the name of "tradition." While megaliths like Stonehenge and the carved white horses are reminders of the old religion, the Mummers' Plays keep the old rituals alive: the St. George plays repeat the ancient death and resurrection theme, while the Wooing plays (or Plough plays) enact the residues of the sacred marriage. Animal disguise is also carried on in many rural areas of which the Mari Lwyd of South Wales, the Old Hoss of Padstow (Cornwall) and the Sailors' Horse of Minehead (Somerset) are the most famous today.[24]

A further residual form of cultural drama is the dramatic customs and games of children. The English song and round dance game "Old Roger is Dead," for example, is a remnant of both the death and resurrection theme and the sacred marriage.[25]

RITES OF MODERNIZATION

One way in which a new culture demonstrates that it is viable is for its ceremonies to provide a new form of social cohesion and to give the individual a strong sense of social identity. This seems to be the case, for example, with *ludruk*, the proletarian drama of modern Java. In 1963 there were 594 ludruk troupes officially registered in Java; but on major feast days, there were about 300 such troupes performing in Surabaja alone—to a total audience of about 120,000 per night, or about one-eighth of the population of this East Java port. The ludruk provides rites of modernization for an ancient culture in contact with modern industrialization in three ways:

> First, it helps ludruk participants (when I use this term, I mean spectators as well as actors) to apprehend modernization movements in terms of vivid and meaningful *symbolic classifications*; second, it seduces ludruk participants into empathy with modes of *social action* involved in the modernization process; third, it involves the participants in aesthetic

forms that structure their most general thoughts and feelings in ways stimulating to the modernization process.[26]

It is a very popular theatrical form which, in addition to its aesthetic appeal, has evolved as a major way in which members of a dominated culture can adjust to one that dominates it.

Analysis of Dynamics

The dramatic qualities of rites of intensification and passage overlap considerably. Indeed, in many traditional societies a performance of a particular ritual myth may have elements of both within it.[27] Primarily, however, the concept of these two types of rites is a form of categorization which allows scholars to comprehend the dynamics of specific cultures.

Figure 5 illustrates one method of analysing the dynamics of a culture in dramatic terms. This shows that rites of intensification, rites of passage and the degree of acculturation can each be examined in terms of the life crises of a culture. The life crises between birth and death can be considered in at least three dramatic types:

1/*Patterns of mothering*: Each culture has its own patterns of mothering between permissive and severe, and these are reflected in rituals.[28]

	LIFE CRISES			
	1 PATTERNS OF MOTHERING	2 PATTERNS OF PLAY	3A PATTERNS OF CEREMONIAL	3B PATTERNS OF ART AND THEATRE
INTENSIFICATION				
PASSAGE				
DEGREE OF ACCULTURATION (dominated/ dominant)				

Figure 5: Method of Analysing the Dynamics of Cultural Drama.

2 / *Patterns of play*: Cultures vary as to whether the play of children is permissive or is severely controlled, and these appear to be related to the earlier patterns of mothering. Ritualized forms of play reflect these patterns.[29]

3 / *Patterns of ceremonial, and/or art and theatre*: The separation of art and theatre from the ceremonial ritual myths has only occurred in modern cultures (that is, from the Renaissance). Prior to that in Western Europe (as well as in many contemporary cultures elsewhere) all aspects of artistic expression were part of the people's ceremonial life. In medieval Europe, for example, the great Mystery Cycles were originally an inherent part of religious ceremonial; only in their later stages did they become increasingly secular. Modern traditional societies do not have a separate category for "art." Many find it difficult to understand why tourists collect their ceremonial objects which, by their very nature, are useless when separated from their ceremonial use. As the Balinese say, "We do not have any art, we just do everything very well."

Each culture has its own patterns of ceremonial and/or art and theatre. With hunter/gatherers there is *only* ceremonial which is always sacred. Modern industrial cultures make a categorical difference between ceremonial rituals (which can be sacred or profane) and those of art and theatre (which are almost entirely secular).

This method of analysis can be illustrated by the three Amerindian peoples who inhabit Vancouver Island: the Southern Kwakiutl to the north; the Nootka to the west; and the Coast Salish to the south and east. The two former have occupied their tribal lands for thousands of years, and are traditionally fishermen and whalers. The Coast Salish were relative newcomers to the coast when Captain Cook appeared off Nootka Sound in 1778. They were primarily river and in-shore fishermen. All three groups also engaged in hunting and gathering.[30]

Analysis of the dramatic dynamics of these people show that, prior to white contact, the Coast Salish were dominated by the other two groups. Aboriginally, the Coast Salish had only two major ceremonial forms, the "spirit dance" and the feast. They used no masks but, just before white contact, they had taken over some of their neighbors: a group near the Southern Kwakiutl (the Comox) had incorporated some of the masks and the ceremonials of their northerly neighbors; others adjacent to the Nootka had taken over the latter's "crawling wolf" performance where the actor crawled on all fours and wore a snapping mask of a wolf. In addition, during the early nineteenth century, the whole Coast

Salish people was pervaded by a new and original mask (the only ceremonial mask they created) in imitation of their neighbors: the gigantic *Xwe-Xwe* mask which, in a kind of cultural feed-back, became acculturated to some of the Southern Kwakiutl.

Prior to white contact, all three peoples had patterns of mothering and of play that were much more lax than in European cultures. Yet there was a difference: the Coast Salish were more permissive compared with their neighbors.

From the late eighteenth century, the immigrant English-speaking culture became increasingly dominant over all three indigenous peoples. The white culture had its own rites of intensification and passage (largely Christian) and there were real attempts to destroy the ritual-myths of the Indian peoples—in economic, social, political and even punitive ways. By the 1920s the ceremonial life of the Indians was at a very low ebb and they were suffering severe cultural distortion: patterns of mothering and play were much more inhibiting, the population was decimated, many were living in poverty in white communities, and the great dramatic ceremonies were performed rarely and in secret.

Since that time, however, the Indian peoples have shown signs of adapting their original way of life within the dominant culture. While patterns of mothering and play have maintained much of the severity of the whites, there has been a steady resurgence of ceremonial life. Yet the same people who engage in dramatic ceremonies can also be fully professional artists in the white man's world. Many Indians worship as Christians on Sunday morning and attend traditional ceremonies in the longhouse all through the Saturday night. A Coast Salish Indian who is a taxi-driver in the modern city of Victoria can, from Saturday dusk to Sunday dawn, be a "spirit dancer" and be fully possessed.

A culture that has been isolated from others for a lengthy period of time can develop strong ritual patterns. We can illustrate this in two cultures: the Southern Kwakiutl and Nootka in prehistory, and in late nineteenth-century Britain (as compared with the rest of Europe) where there had been considerable isolation and ritual stability for a long time. Middle-class patterns dominated British culture: the ancient pagan rites were only pursued in remote rural areas while contact with the peoples of the Empire had been as the dominant culture. A century later, however, after two world wars and the collapse of the Empire, successive waves of immigrants from the West Indies, Africa and Asia have broken down many of the cultural rituals that appeared very stable only years before.

When culture contact occurs, two major patterns emerge:

1 / the dominant culture assimilates some of the dramatic traits of the dominated culture (as the Southern Kwakiutl absorbed the *Xwe-Xwe* mask of the Coast Salish, and as Christianized Britain absorbed paganism);

2 / the dominated culture remains in some subsumed form, either as an underlying strain within the major culture (as has happened with some Indian rituals in British Columbia, and as with rural folk festivals in Britain); or as a strong sub-culture within the dominant group (as may be happening with more remote Indian groups on Vancouver Island, and as with some West Indians in modern British cities).

Developmental Stages of Cultural Drama

Dramatic and Theatrical Criteria

Within the rituals of any culture, there are specific dramatic and theatrical criteria which enable us to "map" its development: acting, acting area, costume and decor.

ACTING

The nature of the performer and the style of acting used varies from culture to culture. In a tribal culture, everyone engages in the religious rituals in one way or another; even when a specific group is performing (as with secret societies) they are doing so *on behalf of* the whole community while the others, *witnessing* the performance (in the biblical sense), are sharing in it. In the ancient agricultural societies of the Near East this changed and king-priests became the actors of the rituals, some of them "secret" and hidden from the people; in Athens during the 5th century B.C., this evolved into the first theatre forms of tragic, comic and satyric plays as religious performances. Thereafter the male professional actor emerged, followed much later by the actress.

Styles of human performance vary between the poles of possession and distancing. Shamans and hunters dance in possession; their acting is called *mimesis*—simple imitation of the "spirit" without necessarily any outward appearance of what is being imitated. Priests in the ancient Near East steadily decreased the level of possession and increased distancing from the role; at this stage, *mime* evolved—the imitation had to be an accurate reflection of what was imitated. In contrast, modern European theatre actors have increased their distancing from the role, some less (as with Stanislavsky) and some more (as with Brecht).

ACTING AREA

The nature and shape of the performance space varies with cultures between *arena, open* and *end* shapes.

Most tribal societies dance in arena shapes, in the middle of a group of non-performing "witnesses" who completely surround them. The most common is a circle of approximately 50-60 feet in diameter,[31] although other shapes occur, such as the square or rectangle with the audience on all four sides. Modern Coast Salish Indians dance in a circle around central fires on the earth floor of a longhouse, while the Marshfield Mummers perform their play in various circles as they proceed from station to station in the village of Marshfield, Gloucestershire, England.

Open shapes are horseshoes or semicircles where the actors have their backs to a screen, curtain or wall of a temple and the audience sits or stands around them in a semicircle. This was the shape of ancient Near East performances and the theatres in Greece and Rome. Similar shapes are used today amongst the Southern Kwakiutl on Vancouver Island, with the Kathakali theatre in Kerala, southern India, and in the great Tibetan festivals.

End shapes are those where the performers act at one end of a large space and the audience stand or sit on one side only. Sometimes the audience is raised and the performers are at floor level; at other times, the actors are on a stage and the audience are on the flat; at other times, as with modern Western playhouses, both actors and audience are raised but at different levels. In many modern playhouses, a proscenium arch is sited between the actors and the audience so that the latter look through "a picture frame" into the performance. Proscenium arches developed in the Renaissance when they were sited half-way back on an open stage; only by the middle of the nineteenth century was the forestage abolished and all action placed behind the arch.

COSTUME

The nature and style of the decoration of face, head and body varies from culture to culture. Tribal cultures use facial painting, masks, tattooing, scarring, headdresses and costumes for the purpose of "being" the particular spirit that they enact. Each part of the decoration is an attribute of the specific spirit. In agricultural societies, ancient and modern, masks and costumes are hieratic: priestly decorations that represent the awesome power of the gods. Attributes that are worn or carried become symbolic. From the Renaissance onwards, Western European cultures have increased the realism of the costume. In Elizabethan England, *Julius Caesar* was performed in contemporary dress, but by the nineteenth century, accurate Roman costumes were used.

DECOR

The nature and type of scenecraft and effects varies according to each culture. Tribal peoples view the acting space as "a place of power"—the abode of the spirits. Thus any scenecraft is purely functional on behalf of the spirits. The longhouse of the Coast Salish is viewed as an *imago mundi* which the spirits actually inhabit during the performance; thus scenery is hardly ever used, except with the *Xwe-Xwe* dance where the performers usually wait in a small "tent" made of cloth in the corner of the longhouse.

Once a society is economically based upon the harvest (of the land or sea) decor can be used whereby the *imago mundi* of the performing space symbolically represents the world of the gods. Thus the Attic theatre developed the *skene* building to these ends, using doors, curtains and other items in a symbolic manner. Likewise, the Southern Kwakiutl (who harvested the sea, and whose abundance of food enabled them to have the leisure to develop their ceremonials) used remarkable decor and effects for highly complicated illusions: masks that opened to reveal other masks within them, puppets that moved and flew around the longhouse, decapitations and burials, moving monsters that filled the whole end of the longhouse, painted curtains, and large screens that divided into four (the bottom two disappearing into the ground and the top two sliding sideways) to reveal another scenic effect within.

From the Renaissance to the present day, Western European styles of theatre have increasingly become realistic. These industrial societies increasingly developed the ability of machines so that, more and more, decor and effects have become nearer to real life.

Cultural Dramatic Stages

These four criteria can be related to the dramatic dynamics of a culture and a series of developmental stages of cultural drama and theatre emerge:

Tribal cultures;
Agricultural cultures; and
Industrial cultures.

This is illustrated in Figure 6.

It should be emphasized that these three developmental stages,

CULTURE STYLE	RELIGION	PER-FORMERS	ACTING STYLE	ACTING AREA	COSTUME	DECOR	HISTORICAL EXAMPLES	MODERN EXAMPLES
TRIBAL CULTURES oral media	Supernatural beings. Ritual myth of creation. Shamanism.	The People. Sharing with the community.	Possession. Mimesis.	Arena circle. Audience in 360°. Places of power.	Face painting. Masks. Magical attributes & dress	Simple symbols in circle as "the centre of the world"	Paleolithic.	Siberians, Ainu, Inuit, Bushmen, Australian aboriginals, Amerindians (most).
							OVERLAP WITH AGRICULTURAL	Pueblo Indians
AGRICULTURAL CULTURES oral & written media	Seasonal ritual myths. Gods. Priests.	King-priests, assistant priests. On behalf of the community.	Mix: possession/distancing. Mime.	Open horseshoe. Audience on 3 sides in or in front of temples.	Hieratic masks & costumes. Symbolic attributes & dress.	Complex illusion. Representing the life of the gods.	Mesopotamia, India, Egypt, Greece. Classic India, China, Japan. Maya, Aztec, Inca. Middle Ages.	S. Kwakiutl Indians, Bali Witch Play, Kathakali, Tibet Festival Drama, Royal Theatre of Cambodia.
							OVERLAP WITH INDUSTRIAL	Noh & Kabuki, Peking Opera.
INDUSTRIAL CULTURES print & electronic media	Secular.	Professional actors & actresses. Communication with audience.	Distancing. Realistic.	End (incl. proscenium). Audience on 1 side in secular playhouse.	Realistic appearance.	Realism. Representing everyday life.	Develops from Renaissance to 20th century Europe & America.	Modern industrial theatre, film, radio & television.

Figure 6: Cultural Development of Drama.

like those of personal development, are not absolute categories into which any type can be slotted. Rather, they represent a cultural typology of three abstract or ideal types to which any real culture can be related. Each culture, like each individual, remains unique and few existing cultures would perfectly match one of the types. Nor does this typology imply a hierarchy of culture styles. There is no intention of suggesting that one culture is better or worse in its drama than another—merely that there are some basic differences between them.

Finally, although historical and modern examples are given of the three culture styles within the typology, each of the examples has radical differences from the next. Thus, although many Siberian peoples and most Amerindians share specific dramatic traits as tribal cultures, they each have individual traits not shared by others. These differences will be demonstrated in an analysis of cultural dynamics (as in Figure 5) rather than in a typology (as in Figure 6).

Conclusion

Developmental Drama is the study of developmental patterns in human enactment. This chapter has outlined the dynamics and developmental stages of the human drama both in terms of the person and in terms of his cultural context. The overall parameters of this study are given in Figure 7.

The concept of Developmental Drama is useful in a variety of ways. First, it has direct bearing upon education in the widest sense of the term. The process of human learning from birth to death, conceived in a dramatic context, is a productive and positive framework. It assumes that *homo sapiens* is an intentional species which re-creates meaning out of experience. The onus for learning is therefore firmly based upon the individual person. Second, the concept of Developmental Drama has particular implications for the use of dramatic education within all educational institutions. Dramatic action is a vital way to approach the specific learnings required in schooling; thus it is directly related to motivation (see Chapter 2), the transfer of learning (Chapter 3), instruction (Chapter 4) as well as the nature of curriculum. A teacher in Victoria, British Columbia, can within the same classroom have children from a variety of cultural backgrounds: various European groups, several types of Indians, and Chinese from Hong Kong and Taiwan. Similarly a teacher in one of the great multicultural cities of the world can have a classroom of children from multifarious cul-

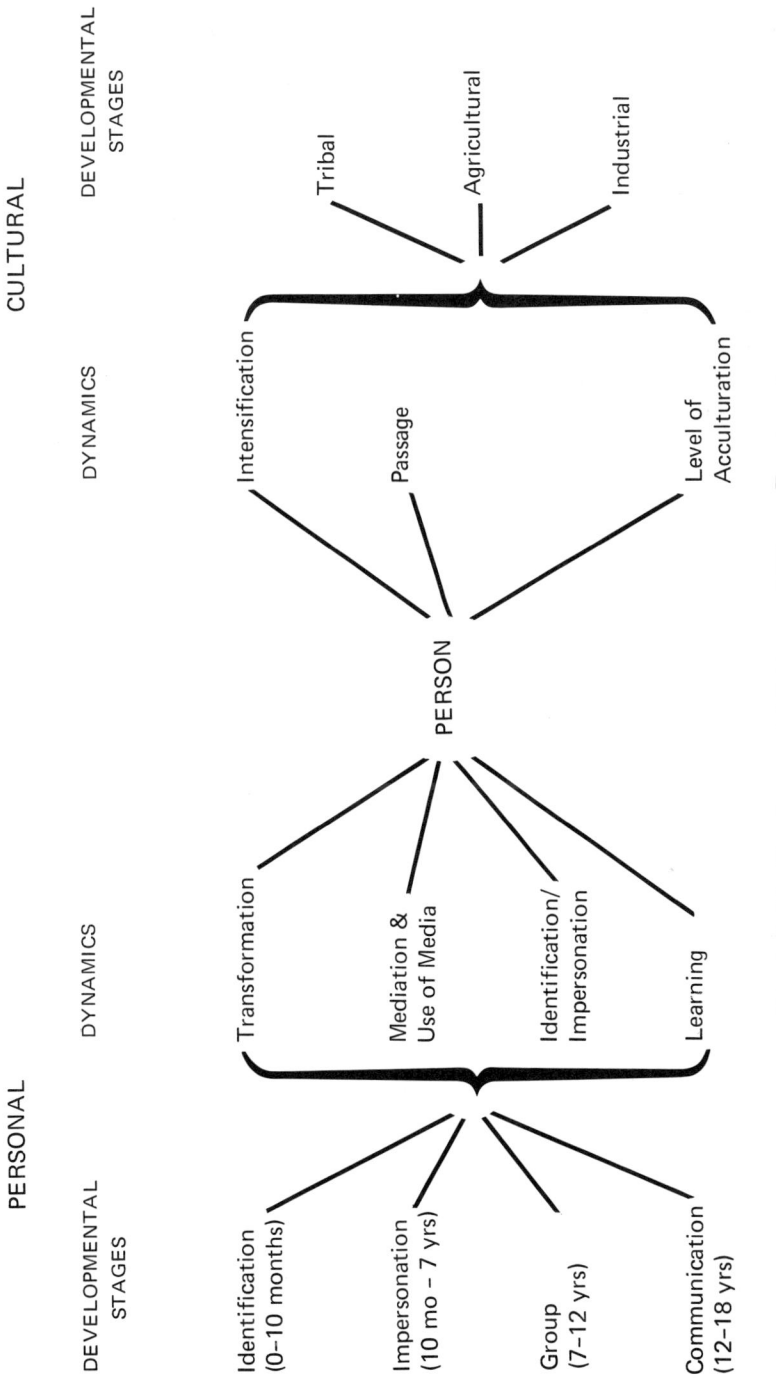

Figure 7: The Developmental Patterns of Human Enactment.

tures.[32] Unless he or she understands not only the personal nature of drama but also the ethnological backgrounds of these diverse students, the teacher can vastly misconstrue students' natural dramatic actions. Third, the concept of Developmental Drama can be seen as an underpinning to the nature of theatre. The human dramatic process outcrops as an art form in theatre—plays performed in a playhouse—together with its substitutes in electric media (radio, film and television). Theatre is the art form of the dramatic process that is studied by Developmental Drama.

By re-playing his experience, the human being re-cognizes it— in other words, re-creates it so that it is given genuine meaning both personally and culturally. Thus, in the final analysis, *we* are responsible for human existence.

Chapter 2
Human Dynamics: Drama and Motivation

"The central nervous system is not normally inert, having to be prodded into activity by specific stimuli external to it. Rather it is in a state of continuous activity."
—*R. A. Hinde*

"What motivates the student to learn?" is a classic question in education. But it always puzzled me when I was a teacher of drama and the arts in schools. During spontaneous drama lessons, I rarely had to consider the question. Almost every child I have ever taught seemed to be self-motivated. Unlike some other teachers, I did not have to think up methods to create motivation in the students. Whether improvising in social studies, or spontaneously dancing, or creating "soundscapes" with a tape recorder, their enthusiasm and interest was obvious and, on occasion, their concentration could be electrifying.

The situation was similar when I was teaching the other creative arts. It was less so when I was concerned with artistic appreciation, and least in non-arts subjects such as mathematics and science. Why? I thought for a while that it was because I taught some things better than others. However, as I listened to teachers talking, questions of motivation hardly ever occurred in conversations about the creative arts. When creative arts teachers (as opposed to those who taught arts appreciation) did raise problems of motivation they were often more concerned with the sequencing of knowledge rather than with spontaneity—with insisting on the skills the students must know (it was said) rather than allowing skills to emerge according to need. A related problem was with those teachers who assumed that "drama" was synonymous with "theatre" and tried to teach theatre skills to the many when they were appropriate only for the few. With these exceptions, motivation was not a prime issue amongst creative arts teachers. Yet it was a constant element in the talk of other teachers. Why?

It was not that the interests of teachers determine student motivation. After all, I was just as interested in history as in visual art. Also, one of the most committed and learned geographers in my experience could never capture the interest of his classes.

Was it the emotional climate of the classroom? Was it, perhaps, that students who constantly write and listen in other classrooms secure relief when they can sing, dance, act or paint? All these factors have some relevance, no doubt, but they do not reach the crux of the question.

Clearly there is something about spontaneous dramatic activity (whether as subject or method) and the creative arts in general that provides a motivation to learn which is concentrated and persistent, and which provides learnings in other content areas through transfer. Also, these qualities are not necessarily present in other curriculum areas to the same extent and the same degree.

This chapter will examine some of the concerns raised by this issue. I shall first look at the most important of the theories of motivation in order to see what assistance they can be. Thereafter, I shall examine imagination and dramatic activity in the context of motivational theory. Finally, I shall attempt to draw conclusions for the practice of education.

Theories of Motivation

Can theories of motivation help us? A survey of those most currently used in education—experimentalism, ego psychology, competence theory and holism—shows that while each is a partial help, no single theory appears to cover all cases.

Much depends on the model used. For those in experimental and Freudian psychology, it is a *machine*: the human being is viewed as an inert mechanism that requires fuel (drives, instincts) to activate it. For competence theorists, motivation is provided by *an attitude of mind*, a particular mental quality. For holists, motivation springs from the inherent *human ability to develop potential*. None of these theories can account for all cases. Also, as we shall see, each is inadequate to account for the inherent motivation of spontaneous drama and creative arts activities.

Experimental Psychology

Carlyle described the nineteenth century as "the Age of Machinery in every outward and inward sense of that word." Out of John Stuart Mill's mechanistic empiricism has evolved the classic position of modern experimental psychology: that nature is inert and people only engage in purposeful activity if they are driven. Primary drives (hunger, thirst, sex and the avoidance of pain) are thought to link by association to secondary drives (money, good marks in school, etc.). Teaching therefore becomes the rewarding of secondary drives. When this does not work, harsh punishment is meted out so that the student will avoid pain. On this view, the difference between the educational attitude of Mr. Squeers and B. F. Skinner is one of degree.

For simple mechanists, instincts determine drives and motives and this has support from animal psychology. Others vary the theory: drive is the spark that activates the nervous system, which is described as "an engine but not a steering gear"; or there is said to be a general drive which can be altered by individual drive manipulations.[1]

Most modern experimentalists consider that goals are reinforcers.[2] Teachers who follow these theorists use positive reinforcers to increase the future possibility of a response, and negative reinforcers to decrease it. The Puritan, John Milton, put it another way:

What reinforcement we may gain from hope
If not what resolution from despair.

Others say it more subtly: Skinner relies on the effects of stimuli upon behavior; Hull, on the other hand, attributes all reinforcement to the single mechanism of drive-stimulus—or, as Miller and Dollard have put it, non-reward is punishment while relief from pain is a reward. But such a puritanical statement is open to two serious criticisms: while anxiety can help immediate repetitive learning, it can reduce permanent long-term learning;[3] and anxiety can cause moral confusion—or, as Saki said, "I think she must have been strictly brought up, she's so desperately anxious to do the wrong things correctly."

Even experimental studies have shown that punishment does not necessarily rob an act of its inherent fascination for either children or adults. It is only when an act or an object is no longer felt to satisfy a positive need that it ceases to be of interest. What punishment may do, instead, is to make a person choose a behavior that is circumspect.[4]

Yet it is true, as Henry Reed wrote, that "If one doesn't get birthday presents it can remobilize very painfully the persecutory anxiety which usually follows birth." Less categoric views of reinforcement are therefore more helpful: that novelty is motivating; that reward systems are built into the brain; and that incongruity provides significant motivation—in moderation, as too much may be overwhelming and too little is boring.[5] Carlow shows that the use of incongruity requires greater teacher sensitivity to the student's needs than is the case with more extreme experimental theories.[6]

Sensory stimulation can be a major determinant of reinforcement.[7] In other words, motivation is not an unsophisticated drive mechanism, nor should it be used as a moral excuse for punishment. Rather, it is a highly complex issue involving the relationship of teacher and student, the nature of incongruity, and a dependence upon the individual's sensory awareness.

However, it is Mowrer who, by injecting concepts from ego psychology, provides a synthetic experimental theory which relates directly to spontaneous drama and the arts. The only way in which reinforcement can be effective, he says, is through *identification*—"reward from another organism, or 'parent person'." He gives a "two factor theory": continuity, where the learner becomes "glad to see" the teacher, so that the teacher's presence has secondary reward value; and reward, where the student models himself upon the teacher which, also, is rewarding.[8] While these factors have their place in creative arts education, they are best examined in the context of ego psychology.

Ego Psychology

Freud considered that the human machine was motivated by the fuel of instincts: until 1914, he said these were sex and hunger; later they became love and hate. While we may not agree with Julian Mitchell that "Freud is all nonsense: the secret of neurosis is to be found in the family battle of wills to see who can refuse longest to help with the dishes," his theory of instincts is unrefined.

More importantly, Freud said that the values of the model are internalized in two forms of *identification*: developmental, where through fear of losing the mother's love, the child introjects her qualities; and defensive, where through fear of punishment, the child identifies with the father in the Oedipus complex.

As developed by later workers, these two forms have implications for dramatic play. In developmental identification P. D. Courtney's concept of mediation is significant: in the child's mind, the mother becomes the link, or mediator, between his wants and their satisfaction. In other words, the mother's attributes take on secondary reward value so he comes to identify with her. As Gabriel Fielding put it, "Men fight in the last resort to impress their mothers."

Others have proposed that defensive identification becomes an independent motivation. By impersonating the aggressor, the child transforms himself from the person threatened into the person who makes the threat—which is not merely identification but also impersonation.[9] We shall examine the significance of this later.

However, ego psychology can only attribute aesthetic motivation to sublimation. Art, for Freud, is merely the redirection of neurotic fantasy into more productive fields. But art really cannot be accounted for by an appeal to something else. Art, quite simply, *is*. "The whole of art is an appeal to a reality which is not without us but in our minds," as Desmond MacCarthy said, yet this reality is not primarily neurotic. It is ruled by imagination, as we shall see.

Competence

Robert W. White said that human beings have an inherent drive towards competence, and this is the basic motivation in all things. He showed that there is support for this from a variety of psychological fields: from experimentalism—as curiosity, exploration, the need for activity, and manipulation; from ego psychology—as mastery, success, motility, and initiative and industry; and from general psychology—as novelty, stimulation and excitement, the visceral, the active and the sensory, hedonism, and the ability to maintain relations with the environment.[10]

White coordinates all these views and gives a motivational theory of *competence or effectance*. He assumes a drive towards efficiency that satisfies "an intrinsic need to deal with the environment." This is demonstrated in grasping, exploring, walking, talking and thinking—in fact, in any activity that promotes a competent interaction with the environment. The major educational problem with this theory, however, is that teachers find it far too inclusive. As Laurence J. Peter commented, "Competence, like truth, beauty and contact lenses, is in the eyes of the beholder."

At least it has the virtues of simplicity. It leads Sutton-Smith to say that "effectance motivation would seem to be at the root of competence as a personality trait."[11] Human beings need to *act* in order to produce an effect, and this ability is strengthened by early encouragement and independence—which increases motives to learn in school.[12] This personality trait can be accelerated by spontaneous art; pre-school children who engage in such creative activities become less dependent on their parents, and ask for less help from them.[13] Children who are encouraged by their mothers to act effectively achieve more in school, and this persists throughout life.[14]

Competence theorists advocate an education that is based on intrinsic motivation—a system of self-reward.[15] Spontaneous drama and art activities assist such a process. Yet if motives are to be deeply embedded in the personality they must be autoplastic: they must be affective before they are cognitive, ontological before they are epistemological.[16] This leads us naturally to holism.

Holism

Holistic thinkers approach motives from a total human spectrum. They do not acknowledge any isolated drive or instinct, and they deny dichotomies. Goldstein said that there is a total human motivation towards completing what is incomplete—what he called "self-actualization."

The holistic tradition has grown in importance in the latter half of the twentieth century. Adler in his later years approached this position. Carl Rogers believed that each organism has a tendency to express and activate all its capacities. And Assagioli assumed that all higher motives contained an aesthetic component. On this view, learning occurs when:

1 / the student is faced by a problem that is meaningful to him;

2 / the teacher is congruent in the relationship;

3 / the student experiences the teacher's congruence, acceptance and empathy.

This centring upon the student's personality is far from the experimentalist's reward and punishment.

Maslow states the classic position on motivation. For him, the experimentalist starts from animals and Freud from the mentally sick. He, in contrast, begins from mental health—from those who are self-fulfilling. Motivation is total: a person's whole being is motivated, and it is unusual to have merely one motivation. Motivations are made up of a complex of needs, of which there are two broad types: (1) basic needs which only become motives when they are deficient—the physiological, those of psychological safety, love needs, esteem, self-actualizing needs, curiosity, and the aesthetic needs which build a healthy self-image; and (2) meta-needs to which all human beings should aspire—wholeness, perfection, completion and the like. Because motives are made up of a complex of such needs, Maslow emphasizes an education that develops potential: to be more human, to understand the self, and to relate to others.

Clearly, while ego psychology merely helps us to relate drama and identification, and competence theory lacks specificity, holism gives importance to the motivation provided by drama and the creative arts. Brian Way agrees with Maslow when he says that spontaneous play and drama develop more of people than of drama, and that all educational activities should "start from where we are." Drama aims to see reality whole. Creative arts assist self-actualization in specific ways: they simultaneously develop self-discipline and, within the objectives of the lesson (a safety need), they provide freedom of choice. When the teacher provides the "What" and the student the "How," a mutual respect grows between teacher and student: the child's "internal wisdom" is respected, and he learns both an internal discipline and a respect for others—which is the basis of a value system. The group creative arts (drama, music, dance) are genuinely social; they encourage a respect for the creation of others, unselfish cooperation and generosity. While dramatic skills are significant, they are less important than the development of judgment, taste, knowledge of how to live—the attributes, in fact, of the self-actualizer.

Maslow and advocates for the creative arts would agree that aesthetic needs are key to the self-actualizing process. This is a belief in creative activity as a necessary component of human existence. In this spontaneous context, aesthetic percipience also becomes motivating:

> The end product of aesthetic perceiving, of non-abstracting, is the total inventory of the percept, in which everything is apt to be equally savored, and in which evaluations of more important and less important tend to be given up. Here greater richness of the percept is sought for rather than greater simplifying and skeletonizing.[17]

In such ways, holism supports drama and creative arts in order to satisfy needs. Newer studies have amplified these issues. Severin has discussed the relation of drama and self-actualization, while Huntsman studied the effect of improvisation upon the self-actualization of college-age students. She concluded that it had a positive influence on their self-confidence and spontaneity, but less impact upon their self-worth and ability to relate to others.

Yet holism does not account for *why* drama appears to have greater motivational force than other approaches. Perhaps some help can be given by two modes that are allied to holism, the gestalt and the existential.

Gestalt thinkers place everything in the context of the present *now* seen as "figure and ground," denying categorization. In other words, we apprehend things not in categories but in relationship to one another—and in immediate experience. Children draw what they *see*, not what they *know*. For Gestalt thinkers, therefore, existence is meaningful first in direct experience and only secondarily through comprehension; "sense" comes before "making sense." The "hands on" experience of creative arts is prior to intellectualization.

For existentialists, motives depend upon the inner "reality" of the individual; consciousness is whole and goes beyond supposed dichotomies (body/mind, affective/cognitive, intuitive/rational, etc.). Thus who a person *is* motivates his explorations of the world.

While education is the encounter of student and teacher, the students' learning is motivated by three things: their Being, their encounter with the subject matter, and their encountering of each other. It is implied that those methods and subject matters which touch inner "reality" will produce the greatest motivation; but what these are in motivational terms is not stated by existentialists. Despite the fact that many existentialists are also artists (specifically, dramatists), nowhere is it said that artistic spontaneity has the closest possible relationship with our inner world. The nearest they can get is when Rollo May says that a sense of self must precede "doing" and that doing occurs before thinking; and when Winnicott can postulate the learning sequence, "I am, I do, I create."

Organism and Imagination

The Organism Model

To account for motivation we need a model that obeys the parameters of life, specifically human life. Such is the model of the living organism. Any significant model in our time must relate to Einsteinian physics: it must, in other words, allow for our individual "frames of reference" of the external world. It must relate to who we *are*. It must also obey the findings of biology. This demonstrates that any organism is a unified whole which has tension between its allied parts. That this tension has specific human effects is shown by modern psychobiology:

> Evolution appears to be more than the mere product of chance governed by profit. It seems a cornucopia of *evolution creatrice*, a drama full of suspense, of dynamics and tragic complications. Life spirals laboriously upwards to higher and even higher levels, paying for each step.[18]

Just as the atom has within it component parts which, if split, release great energy, so the organism has fields of force and energy in its very nature. Chinese philosophy holds that there are two organic energies in polar relationship to one another. Most modern Western thinkers would accept the fundamental proposition that energy is involved in all the processes of life—in moving, feeling and thinking. Even the experimentalist Hebb recognized that all depends on the natural activity of the nervous system; that the nerve-cell has no need for external excitation to become active. Nuttin has rephrased the issue this way:

> This active, persistent and selective purposiveness which characterizes behaviour is the basic motivational phenomenon which appears in many forms according to the kind of conduct (innate or acquired, for example) and the level of the development of the organism. This conception implies that motivation is at the same time a source of activity and of direction; or, more precisely, it defines conduct as a directed activity. These two aspects, the dynamic and the purposive, have too often been separated in the study of motivation.[19]

This indicates that, provided the right environmental conditions satisfy basic needs, the human organism contains the energy that gives it motive. That each organism differs is axiomatic: individual differences depend on unique mental structures. Thus each person will display different motives. Yet, insofar as all human beings are organisms, they will have common and shared motives.

Nissen has suggested that every organ is self-motivating. It has to exercise the functions of which it is capable. In this sense, cognitive motivation would stem from the needs of the cell tissue in the brain and nervous system generally. Its function is "to know" and it tends to act immediately on its knowledge. Years ago, Adler said that some activities occurred through a tendency towards exercise for exercise's sake. But function as an end in itself does not explain the interest in the specific activity or object. In other words, the psychochemical activity of the nerve-cell and the act of knowing are not identical.[20] The organism model can only be explained in terms of imagination and action.

The organism model is directly opposed to mechanist models even though it can incorporate parts of them—identification, for example.

It provides competence theorists with an adequate matrix. The inherent energy of the organism incorporates attitudes like curiosity, manipulation and hedonism. Specifically, it allows for relationships with the environment: the organism acts in order to maintain its own equilibrium between inner and outer—this is

Winnicott's essential point, that play is the human way to relate inner needs and the demands of the environment.

Although not exactly the same as holism, the organism model relates closely to it. The energies of the organism are directed towards satisfying its inherent potential. What provides the frame of reference for our gestalt of figure-and-ground is the specific balance of the energies of the organism. Our inner reality places the greatest significance upon the experiences which relate most closely to our own inherent tensions.

The organism model stresses action. An organism must act by mediating with the environment, and it does so in any one or all of three directions: to change the environment; to generate new encounters; and to shift the focus of sensory awareness.

Action can be direct or indirect. Initial actions tend to be direct and overt, but they change as the organism matures, when they become more indirect and covert. The "hands on" experience is the precursor of criticism and percipience. Within indirect and covert actions are embedded other meanings—those of previous direct and overt actions. It is in the direct act that motivation tends to propel the organism spontaneously, and it is this spontaneity that allows us to make an adequate response to a new situation, or a new response to an old situation.[21]

Activity seems linked to the very life of the organism in the same way as respiration and other biological adaptations. The degree of general activity of the organism can vary considerably according to certain well-defined conditions; of these, the motivational state is usually revealed by increased activity. The need for activity and movement shows itself as soon as an obstacle tries to intervene.[22] To conceive of ways of overcoming an obstacle is, specifically, the province of imaginative thought. It is the nature, style and degree of imagining that characterizes the differences in energies of one human organism from another. Yet imagining is only one of a number of states of Being.

States of Being

Motives arise from Being. They are centred within the tensions of the conscious organism—within the "I am" as related to the world. At the nub of consciousness lies this *relationship*. How A relates to B and C relates to D is not a cause-and-effect relation; it is an awareness of the tensions that oscillate between parts. It enables us to discover our particular powers, whether in the satisfactions of harmony or the dissatisfactions of discord. It is the necessary precondition of all action.

This relationship operates in different modes, in five states of Being: living, remembering, imagining, dreaming and fantasizing.

These are specifically not separate categories. They are overlapping styles of operation which mix according to the needs of the individual organism. Each state works with images and imaginings (see pp. 7–8). It is the use that each state makes of these elements that differs. This is largely controlled by emotions—feeling gives meaning to a state. In this sense we can say that Being is a meaning-giving operation.

Dreaming, remembering, living and imagining interrelate productively and contribute to each other. Fantasy does not; it draws off energy that could be used in other states. Three are states of time: remembering is of the past, living is of the present, and imagining is of the future. But dreaming and fantasizing are not; both use images formed in the past, but the states themselves are suspended in time.

REMEMBERING

Remembering works with the existing materials of consciousness. It brings back the images and imaginings we have previously created. As a result, it is constantly used by other states. But recall does not simply bring back "the facts." It places past images within the context of the present. In other words, memory is a lesser form of re-play: what we remember is re-created according to the needs of the present.

LIVING

Living is the state with which we work in the everyday world. It has, falsely, all the appearance of being objective. It uses sensory data and tries to analyse them rationally. Yet although the living state has more objectivity than dreaming, remembering and imagining, it places the objective within a subjective matrix. It is set within felt-time and felt-space so that it is Being which provides reason with meaning. In McLuhan's terms, living is as much spatial as linear or, as D. H. Lawrence put it, "Life makes no absolute statement."

DREAMING

Scott Fitzgerald said that dreaming is like living with the mainspring taken out. It uses the undifferentiated materials of consciousness and connects them in metaphoric ways. Dream works poetically or, as J. A. Hadfield would have it, like a drama. It relates inner and outer symbolically; it associates past, present and future in the same manner that poetry uses metaphor. Within dream, however, the self cannot distinguish between subject and object.

FANTASIZING

Fantasy is a dissociated state; it exists for itself. It consumes energy required by the other states yet it does not contribute to them. Consciousness, Peter Redgrove says, "does not need to spend itself on fancy and the empty air." But fantasy becomes the dominant state for some disturbed persons.

IMAGINING

Conan Doyle said that if there was no imagination there would be no horror: it simply could not be conceived of. Imagining is the uniquely human state. Human beings can suppose; they can postulate, create designs or theories and test them out, and even reject them if they fail. Even in abstraction they can compare possibilities.

The major characteristic of imagining is "as if" thinking. This is based on the ability to "put oneself in someone else's place," which is essentially a dramatic act. It can lead us to see both sides of a question, and the tensions between them. Eventually it can lead us to envisage a whole variety of possibilities within a situation.

Imagining is the prime mode whereby we relate subject and object. It takes elements of the environment and re-creates them subjectively. Thereafter, all other states can work with the results. By re-creating the objective, it is the foundation of symbol formation.

Imagining plans for the future. It sets up possibilities and tries them out in action, overtly or covertly. It eclectically uses elements from all other states, unifying them into new elements. By focusing on possibility, bringing about actions that are future-oriented, it also re-creates genuine human meaning. Imagining creates meaning in a unique manner. We transform elements of the environment into images which are then grouped and combined in particular ways. Mind then gives these imaginings meaning: it gives direction to the organismic tensions and provides a focus for their energy. Thus *imagining provides the dynamism for areas of new possibility, for overcoming obstacles, in which varieties of new imaginings can work.* This is the essential motivational quality of re-play: it re-creates the images of experience within an imaginative context so that we can conceive possibilities.

Imagining always relates the self to the environment through an act. This can be looked at in different intellectual perspectives. For

Piaget human action is the raw material for all adaptation, and even abstraction is an action. Whereas Piaget is largely concerned with cognitive structures, the perspective of Witkin is somewhat different. He is primarily concerned with affective and aesthetic structures. He shows that when imagining is externalized, it results in expressive form. Yet it does so in a particular way, as Witkin puts it: "It is the child's direct sensing that both guides and controls the expressive act until it is recalled in an expressive form, a feeling-form."[23] The significance of what Witkin says is important: sensory perception becomes re-called (as images) when it is re-played; and this re-playing, or re-creating, is an expressive form—a form that has an emotional basis. The aesthetic forms used in drama and the arts, in other words, are primarily emotional rather than cognitive; yet they have a mixture of both. But the "hands on" experience (as within spontaneous drama and the creative arts) is important for an additional reason: it grounds cognition in the self through its affective and aesthetic qualities. In John Masefield's words, "We must re-create the arts or die."

Two things follow from this: the creative has a more direct impact upon the self than the critical; and the "hands on" experience will lead to stronger motivation and more permanent learning than the experience that is purely abstract. In other words, school learning should be based, first, upon the affective and the aesthetic, and only secondarily upon the abstract, if students are to be highly motivated to learn. This is significant for implementation, as we shall see below.

The Identification/Impersonation Complex

Of the states of Being, imagining is the kernel for all specifically human developments. Yet *both the imagined thought and the action that results are dramatic in character.*

We have already seen that the human organism directly links the imagined thought and the expressed action, but this develops in a particular way with maturation. Infantile identification is the basis of symbolic thought. Thereafter, developmental identification enables the baby to "put himself in someone else's place," while defensive (projective) identification permits him to form primitive symbols. This develops the use of "mediate objects" resulting in the primal act at ten months old (see p. 12 above). It is this primal act which becomes the prototype for all later adaptations. From then on, re-play develops as an acquired skill. We continually improve and enrich our abilities to re-create the world in our imaginings and re-express them in actions. The structure of imagining and of action is, in both cases, double: both contain the oscillation between parts, the tension that is characteristic of the organism.

Another perspective on the Identification/Impersonation Complex is provided by experimental psychologists. They tend to regard identification and impersonation as the result of social motivation—that is, as derived from certain physiological tendencies by secondary reinforcement. On this view, the individual seeks the company of others because they have satisfied his need for food; then, by a process of generalization, the bond that unites an individual to another who has satisfied his needs is extended to others of the same species. Nuttin says:

> The fact that the child finds satisfaction of his many needs through the adult doubtless creates very special affective bonds between them. However, the facts show that to explain the social tendency in terms of satisfaction of primary needs is not plausible. . . . Spitz's systematic observations (1945) tend to show that the satisfaction of organic needs does not suffice to develop social contact in children. Although during hospitalization the child receives all necessary care and the satisfaction of "primary" needs from adults, large gaps in the social and emotional contacts of the child—and even in his intellectual and physical development—become apparent through the mother's absence. A more complicated network of human interaction would therefore seem indispensable and valuable *sui generis*.[24]

The most effective answer to this problem given by experimentalists is that of Mowrer (see p. 46 above). This, in effect, is an acknowledgment of the Identification/Implersonation Complex, though in a different language style. In contrast, the study of D. B. Cook demonstrates the effects of maternal personality and language style upon mother-infant interaction and the resulting modelling that occurs.

Imagination and Energy

The organism model permits us to see that it is imagining which is the source of human motivation. The tensions within any organism create an energy flow. The tensions within Being are made even more energetic by imagining and the resultant actions. "As if" thinking requires a leap into the unknown, into the milieu of possibility. It commences with the baby's imagining that there is a "me" and a "not me" which are related by "mediate objects."

Life itself is inherently energetic. Niels Bohr argued that the ultimate nature of matter could be regarded as waves *and* particles; these must be viewed in alternation since it is impossible to see oscillating "sides" simultaneously. Atomic physics, electricity, the biology of the cell and DNA—all demonstrate that oscillation between component parts emits energy.

It is the tension between oscillations that leads the human organism to explore, to attempt to master, to lead towards competence. It is imagining that requires satisfaction of safety, love, esteem, self-actualization, curiosity and aesthetic needs. *Without the ability to imagine, these needs could not be envisaged.* Of course, physiological needs still have to be satisfied, but the dynamism that is specifically human originates in imaginative tension.

Imaginative tension, the oscillating dynamism between the parts of Being, is not the same as the dialectical synthesis of opposites of Hegel and Marx. Dynamism is not a matter of mere opposition. It involves both negative and positive attraction. Blake put it aptly when he said

> Negations are not opposites;
> Contraries mutually exist.

Thus it relates to synergy:

> Synergy is a state of mutual enhancement between two or more helixes, so that their respective segments are developed and strengthened. It consists of an affective and intellectual synthesis which is *more* than the sum of its parts, so that each party to the interaction can win a "return on investment" that is greater than the competence risked. Abraham Maslow has argued that synergy applies not only to the relationships between people and groups but that synergy *within* the person promotes a synergy *between* persons and vice versa. Translated into the terms of the helix this means that *all* segments of both helixes can ideally achieve an *optimal organization of strengths that will lead the double helix to "spiral upwards."*[25]

The fecundity of synergy can be discussed in a variety of ways: in the relation of inner and outer; the unity of contraries in dialogue; the fusion of "I" and "Me"; and the unity of subjective and objective that is basic to existentialism. Writers as diverse as T. S. Eliot and Marshall McLuhan acknowledge the fecundity of the paradox, while Koestler discusses creativity in similar terms as "bi-sociation."

That this is physiologically based is demonstrated by the fact that the brain has two modes of consciousness: the verbal, rational mode, and the mode of holistic mentation. The dynamism between them is of synergy because the corpus callosum joins the two hemispheres of the cerebral cortex and creates a unity which is more than the sum of its parts. The left hemisphere, concerned with logical and analytic thinking, is connected to the right side of the body. The right hemisphere, connected to the left side of the body, is simultaneous and relational, and is primarily responsible for our orientation in space, artistic endeavor, crafts, body images and the recognition of faces. However:

> When a tachistoscope is used to introduce information to only the right hemisphere and either a nonverbal or a verbal response is required, the nonverbal response comes more quickly than the verbal one. A verbal response requires the information to be sent across the callosum to the left hemisphere which takes some time. This indicates that the normal brain does indeed make use of the lateral specialization, selecting the appropriate area for differential information processing.[26]

In other words, not merely does the operation of the brain generate synergy between poles, but "hands on" experiential activity is the primary mode; only at a secondary level does this relate to the analytic.

But the brain also functions in a vertical direction. P. D. MacLean has shown that there are fundamental differences in anatomy and function between the lower and the upper brains: between the archaic brain structures which humans share with reptiles and the lower mammals, and the specifically human neocortex. The former (the limbic system) controls instinctive and emotional behavior. But the neocortex controls intellectual and rational thought, and provides human beings with language, logic and symbolic systems. MacLean has shown that there exists:

> a dichotomy in the function of the phylogenetically old and new cortex that might account for differences between emotional and intellectual behaviour. While our intellectual functions are carried on in the newest and most highly developed part of the brain, our affective behaviour continues to be dominated by a relatively crude and primitive system, by archaic structures in the brain whose fundamental pattern has undergone but little change in the whole course of evolution from mouse to man.[27]

In other words, the intellectual and rational activities of human beings are subject to emotions over which they have but limited control.

The picture presented by the physiology of the brain is significant for motivation and learning. The double poles—relational/analytic, and emotional/rational—show that the oscillations of mind are multidimensional. The dynamism between parts is far from linear: it is a complex unity whereby the poles are in tension, pulling apart and pulling together simultaneously. Thus imagining can provide us with multiple meanings at the same time—the paradoxical and the symbolic. This also accounts for the double meaning of the re-play: the actor is understood to be both himself and another.

The organism model, with motivation centred in imaginative action, provides us with a theoretic tool which obeys the conditions of human existence. It incorporates those aspects of previous theories which appear to work in educational situations and, in particular, provides the competence and holistic theories with the necessary honing edge for teachers to use them effectively with their students.

Symbols and Their Applications

Icons, Symbols and Signs

Imaginative action has two levels of meaning: what is meant *directly*, and what is meant *symbolically*. It not only exists as an everyday action (a painting consists of a canvas, brush strokes and paint) but at the same time is a *re-presentation* of my thought (the painting symbolizes my imaginative state). Imaginative action always has double meaning, just as *Hamlet* is not merely about the events in Hamlet's life but also about their symbolic significance to humanity.

Symbolization has a variety of forms which emerge as the human being develops:

1/*icons*—undifferentiated double meanings where the symbolization is primarily emotional;

2/*symbols*—double meanings, partially affective and partially cognitive, that are metaphoric in character;

3/*signs*—double meanings where an abstraction has a one-to-one relation with a variety of particulars.

These forms of symbolization are used in a variety of ways. During maturation they emerge as follows: through play, as icons; through art, as symbols; and through abstraction, as signs. These are not isolated categories but overlap in a number of ways.

In the first months of life, the baby works with proto-icons: half-formed and partially resolved symbolizations. Then, in the primal act, the 10-month-old child acts "as if" he is himself or his mother. This is the first complete act of re-presentation. His play medium is his self—his movements, his sounds, and his Being—all together as "a costumed player." This is the model to which all later forms of representation refer. The primal act gives the child his first complete control over the environment, and this is crystallized into "the icon of himself."

As the child develops the icons of play, he increasingly experiments with his control over the external world. He does so in a "whole" manner: he mingles apprehension and comprehension, emotion and cognition, according to his own will. There is no external compulsion upon him to complete his play, to produce products. If he does so, all well and good. If he does not, that is fine too. The icons of play are not so obvious as the symbols in art where products are aimed for. That icons exist, however, is demonstrated from psychotherapy where play can be interpreted as symbolic of the inner world. But such iconic activity is never fixed once for all; it cannot provide us with a universal explanation; nor can it reveal a cause-and-effect relationship. The symbolization of icons shifts and moves. It is often fragmentary and elusive. In this sense, play is the increasing *attempt* to objectify the self.

Art is the successful *achievement* of this. The symbolization is concrete. Artistic symbols, like the icons of play, are "whole." Yet they are primarily of feeling and of apprehension. Only secondarily are they of comprehension, of cognition. Even more than the icons of play, the symbols of art are rich and multi-layered. They contain referents, but go far beyond them. They become so fecund that it is impossible to express their full meaning in logical statements. Any logical statement of a Rodin sculpture, a symphony of Beethoven or a play by Shakespeare can only be partial and will miss its essence, its "whole."

The wholeness of a symbol lies in the quality of its double meaning—affective and cognitive. Everyday language recognizes this quality through such terms as "flying saucer," "eye of a needle," and "ear of corn." What is involved is a kind of *contrary recognition*. Thus when Hamlet persuades Polonius that a cloud is like a camel, then a weasel, and then a whale, he recognizes a cloud contrary to the fact that it looks like other things. The symbol or metaphor unifies the contrary meanings into a new gestalt that goes beyond them both.[28]

Signs, on the other hand, are arbitrary. They are abstractions. They have a one-to-one relation with any referents one may choose. Bertrand Russell indicated that "mathematics may be defined as the subject in which we never know what we are talking about, nor whether what we are saying is true." Thus $1 + 1 = 2$ applies equally well to cabbages and kings. Because signs are abstract, they are specifically not fecund of themselves. Yet just as artistic symbols emerge out of the icons of play, so do signs. But these latter two forms of symbolization emphasize the different components contained within the icons of play: art the apprehensive, and abstraction the comprehensive.

Here we reach the crux of the matter: *motives vary with the style of symbolization used.* That is to say, play is deeply motivated, art is well motivated but less so than play, and abstraction is least motivated. Play is deeply motivated because its icons refer directly to the oscillations of the inner—the organismic tensions of Being. The symbols of drama and the creative arts emerge from play. Art actions result in symbols that are affectively based; thus the motives to pursue them are almost as strong as those in play.

But the world of signs provides less motivation. Whereas symbols retain a deep relation to the organismic tensions of Being, signs make this relationship more tenuous. The symbols of art and religion have emotional intensity: the paradox and the metaphor retain a tension between their parts. Signs only do so abstractly. As we have seen, they can relate to widely diverse referents. When 1 + 1 = 2, should a child make 1 + 1 = + then he has given it symbolic meaning and destroyed its abstract reference. In terms of math, he is "wrong." In one fell swoop, he has returned the world of signs to that of symbols. Yet signs are not entirely devoid of tension. Einstein himself acknowledged that his own abstract thought was "toying with concepts." In other words, the distinction between the icons of play, the symbols of art and the signs of abstractions are really matters of degree rather than precise categories.

Symbolic Applications

Symbolization looked at in such a way can affect specific practical fields. In terms of schooling, motives are greatest when using the icons of play. Further, the symbols of drama and the arts are liable to produce greater motivation than the signs of abstraction. This indicates a hierarchy: play icons/artistic symbols/abstract signs. In normal maturation, the child proceeds through the hierarchy so that the motives of one are built into the next.

A learning retardation at any level, therefore, requires a return to an earlier form of symbolization to resuscitate motivation. The student with problems in, say, calculus will have increased motives if the work to be learned can be set in the context of symbols or icons. This also applies to retardation in media. The student with difficulty in two dimensional media (say, reading) will have increased motivation if his work is related to earlier media (say, three dimensions) as illustrated in Figure 3 of chapter 1. These reinforce earlier learnings, relate what is new to the "I am" experience, and ground what is to be learned in the Being of the student.

In terms of emotional disturbance, much depends on relating frustration to the level of symbolization. Dollard and "the Yale group" consider that all frustration is a motive for aggression: frustration provokes aggression, and this aggression can be cathartic. Aggression is increased according to the intensity of the frustration or when it stems from another person's act which is seen as arbitrary rather than reasonable. Aggression is also related to punishment: children whose aggression was severely punished at home tend to be more aggressive than others in their play. All these types of aggression tend to be worked through symbolically. Those who have been severely punished also tend to increase their aggression in imaginary activity.[29] In terms of diagnosing what method is to be used, therefore, the teacher might well work backwards from signs to icons, using the levels of media in Figure 3. This is a prime method in dramatherapy (see Chapter 7).

Tension, as opposed to disturbance, can also affect motivation in almost anyone. Play icons and artistic symbols have a particular value in displacing or dissipating such tension. Visual art has a better displacement value than verbal activity[30] and, generally, earlier media levels displace tension more readily than later levels (Figure 3). However, the substitutional value of symbolization also depends on how close it comes to reaching the goal of the original task.

Specifically, application of such a methodology encourages motivation in practical fields. It brings the individual face to face with the dynamism of his imagining organism through the vitality of icons and symbols.

Implications for Curriculum

That motivation is organismic, is based upon identification and impersonation, and varies according to the dynamics of symbolization, provides implications for curriculum. I shall leave questions of implementation and teaching strategies to Chapter 4, and I have dealt with how program planning and design are affected in my book *The Dramatic Curriculum*. But how does the concept of organismic motivation bear upon general questions of curriculum?

The Primacy of Feeling

Acquisition of knowledge must be grounded in Being if it is to be effective. No skill or knowledge is acquired in the abstract, as separate from the student's existence. If it is true, as Sir John Newsome said, that "*all* education is, in a sense, vocational, vocational for living," then it has to relate to the essence of our selves.

The feeling world is primordial. The good math teacher will relate both the mathematical concept and the specific problem to the student's Being; he will base the necessary abstract signs upon meaningful icons and symbols. Human rational processes hinge upon, and develop out of, the "I am" experience.

The Pedagogic Encounter

Schooling takes place in the encounter of student, teacher and materials. But how can the teacher distinguish between approaches that assist the "I am" experiences from those that do not?

The essential quality of the learning experience is that it is dramatic. The teacher's stance should be that of a dramatist (see Chapter 8) and this will awaken the student's dynamic feelings, attitudes and values. The teacher becomes a model for the student who will come to dramatize his own experience. To share a common meaning provides a mutual identification of student and adult, and impersonatory factors result. Mutual co-discovery means mutual co-existence. Without such mutuality, no curriculum can be effective because it will not relate to the intrinsic motivation of the students.

Uniqueness

Each student must be treated as unique. The "system" of school—with large classes, mechanistic methods of learning where teachers provide in-put and students give back out-put—mitigates against this, and teachers must take risks to preserve uniqueness. A program that encourages such uniqueness will satisfy the conditions asked for by Phenix: the engendering, gestating, expecting and celebrating the moments of singular awareness and illumination.[31] It will also satisfy two other conditions: it will regard a student's individuality as appropriate to his developmental stage; and it will "start from where you are" for both student and teacher. Such a climate in a classroom will provide each individual with freedom without anarchy. Thus the student finds his own ability to be self-motivated.

Approach to Materials

The student must encounter materials in ways that, appropriate to his maturational level, learning can occur with ease. For the strongest motivation to occur, materials must engage his feeling world, motivate his spontaneity, and allow him to re-play from the materials so that conceptualization can take place.

Materials must relate to the student's icons. By doing so, they release his innate synergy and motivation, and learning becomes authentic. This permits the re-play of the student: it encourages his spontaneous and expressive actions, and learning results from the imaginative transformations of the materials. They become incorporated into his re-creation of a world structure. Thus he can relate to, live with and control these materials in his own unique manner. Put another way, materials that encourage self-motivation are also socially dramatic: as they relate to the student's interpersonal encounters, he re-plays them and so becomes motivated by his inner structure in relation to the world.

On the other hand, materials that are based on mechanical and abstract learning tend to dominate the student. He does not need identification with the teacher so he and the teacher do not coexist and learning is inauthentic. This affects evaluation which, in order to be authentic, must be responsive.[32]

Re-Play and Symbolization

The play approach is fundamental to any humanly based curriculum. The origins of symbolization indicate that the motivation of the human organism responds, primordially, to play icons. The icons of play must be built into all learnings intended by a program. Play reveals objects as they are: it makes referents immediately apparent—and to the whole consciousness of the student. It allows the student to incorporate the everyday world into his self.

Re-play with young children consists primarily of spontaneous drama and the creative arts. They provide both iconic and symbolic learnings. Their symbols are energetic. They provide the "I create" which reinforces the "I am" and "I do" of icons. Both icons and symbols provide double meaning: icons lead to affective and everyday meanings; symbols provide affective and aesthetic meanings. Symbols not only re-emphasize self-worth and action (in relation to referents), they also lead to re-creation and conceptualization. It is rare for a child of 3 to attribute any significance to his scribbles. If he does so (and this only happens in 10 per cent of cases) he always says afterwards *what* he has drawn. By 4 years old, some will explain what the drawing will represent while the activity is taking place, but others form a definite idea of *what they are going to do* before beginning. By 5 years old, 80 per cent work out their plan before they start, while 100 per cent of 6-year-olds do so.[33] In other words, there is a growth from the direct experience of play icons at the 3-year-old level to symbolic representation at 6 years old, at least with drawing. This growth is universal in all forms of re-play although there are differences in development, first, between specific media and, second, in different cultures. In terms of motivation, it should also be noted that the growth from icons to symbols involves the student *setting himself a goal*.

The process continues with adolescents. They are beginning to cope with abstraction which is based upon signs. Yet this has particular difficulties for them. For signs, abstractions and theories to be meaningful they need to be grounded within the felt selves of the adolescent. For him, knowledge has no significance unless it is grounded in his own reality.

The adolescent needs to temporalize and spatialize from his own centre. He is not an independently functioning adult, nor is he a child. Unless he has adequate returns to the felt world (through the icons of play and the symbols of re-play), he can feel oppressed by objective and abstract data. This is when alienation occurs. In a totally cognitive and mechanist environment where only abstract data are acceptable, feelings and moods can be considered inappropriate. Far too many secondary teachers think that "emotional education" should not enter their classrooms. Thus adolescents can develop what Rollo May called "schizoid symptoms": the so-called "irrational emotions" brought about by living by rote in a memorized world. Significantly, the danger is always proportionate to the academic proficiency of the student.

The problem is further complicated because adolescents feel that their time in school is a waiting period. Their inner felt world views action as only minutes ahead, yet what is being learned can only be effective in some remote future. When learning becomes so divorced from the immediate referents of play and the symbolic re-plays of spontaneous drama and the creative arts, the future seems indifferent and the present unimportant. Then teachers will say that students lack motivation for schooling.

Resuscitation under such conditions is only possible by returns to icons and symbols through the activities of play and re-play. Then the arts are therapies: they ground the Being of adolescents so that they can relate abstract signs to their felt world.

This may be true of adolescents in general, but how do we account for individual motivational differences? Fluctuations in the level of aspiration seem to be bound up with the dynamic personality structure. The study of Hoppe showed differences in two students: the first, who experienced one failure after another and was obliged to lower his level of aspiration during the test, began each new task with higher motivation than any other subject; the second, who had an average number of successes, had the lowest level of aspiration in all tests. Generally speaking, the level of aspiration in industrial cultures rises after success and drops after failure. Furthermore, students almost always aim at a higher goal than that which they successfully achieved in a previous task. It seems, therefore, that individual motivational differences are due to both personality structures and levels of felt success.

In addition, there are some variants amongst disturbed persons. Some (neurasthenics and dysthymics) tend to set themselves higher levels of aspiration than average people, while hysterics have a very low level of aspiration, often setting themselves a lower level than the one they have just reached.[34]

The Multi-Disciplinary Approach

A multi-disciplinary approach to curriculum results from these considerations. Students require comprehensive experience—both apprehension and comprehension within a *felt* context.

Spontaneous drama and the creative arts are the nub of a multi-disciplinary program. The synergy inherent in their icons and symbols is the foundation for the self-motivation of students. Thus:

> We can say that art finds its roots in the *freedom* to vary indefinitely the relationship between language and reality—the freedom inherent in the possible (not necessary) character of this relationship. Art explicitly and deliberately uses this freedom which man, outside of art, uses only occasionally and partially and always under the influence of external conditions and circumstances. . . . Art always has a liberating function; and this liberating function is what is commonly called creation. The symbols (and by these symbols I mean not only words, but forms, colors, masses, sounds, etc.) can be varied indefinitely in their meaning by artistic activity.[35]

The symbolism of re-play provides the freedom of the possible. It codifies and encapsulates imagining. And it is imaginative possibility that activates human motives which range across so-called subject matters.

Different styles of multi-disciplinary modes using the arts have been described by Lett, while ways of implementing them in galleries have been discussed by Parres. Both show that motivation is helped by this approach.

In what way does this occur? In a revealing study of hundreds of British children, Witkin related the cognitive stages of development as described by Piaget to affective and aesthetic maturation. He demonstrated that students developed the following qualities:

Pre-adolescents:
contrasts, semblances, harmonies, discords — corresponding to the "four rules" of mathematics

Adolescents:
polarities, identities, syntheses, dialectics — corresponding to the abstractions of scientific thought

Witkin commented:

> All describe ordering in the sensate experience at the level of sensate totality (and thus) this is ordering in respect of "wholes" rather than ordering between individual sensate events.[36]

Put another way, these are *feeling* qualities. They are also qualities of *relationship*; yet this relationship is specifically not of a cause-and-effect type; it has the same affective and aesthetic qualities possessed by the symbols of art. From Witkin's work we can see that these qualities are the bedrock for the development of scientific thought as explained by Piaget.

Ordering in symbolic "wholes" is what characterizes all artistic activity. It is a holistic type of thinking that unifies what has to be learned. The freedom of artistic symbols relates to more than one meaning for the referent and thus allows motivation to range over subject matters. In this sense, spontaneous drama and the creative arts can provide curriculum with meaning.

Drama is the kernel of all of the arts. We have already seen that the primal act is the generic origin of all artistic media. But, as Morris indicates, it is also the most powerful in its motivating qualities:

> Drama, it seems to me, is perhaps the most powerful of all the arts in evoking existential awareness. In dramatic interpretation, the pupil can literally assume the role of the existential actor, making clear to himself—in the act of making something clear to his audience—what he considers the most important of his own subjective feelings. How one interprets a role inevitably reflects how one views his own life and its meaning in the world.[37]

Spontaneous drama can become a motivational touchstone for program content. Should the teacher and the student approach a multi-disciplinary curriculum from the position of re-play, the student stands independently. He portrays the world in a specific medium, but *as he sees it* and not as his peers or teachers see it. In such circumstances, the teacher is

> arousing the pupil to artistic expression which the teacher cannot anticipate. The teacher does not know in advance what he is after; all he knows is that it is important for the pupil to *feel* his own experience

through the medium of his paintbrush or carving knife or cutting tool. *What* the student creates is less important than that he *does* create something which he can see as his own artistic statement about his experience.[38]

When this happens, the student is synthesizing (within his expression) the feeling-form in relation to the materials. This learning, however, must be clearly distinguished from *catharsis*:

> The cathartic effect attributed to acts of pure emotional release must in any case be distinguished from the complex of emotional responses into feeling-form. . . . Feeling-form is the product of subject-reflexive action in which the disturbances wrought within the individual are projected in a medium which recalls them. There is no recall in emotional responses, however. These are simply subject-reactive.[39]

The motivational quality inherent in spontaneous drama is not primarily in the release of emotions. Nor, in contrast to many current situations in schools, is it a study of verbal material *about* the world that lies beyond the student. It is to "lay bare the nerve endings of one's emotions"[40] and to re-play one's experience within what Witkin calls "the intelligence of feeling."

Conclusion

Motivation is organismic. Centred upon the creative imagination, it becomes synergetic in action. This provides the experiential icons of play. In spontaneous dramatic activity, the experience is replayed. It is self-motivating because it is the organism's way of creating meaning out of experience. If schools do not permit dramatic action to infuse the learning of students, a great risk is taken. Students will tend to learn information by rote because "it is the acceptable thing to do." Then schools risk the inevitable results: students become uninterested, bored and even anti-social. In contrast, if drama infuses the whole curriculum, students can become enthusiastic, excited and self-motivated about their learning.

Currently, this view of motivation does not hold sway in all schools. For too many teachers and educational administrators, mechanistic theories of motivation prevail. As Shaw once said, "For four wicked centuries the world has dreamed this foolish dream of efficiency, and the end is not yet." But if teachers want students to become self-motivated, to come to love their learning as they love life itself, they must set what has to be learned in a dramatic milieu. All genuine learning is unified when it has meaning for each unique individual. Or, as Shaw also said, "Every scientist must be a metaphysician."

Chapter 3
Drama and the Transfer of Learning

> "You are the music
> While the music lasts."
> —*T. S. Eliot*

Quiet revolutions eventually bring forth thunder. This has happened with drama in education. However, although Ernest Bramah said that when struck by a thunderbolt it is unnecessary to ask its precise meaning, in this instance there are some problems that need clarification. One such problem is the relation of spontaneous drama to the transfer of learning.

In its beginnings early in this century, drama in schools all over the world was equated with theatre; it was entirely associated with the extra-curricular production of plays. But things have changed radically. Drama as *spontaneous* action is now assuming a major role in the learning of students. It first took root in Britain. Two colleges began to train teachers in such methods in 1948; by 1968, one-third of all the teachers in the country could take it as an option, and the government had issued a very distinguished report which gave the subject authority.[1] The teaching of spontaneous drama spread rapidly throughout the Commonwealth: for example, in 1977 over 150 high and technical schools in Victoria, Australia, offered it on the curriculum,[2] and in Canada graduate degrees could be taken. In the United States, where "the cash value" of ideas led "creative dramatics" towards production of plays, the growth was slower. However, recent events demonstrate an increasing change of attitude towards process rather than product.

The essential quality of this approach to education is that learning is set within a holistic and human context. Drama "is more concerned with the development of people than the development of drama."[3] It has *intrinsic* values. The very action of spontaneous drama is good in and of itself: "We teach *the value of action*."[4]

As drama is the key way to *represent* experience, ability in the former enhances the latter—thus symbolism and abstraction develop. With very young children, dramatic play *creates* the relationship between our inner world and the environment. This not only assists social development but also forms our "world view," and this search for a balance between inner and outer (adjustment) continues throughout life.

The usual methodology is to "start from where we are." The teacher provides the framework and the stimulus (the "What?") and the students make creative choices (the "How?"). With young children, for example, Peter Slade may play a drum:

> "What does that remind you of?" (the "What?")
> "Horses!"
> "How do *they* move?" (the cognitive question)
> "Like this . . ." (the "How?")
> "Right, let's move like that, then . . ." (*drum continues*).

With adolescents, Dorothy Heathcote might ask whether their improvisation will be of the past, present or future. Thereafter, continuous alternative questions are asked, leading them to their own creative choices as to the nature of action. Within such a methodology, the teacher is always an active agent for change, but the student is responsible for his own existential choices and, to invert Pierre Mendès-France, "to choose is to govern." Skills are not taught from some predetermined standards or program but when they are "asked for"; that is, the teacher "reads" the sub-text of the student and supplies skills as they are needed.

It is clear that the intrinsic values of spontaneous drama, when allied to such a methodology, have resulted in the immense popularity of drama when it is viewed as a subject. Unlike Willy Loman who was "liked, but not well liked," spontaneous drama is almost universally enjoyed. When people are responsible for their own activities, they feel a relationship to their own inner needs. Education which relates directly to the personality is immediately effective. Moreover, as dramatic activity is inherently self-motivating, the concentration, sincerity and absorption of students of all ages can be extraordinary.

However, it has also been claimed that spontaneous drama in schools has *extrinsic* values—that is, it has values for purposes other than the activity itself. Some have supposed that drama can transfer learning to all subjects in the curriculum. Others have claimed that the arts, including drama, are basic to "the basics," or that drama is a key method for learning language arts, social studies, second language learning, or even political and economic awareness.[5]

Transfer of learning is assumed by most contemporary teachers of drama, and in two ways: generalized existential learning; and specific items of learning. Goffman considers that human acting is the presentation of Self, and drama teachers assume this to be the case whether the presentation is in life or in simulation. For example, most would accept the transfer validity of an adolescent student improvising a job interview; they would argue that the student's simulated actions will influence (presumably for the better) the real actions that occur in the life interview.[6] Many similar practices in dramatic education make the assumption that a wide range of existential learnings can transfer from enactments. This is then extended to the ability of drama to transfer specific items of learning and therefore to conclude that it is a sound methodology for most of the curriculum.

Moreover, as an approach to education, spontaneous drama has come to incorporate a great many previous approaches and provide them with bite. It has influenced the project method of the English primary school by giving it focus. It has incorporated "learning by doing" by turning it into "learning by acting" and thereby given Dewey's "collateral learning" the significance of being dramatically *felt* in order to be of value. It has assimilated many "creativity" approaches by considering that what is creative is original to the individual (but not necessarily unique) in that his imagination is expressed dramatically. As ancillary techniques, it can use elements of role-playing and encounter training. It has direct relationships with aesthetic education, and it can be used as a basis for affective education. Such extensions make it difficult to think of any adult behavior that could not be affected by earlier dramatic actions.

But is the basic assumption true? Can, in fact, most of what is learned within dramatic experience be transferred to other forms of learning? To my knowledge, there are no empirical studies of drama that can support this claim. There is, however, no dearth of general psychological studies on the transfer of learning. As Henry Ellis has said: "We might, in fact, regard all studies of learning beyond a very early age as studies on the transfer of learning."[7] This chapter, therefore, will examine the relevant psychological literature on the subject, and attempt to make relationships to the use of drama in modern education.

Background to Transfer

Education

Instances of transfer occur in many formal learning situations. For example, having mastered one foreign language, such as French, one may find it easier to learn a second and related language, like Spanish, although this may not always be the case.

In the past, it was assumed that a formal discipline provides transfer of training. Thus Latin and mathematics were regarded as vital because they strengthened reason and memory. However, early studies failed to find evidence of this.[8] Moreoever, as H. G. Wells could say: "We were taught as the chief subjects of instruction Latin and Greek. We were taught very badly because the men who taught us did not habitually use either of these languages."

Although educators abandoned formal disciplines as methods of transfer, it was still considered that a student could "generalize" his experience from one situation to another.[9] Students were therefore asked to consider features of problems which could be generalized to different situations.

None of these theories was satisfactory. Modern psychology requires explicit criteria before accepting theories of transfer.

Psychology

In recent years, there has been an increased interest in transfer. This has been summarized by Henry Ellis whom we will follow here. He shows that contemporary research has been less interested in *whether* transfer occurs than in *why* it occurs. He states the current view of empirical psychology about transfer as:

> Transfer of learning means that experience or performance on one task influences performance on some subsequent task. Transfer of learning may take three different forms: (1) performance of learning may *aid* or facilitate performance on a second task, which represents *positive transfer*; (2) performance on one task may *inhibit* or disrupt performance on a second task, which represents *negative transfer*; and (3) finally, there may be no *effect* of one task on another, in which case we have an instance of zero transfer. *Zero transfer* can occur either as a result of no effect of one task on another, or as a result of equal effects of positive and negative transfer that cancel out.[10]

Clearly, transfer is very pervasive. It is found not only in cognitive tasks or motor skills but also in feelings and attitudes. We will now examine those aspects of modern psychological findings that are relevant to dramatic education: non-specific transfer, specific transfer and general factors.

Non-specific Transfer

Current behavioral psychology distinguishes between non-specific and specific transfer. Non-specific transfer is said to occur, not because of any particular features of the task, but because of more general characteristics. Many of the claims of dramatic education for transfer of learning would, at least in the current literature, be regarded as claims for non-specific transfer.

There are three factors of non-specific transfer that can be considered in relation to drama in education: learning to learn, warm-up and mediation.

Learning to Learn

It is a commonplace that people improve their ability to learn new tasks or skills if they have practised similar tasks beforehand. This is usually known as learning to learn; it occurs in many instances, from verbal learning to problem solving, and is one case of non-specific transfer.

Early trials are necessary to establish a learning habit[11] or, as Julian Huxley put it, "Sooner or later, false thinking brings wrong conduct." The early experiments of children's play, constantly repeated, become habits of mind and action. It is assumed by the literature of both psychotherapy and educational drama that play is the young child's natural way to learn, and should be encouraged. The real actions within play must precede the symbolic actions of learning[12] which build the structures of new thought. From this, it is possible to theorize that the inner imaginings expressed within the repetitions of dramatic play are basic for all forms of later learning. We could rephrase this perversely, like Hilaire Belloc, as: "For deliberate and intentional boring you must have a man of some ability to practise it well, as you must to practise any art well."

Insight is probably related to this process: it may well be the result of extensive early practice on related problems and may lead to the development of personal characteristics.[13] As Whitehead said, "All men enjoy flashes of insight beyond meanings already stabilized in etymology and grammar." Play is continual with young children. We may assume that learning to learn through dramatic play provides the basis not only for conceptual structures but also for intuitive knowledge.

Paul Stevenson, in examining insight in spontaneous drama, has shown that it is specifically functional:

The continuing modification of our reality systems on the basis of what we experience (new or second-hand) is the real basis of learning. When such a structural modification occurs, we can say that we have achieved "insight." We know the universe a little better. Our reality system is that more in tune with the vast unknown. We will then continue to live our life *in the light of* the new learning. From the moment of "insight" on, we will set our goals, plan our time and direct our energies knowing something new. If we do not *act* on what we know, it means that we do not really *know* it at all. Insights without the skills required to act on them are therefore not really "insights" at all.[14]

Insights achieved through drama, in that case, are built upon *the use* of previous insights. The more early experiments through drama, the more likely subsequent insights will be.

Warm-Up

Warm-up is more short-lived than learning to learn. It refers to immediate personal adjustments that carry over from one task to another and facilitate learning. Thus it is easier to recall word lists if they are practised quickly, but it is more difficult if such practices are delayed.[15]

Warm-up is normally a component of all spontaneous drama sessions. Teachers begin with exercises in sensory awareness, providing the general motor adjustments necessary for optimal performance. Where drama is used with other subject areas, the warm-up may be related to specific learnings: for example, in history, language arts, business, and a range of other subjects.

Mediation

Experimental psychologists use "mediation" in a different way from that discussed on pp. 5-9. They equate it with transformation—the transformation of perceptions and thoughts into actions. Learning that allows for this is more effective than that which does not.[16]

It is axiomatic in drama teaching that what is being fostered is the students' imaginative transformations and their resulting actions. As Rilke says, "Our life passes in transformation," which is merely another way of rephrasing Shakespeare's:

> as imagination bodies forth
> The forms of things unknown, the poet's pen
> Turns them to shapes, and gives to airy nothing
> A local habitation and a name.

It is the purpose of the drama teacher's "What?" to allow the student's transformational processes to choose from his perceptions and create imaginings which are then externalized, again through choice, by acting. The teacher intends that the ideas to be learned will associate with the student's previous experience. Through the student's choice of imaginings and actions, these ideas will be learned faster and more efficiently than by rote or mechanical methods.

Those who advocate the power of transfer through education have transformation as the crux of their argument. It is this which occurs between the "What?" and the "How?" It centres upon imagining, itself given meaning by the Identification/Impersonation Complex (see pp. 55-56).

Further, learning will be more efficient if the open-ended approach of dramatic education is followed rather than the analytic methodology of the field known in the United States as "creative dramatics." Thus:

> It seems probable that actors, like children, first perceive salient *gestalts* and then attempt to reproduce them. If that assumption is correct, the methods of teaching creative dramatics may be faulty, as they tend to emphasize analysis as a means for understanding roles, rather than more generalized or original reactions to the totality. It could be that proponents of creative dramatics falsely proceed from the part to the whole rather than the reverse. The child's excited, if caricatured, representations may be the more proper starting point.[17]

Specific Transfer

Specific transfer is concerned with elements of tasks that can be transferred. In the psychological literature, those which have particular importance for dramatic education are task similarity, stimulus predifferentiation, time interval between tasks, degree of original learning, and the variety of previous tasks.

Task Similarity

The degree of transfer of learning is affected by the similarity between the original and transfer tasks. In general, the more similar the two tasks, the greater the amount of positive transfer. Thus international traffic signals make it easier to obey traffic signals when travelling in those foreign countries using them.

With adolescents, for example, spontaneous dramatic activity centres upon impersonation, and to act "as if" one is another person in a task is liable to help when tackling the task in reality. In N. F. Simpson's words:

MRS. EDO: Sid just had another bad night worrying about being so different from the people he sees round him.
MRS. MESO: Has he tried resembling anybody?

Thus it would seem likely that a student improvising a job interview would transfer learning more easily to a real interview than, say, to crossing a real road. In other words, positive transfer seems more likely when the *subject-content* of the dramatic situation is similar to the *subject-content* of the life situation.

Yet, in addition, transfer can also occur according to similarity of *drama-content*. As a first example, we can take verbal fluency and confidence. A drama student can transfer such an improvement to other situations, such as talking with strangers, acquaintances, teachers, etc. Gesture is a second example. A student who learns to express himself more completely in gesture during drama teaching may transfer that increased ability in a variety of ways: to life situations as a whole; or to expression in another medium (e.g., paint or three-dimensional modelling) which requires bodily movements similar to gesture.

Yet the implications of task similarity within dramatic education are not simple. Similarity itself is a complex variable. Dramatic action is a holistic and complex medium. Thus, although the relationships are not simple, the implications for transfer within dramatic action are considerable. One example of this complexity can be considered. It is axiomatic in the psychological literature to consider that transfer may vary along dimensions of either stimulus or response similarity. It has been shown in terms of dramatic education that it is possible to equate stimulus with perceptual awareness, and response with dramatic action. If this is so, then it is possible to conjecture:

1/Increased awareness in one perceptual mode (e.g., sight, sound) brought about within dramatic action, may transfer to increased ability in another perceptual mode.

2/Increased awareness in one or more perceptual modes may transfer to increased ability in dramatic action (in subject-content and/or drama-content).

3/Increased ability in one aspect of drama-content (e.g., movement, speech, impersonation) may transfer to increased ability in another aspect of drama-content and/or subject-content.

4/Increased ability in one or more aspects of dramatic action may transfer to increased ability in one or more perceptual modes.

Further, it is possible to ask subtle questions of any of these four conjectures. For example, at what age does impersonating a policeman, when compared, say, to impersonating an abstraction like "fire," increase transfer ability in one or more perceptual modes? Questions such as these may open the door to valuable research studies.

As far as I know, no such empirical studies exist. However, detailed studies about task similarity do occur in experimental psychology[18] from which the following principles can be discerned:[19]

1/*Where stimuli are varied and the response kept identical, positive transfer increases with increasing stimulus similarity.* Thus we would expect considerable positive transfer from checkers to Chinese checkers, because the conditions of the games (the responses) are similar, and even though the pieces and rules (the stimuli) are different, they are much alike.

This corresponds to many current practices in dramatic education. It is common, for example, before approaching dance-drama to have prepared students by teaching elements both of dance and of drama. It is also common when drama is used as a method of teaching other subjects: for example, Witkin indicates that drama and art teachers should

> ... use a number of quite different stimulus forms to evoke the same sensate problem. In this way, the pupil is liable to transcend the particular forms used to set the problem by grasping the resemblance between the forms, the "gestalt" they have in common.[20]

Thus the teacher of language arts might use a variety of drama stimuli (say, improvisation, dance-drama and creative "soundscapes") for one language response; a history teacher might use different creative approaches from all the arts (say, creative music, creative art and creative drama) to approach specific learnings in history.

2/*If the responses in the transfer task are different from those in the first task, then the greater the similarity of stimuli, the less the transfer.* Thus if the rules about traffic lights were changed, if "Go" were orange instead of green, we would expect difficulty in learning the response because orange and red (stimuli) are similar.

Drama teachers leading students to other subject matters acknowledge this problem in transfer. Thus, for example, when improvisation is related to social studies (say, life in a foreign land), and the normal outcome is the students' independent research followed by writing a diary about people in that land, it is not common practice in the session immediately following to create improvised dance-dramas which relate to research and diary-making. Both forms of dramatic activity can be used as stimuli under different circumstances, of course, but their close similarity, used in proximity, is liable to make transfer learning difficult.

3/*If we keep the stimuli identical in the initial and transfer tasks and vary response similarity, positive transfer will increase with increasing response similarity.* Thus we would expect greater transfer from tennis to badminton than from tennis to baseball because responses are more similar in the former case (the style of play with racquets) than the latter.

In the same way, if the subject matter to be learned has to do with people's lives (as with the humanities, for example) we might well begin from dramatic activity centred upon impersonation—say, improvisation that develops characterization. After all, as Ionesco says, "Characters in a play don't always have to be bigger fools than in everyday life." History can well be approached through spontaneous characterization and we can expect transfer to occur; it will probably transfer less if we are working towards the learning of algebraic problems. Similarly, we can expect improvisation on abstract themes to relate more quickly to those subjects which are specifically abstract, such as mathematics, than, say, the study of a novel. These three principles correspond to many current drama practices.

Stimulus Predifferentiation

Previous experience with stimulus aspects of a task may have important effects on transfer, of which we will consider two.

Transfer is considerable when the stimulus is the same for the two tasks.[21] Thus drama exercises on sensory awareness of natural things might be related to literary studies about natural things in the novels of Hardy; the movement abstractions of Rudolf Laban might be related to subsequent work on geometric shapes; work on improvisational structure might be followed by the structure of story writing; or mime work in size, shape and weight of imagined objects might be related to similar work in gymnastics.

Learning to attach labels, or names, to stimuli that are somewhat similar can produce efficient learning. However, students do not learn to enrich the stimulus when this occurs.[22] But great care must be taken here. As Clive Bell said, "We are in the age of names and catalogues" and, in such an age, the name can create the fact to our detriment. It is clear from the dramatic literature that when labels are provided so that students can distinguish between movement elements (rhythm, time beat, mood, etc.), the response they make is liable to clearly differentiate between such elements. However, it is unlikely that this will deepen their emotional response to the stimuli, at least in the short run. Whether it will do so in the long run is a matter of conjecture.

Time Interval Between Tasks

When a time interval elapses between two tasks, transfer of learning can vary. Where transfer relies on memory, it will decrease as time elapses between the two tasks,[23] but where it does not, it will remain approximately constant.[24]

Spontaneous drama, specifically, relies less upon the memorizing of the facts within it than upon attitudes, feelings and insight, and their relationship to facts—their inner meaning to the individual. The transfer of learning within drama, thus, remains approximately constant whatever the time between the two tasks.

Degree of Original Learning

The degree of original learning determines the level of transfer. Positive transfer increases with more practice on the original task,[25] and negative transfer is likely to occur when there has been little practice on the original task.[26]

Spontaneous drama in schools is built upon the natural play of children, a form of original learning possessed by all human beings for years before they reach school. All children have great practice in play before school drama builds upon this experience for a variety of learnings through transfer. The drama methodology, therefore, provides a remarkably efficient vehicle for the transfer of many learnings in school.

Variety of Previous Tasks

Transfer increases if there is an increased variety of original training. Only a small increase in the number of training tasks increases positive transfer.[27]

A drama program specifically provides a variety which acts as original training for non-dramatic subjects. Drama teachers eclectically use all media—sound and words, music and dance, paint and sculpture—to enhance the dramatic experience. With such a variety of tasks available, we can expect considerable transfer to other subjects.

General Factors

There are many general facets of the transfer of learning that have relevance to spontaneous drama in education.

Several characteristics of the learner influence transfer. Studies indicate, as we might expect, that more intelligent students show greater transfer ability.[28] More interestingly for our purpose, if a student is poorly motivated he is likely to learn less and reduce the chance of transfer. But motivation is related to anxiety. It has been found that anxiety facilitates simple types of learning but interferes with more complex tasks;[29] students with intense anxiety perform better when facts have to be retained over short periods, whereas students with least anxiety perform better in complex behaviors like synthesis and application.[30] This has considerable significance for drama in schools. Children who enjoy the activity learn more or, as John Masefield puts it, "The days that make us happy make us wise." Drama, being based upon play and upon the organic need to externalize imaginings, is self-motivating. Specifically, it has very low anxiety. Further, drama by its very nature is a synthesizing activity that results in immediate application: it places facts within a context that is meaning-giving and self-actualizing. As a learning activity for other subject matters, it decreases anxiety and, thereby, is of great assistance in complex and permanent learning.

Current educational practice emphasizes problem-solving, teaching students to "think for themselves," to identify problems and come up with solutions. In a sense, studies in problem-solving can be treated as studies in the transfer of learning.[31] As dramatic activity is commonly regarded in the literature as "thinking on the feet,"[32] it might be assumed that there are direct relations between studies of problem-solving and spontaneous drama in schools. Unfortunately, most studies in the field appear to have no parallel application.

What parallels can be made are somewhat tangential but raise interesting questions. For example, transfer is improved when the original task is meaningful and students learn the principle in context rather than through simple role approaches.[33] We may possibly assume, therefore, that drama is an effective learning mechanism because facts relate to the student's "felt world" and are thus meaningful to him.

Summary

This survey of the psychological literature has, of necessity, been brief. However, it demonstrates that, when spontaneous drama is used with other subject matters in a program, we may assume that transfer of learning takes place for the following reasons:

1/It provides high motivation and low anxiety.
2/It is always meaningful to the student: by allowing the freedom of choice inherent in imaginative thought, it creates significance for the learner.
3/It has immediate application because it is a synthesizing activity.
4/It assists students in learning to learn.
5/It stimulates insight.
6/It provides warm-up so that immediate personal adjustments will carry over from one task to another.
7/It can provide certain specific transfers by using:
—stimulus predifferentiation
—learning over long periods of time
—natural play; thus it maintains a high level of learning for school tasks in a variety of media; it provides strength to the original learning which then transfers with ease to subsequent learnings.

It is fair to state, however, that only studies from psychology have been cited. Specific studies of dramatic activity are necessary in order to confirm these assumptions.

Drama as a Method of Learning

Drama has two places in the life of a school: as a subject and as a method. When used as a method to teach non-drama subjects, it can assist learnings in such subjects by enabling transfer to take place. That is, if spontaneous drama is used in the context of, say, a second language, then the language learnings can be enhanced. We have seen in the survey of the psychological literature just how such transfers are liable to occur. Thus:

> Given the opportunities, drama can have an all-embracing relationship in the life of the school. It should be seen as an integral part of the system rather than as a luxurious appendage to the timetable when other curriculum demands have been satisfied. At the same time drama is not an educational panacea. It is one component in the broad process of education.[34]

How, precisely, can drama enter the whole curriculum as a transfer mechanism? If the teacher is responsible for the "What?" then how will he establish the conditions for transfer through the "How?" There are some generalized principles when teaching for transfer.

1/*The similarity between the tasks must be maximized.* That is, "A teacher who hopes to induce much transfer must attempt to teach under conditions which are at least somewhat similar to the ultimate testing situation."[35]

With spontaneous drama this can be achieved through subject-content and drama-content. In the first instance, students might improvise about the Renaissance voyages of discovery in history and then engage in research and writing about the same subject. In the second instance, the shape and structure of an improvisation might be related to shape and structure in a variety of subjects—for example, to natural form in biology or the sciences in general.

2/*There should be adequate experience with the original task.* Work and practice on the original task is a prerequisite for the transfer of learning. This is why play achieves high levels of transfer with young children: they have had extensive practice before they have reached school. Obversely, limited practice with the original task can produce no transfer and, even, negative transfer.

One major implication of this is the need for good and continuous teaching of spontaneous drama at the early stages: "greater emphasis could be placed on those topics that are known to be necessary for the mastery of subsequent course work".[36] But this does not merely apply to early childhood education; for the transfer strength of drama to be effective at all ages, there must be continual practice and achievement. This indicates that it is a necessary component in the broad process of education and that students at all levels need to return to spontaneous dramatic activity in order to ground learning in their beings.

In terms of specific practice, adequate time must be spent on the drama task before attempts are made to stimulate transfer. For example:

> A class of thirteen-year-olds had been working on the theme of coal-mining in the nineteenth century in social studies as well as drama. In the previous lesson they had explored life in a mining community in small groups of their own choosing. In this lesson the teacher wanted to focus attention on the conditions down a mine. He was intending to structure the activity and feed in factual information, and give them the experience of working in narrow passages and shafts.
>
> However, the class arrived unexpectedly at the beginning of break and excitedly announced that they wanted to continue with the previous week's work. During break they eagerly constructed their sets and asked if they could use the studio lighting. They started work straight away as if there were not a minute to lose.
>
> One group consisted of six boys and six girls. They divided themselves into six couples (as decided the previous week) and began acting-out. Each couple was involved in a domestic scene at breakfast. There was little attempt at characterization since they were chiefly concerned

with the typical stereotyped husband/wife roles, and of course, their real relationships. The climax for each couple was the man's departure for work, as this involved kissing the wife goodbye.

Yet although this was the real motivator, it did not prevent the group from exploring other areas, such as working in the mine and the women's life at home, which they did with as much involvement. Towards the end of the lesson they sat down together and discussed the work, which showed that they were equally concerned to pay attention to details of the period, as well as role-play couples.[37]

3/*A variety of examples should be provided when teaching concepts and principles.* One example:

A boy was working with other sixteen-year-olds on an improvisation of the Easter Story. As Christ he was being scourged and vilified by the rest of the group. It was working mechanically but had no excitement within it.

The school choir was rehearsing *Messiah* as part of preparations for an end-of-term presentation. It was decided to try playing the scourging scene against the background of the choir's singing of "Worthy is the Lamb." The result was staggering. Not only did the improvisation become ritualized and climatic but the boy, in the role, began to cry. Others watching him were similarly moved.

When asked about it he said that for the first time he understood how it was that a man who was being ill-treated could feel emotions other than anger and resentment. It should seem that the juxtaposition of the dignity and beauty of the music and the brutality of the event had, for him in particular and others not so acutely, highlighted a basic contradiction in man.[38]

To use the initial tasks of drama and music in such a way is to prepare for good transfer to moral or religious education (most obviously), or to themes in literature (less obviously).

4/*Important features of a task should be identified and, perhaps, labelled.* Young adolescents learning improvisational structure will be able to transfer this to composition if, in both tasks, they have identified a beginning, middle, and end. But identification is not necessarily labelling. The former takes place in modern educational dance and the latter in contemporary dance:

I don't teach them techniques exactly—that's more contemporary dance. There's a subtle difference, you see. There they have special movements which they must do and this is called technique. And they express themselves through set movements—a bit like ballet except more . . . they teach this in some schools.

But in modern educational dance there is no right or wrong movement. *I want them to know whether they're moving slowly or quickly*

> *and whether they're moving in space up or down or forwards and backwards.* But within this context they can move as they wish. They can use which part of the body they like whereas if you said I was teaching them a technique I would also be teaching them how to move in movements. I don't ever give them movements and say now this will be the right movement in this situation.[39]

Labelling and naming breeds "proper" and "improper" skills, whereas identifying allows for spontaneity and encourages transfer.

5/*The teacher must ensure that general principles are understood before expecting much transfer.* Thus:

> This was a sequence of lessons that developed from an initial stimulus by the teacher. He had asked the class of twelve-year-olds to consider the effects on natural order if the sun's properties were to change. This led to a discussion about stars and galaxies and later a movement sequence representing, first, the natural order and secondly, the disruptive effects caused by a meteorite.
>
> In subsequent lessons the class explored the idea in a variety of ways: in pairs as astronomers noting the disruption and discussing it; as groups of individuals whose lives were affected by the change in the sun's properties; as individuals fleeing from cities to take refuge in the countryside, and living in caves and banding together for security.[40]

If the student works through a number of dramatic examples of the general principles, the initial task becomes well known. Preparations can then be made to transfer these principles to the responce task—in, say, the study of science.

These five principles are the basis for the teacher's practice. He must implement these within the context of his encounter with the student.

Conclusion

It is clear that the claim of spontaneous drama to be conducive to transfer of learning is positively indicated by the literature, and that there are specific teaching principles to achieve this.

However, it is fair to say that spontaneous drama, while it can, under certain conditions, provide specific transfer, is most useful as a general climate to encourage such qualities as high motivation, meaningfulness, insight, and learning to learn. Specifically, it allows for transformation. It provides a moral climate for learning. It encourages "as if" thinking that allows for a continuous adjustment to reality. It does so in a "hands on" manner. It has immediate application and involves, as T. S. Eliot has put it, "a recognition, implicit in the expression of every experience, of other kinds of experience that are possible."

In terms of other subjects, it most obviously transfers to the humanities: to the language arts, social studies, guidance, the arts, and second language and literature. Yet it also greatly assists the general principles of the sciences and social sciences by providing practical experience of their underlying meanings. Less obviously, but just as effectively, spontaneous drama can transfer to the learning of abstraction, as in mathematics and science; the dramatic icon of "the costumed player" is the foundation for the learning of symbolization and the eventual understanding of abstract signs.

Specifically, spontaneous drama has application to the basics: to speaking, reading, writing and numeration. The literature shows that dramatic action brings about and reinforces those actions of which it is the origin: sounds, speech, and language on the one hand, and movement, dance and dimensions on the other. The ability of expression in a later medium (say, reading, which is discrimination in two dimensions) hinges upon genetically earlier learnings: those of three dimensions, movement and drama. Thus, the child who is learning to read on the parent's knee is modelling himself upon the parent—acting "as if," a dramatic process—while the slow reader is best placed in a situation where he can ground the reading experience in his being through dramatic actions. In both instances, the kinds of visual discrimination necessary for learning to read are transfer tasks from the stimuli of inner dramatic action. Spontaneous drama in this sense can be overt (behaving "as if") as with young children, or covert (thinking "as if") as with older students, but in either instance, drama is providing an effective transfer of learning.

This chapter has not, of course, *proved* that spontaneous drama is effective in the transfer of learning. As James Stephens said, "Nothing is perfect. There are lumps in it." However, this would apply to most findings in human learning. Meanwhile, spontaneous drama is increasing in all aspects of education at a rapid rate. Its emergence as a major force in learning has been largely unheralded. Unfortunately, until empirical studies demonstrate directly that transfer of learning occurs through dramatic activity, some element of doubt will continue to exist—at least amongst objective social scientists. Until that time, the quiet revolution will continue.

Chapter 4
Drama and Instruction

> "The teacher's role is to harness drama to his own needs. To use it in the way in which it will most aid him in challenging children to learn. Its purpose will never vary, but the activity will vary as the child matures."
> —*Dorothy Heathcote*

Throughout this century, writers on the use of spontaneous drama in schools have claimed that it is a major method of instruction in all subject areas. Unlike theatre, which is usually taught for its own sake, spontaneous and creative drama is a technique also used by teachers in non-drama areas. But is it true that spontaneous drama is an efficient method of instruction? Does human enactment relate directly to learning and, if so, can teachers use it with profit in all aspects of school programs?

In order to consider such questions, we shall examine recent research in instruction and relate this to creative drama as a method: through the parameters of instructional techniques, the context of errors, retention and transfer, specific strategies, and the place of other children within instructional methodology. Thereafter, we shall relate this to a current view of instructional objectives in drama, together with a major study of drama in the elementary school.

Instructional Techniques

Instruction can vary in style between discovery or problem-solving techniques on the one hand, and the heavily guided and structured approaches on the other.

The discovery method as a form of instruction has long been

associated with educators like Rousseau, Montessori and Dewey. Its contemporary advocate is Bruner, who asks that teachers should induce active participation of the learner in the learning process. On this view, instruction is a "discovery-learning" environment which encourages the student to explore alternatives, and the learning that results transfers to related tasks and situations.

The heavily guided approach is in strong contrast. It stresses stringent controls on the learner through the use of commands, prompts or cues. Ausubel proposed learning through the "reception" of material that was presented by the teacher in nearly final form. Skinner advocated instruction that prompted the student's every response, while leading him in a logical way to achieve the desired behaviors. More recently, Gagne said that learning is a step-by-step approach through a hierarchy of prerequisites until the desired learning behavior is obtained. If students are to learn the necessary sequence of learning tasks, then they must be guided in their attempts to respond correctly. Thus Gagne minimized the need for independent discovery.

Numerous other instructional strategies occupy intermediate positions on the continuum between discovery and guided learning. This range of possible instructional approaches has been uniquely described by Mosston. He has shown that the command technique is associated with the structured environment and, within such a framework, students' learning is heavily guided towards specific outcomes. It can, indeed, be considered behavioristic because strong control is exerted over the learner's progress.[1] This would be supported by Skinner who contends that it is easier for the student to respond correctly the first time than it is for him to undo past errors.

In contrast, the discovery approach allows the learner to experiment and to explore solutions to problems. The teacher presents the student with the material in problem form, but does not give him the solution; the learner is then encouraged to discover ways to accomplish the goal and to solve the problem. Those who support this approach consider that it encourages reflective thinking, association and self-direction.

In creative drama classes, the teacher encourages spontaneous dramatic play, creative movement and speech, as well as role-playing. He sets this activity in a framework whereby the students are always directed towards the future; they are engaged in activity that leads them onwards towards possibilities. In Mosston's context, therefore, creative drama is a genuine problem-solving technique. It is indeed a discovery method of instruction which can lead to reflection, association and self-direction.

Within the discovery approach, however, there are a variety of modes, two of which are extremes:
— learning by discovery (or "guided discovery") in which the teacher has prespecified objectives in mind; and
— learning to discover (or inquiry based) where the emphasis is upon how to inquire rather than on what is to be learned.

In the most general terms, we can see this in the literature of dramatic education: the first is advocated by the creative dramatics approach in the United States, and the second by educational drama in Britain. Needless to say, there are many variants in both approaches and in all countries.

Errors and Retention

The common teaching strategy in creative drama is for the teacher to provide the "What?" (e.g., "Let's be bears," or setting an improvisational framework on the subject of earthquakes) while the students provide the "How?" Although there is some difference between the more open British approaches and the less open American ones, this is basic to the field. However, it raises the problem of errors. If students really provide the "How?" they will naturally make errors before they have refined their skills. Skills are not formally given. Rather, help is given in skills as the students' needs become apparent from their work.

An example is from a creative drama class led by Dorothy Heathcote.[2] A child, in deciding the setting of the group's drama, chose "a village in the county of Coventry." Although it was obvious to Heathcote that the child's knowledge of geography was inaccurate (since Coventry is a city, not a county), she pointed out that *at that specific moment* to correct the child's mistake was not desirable. In her view, what was important was not that the child's extrinsic knowledge was accurate but that the child's conviction within the drama was respected.

But does this provide effective learning? Instructional theorists disagree about the function and desirability of error-making in the learning process. Those who accept the discovery technique state that learners profit from their errors in two ways: first, they develop problem-solving abilities which generalize to future situations and, second, they become more actively involved in the learning process.

In contrast, those who advocate structured instruction suggest that learning, particularly early learning, should be error-free.

Skinner, for example, does not believe that learning occurs when errors are made. For him, trial-and-error learning is inadequate because the student learns nothing beyond, possibly, how to try. As an alternative, Skinner and others ask that learning should be strongly guided and reinforced. Their viewpoint stems largely from animal learning studies. From such a view, Terrance says that error-making leads to emotional reactions and a decrease in transfer ability.[3] On the other hand, there is strong opposition from many to drawing conclusions about human learning from animal trial-and-error studies.

More modern research has shown that errors in early learning have little effect on later learning.[4] Although one study showed that if a student places great confidence in a learned error he can find it more difficult to unlearn,[5] another showed that the older a person is, the more difficult it becomes for him to rid himself of errors.[6]

Error learning is directly related to retention and transfer (see Chapter 3). Numerous studies have examined these in terms of instruction.[7] There is now overwhelming evidence to show that open techniques (such as creative drama) increase retention and transfer more than closed methods (such as the response-confirmation approach). It is true that some researchers have suggested that the transfer of verbal knowledge is more efficient when the initial learning is by prompted methods rather than by discovery techniques.[8] But, contrary to this, others have shown that students engaged in discovery learning are superior in retention and transfer to those using prompted learning.[9] Prompted students are superior in initial recall but not in retention. The crucial factor in the transfer of learning was found to be the increased motivation of students. Characteristically, creative drama is something students *want* to do and, thus, the expectation is that their retention and transfer will be high. However, students are not usually familiar with discovery methods. They are not the most common forms of instruction today, and creative drama is not a universally used technique at present. Consequently, current students will probably need a longer period to use and apply such methods effectively. Discovery through drama is effective in transfer and retention if adequate time is allowed for such processes, and also if the students feel that they are successful within them. Success in discovery is related to effectiveness in discovery.[10]

Guidance becomes more effective as task complexity is increased.[11] In creative drama, more guidance is required with adolescent students than with children—though, as the drama literature indicates, such guidance should be by responding to need rather than by the use of commands. Guidance usually leads to more rapid learning on the primary task of interest than does non-guided learning, and this affects transfer.

There have been many studies on the effect of instruction on transfer learning. Heavily prompted learning seems to have an advantage over trial-and-error learning in early trials. However, with more trials and performance, there is little difference in performance as a result of the methods used.[12] But discovery methods, like creative drama, produce greater transfer than error-free methods.[13] Discovery methods lead to more transfer to a simple task while, with complex tasks, increasing guidance is required.[14] If discovery methods yield better retention and transfer,[15] the implication is that, even if time prevents the total use of discovery methods, it is important to use instruction that is at least partially based on discovery.

There is no reason to doubt, therefore, that creative drama can be effective in learning, retention and transfer. It overcomes any problems associated with error-making by increasing motivation. Although it cannot claim to be as effective as highly structured methods in immediate recall, it greatly assists retention over long periods of time, and it provides greater transfer than guided instruction.

Strategies

In activities that require fixed responses or cues, heavily guided learning may be the most expedient method. The automation of skill may be desirable for some student performances while it is not for others. In fact, it is highly doubtful whether fixed responses are required in many school situations. Some recent evidence shows that the more the task performance is automated, the more difficult it is to make adjustments when necessary.[16]

Most modern educational approaches require methods of instruction which will allow adjustments by the learner. The problem-solving approach is usually described as a method of search and discovery without the benefit of a principle or rule to which to adhere. Would this apply to creative drama?

Depending upon the intention of the teacher, strategies would be used for particular purposes as follows:

1 / If the purpose of learning a skill is *only* for the highest level of performance in that skill, then a guided and prompted method would seem appropriate. This is particularly the case if there is

concern for economy in training time. Under these circumstances, drama would probably not be used.

2/If the purpose of the learning situation is to lead to the application of what has been learned to other related skills and situations, then an open methodology should be employed—some form of discovery, problem-solving, or trial-and-error strategy. In these circumstances, creative drama might be used.

3/Self-paced, closed-loop tasks should be learned primarily through a guided technique for response consistency.

4/Externally paced, open-loop tasks should be learned primarily through a discovery technique such as spontaneous drama to achieve familiarity with diverse situations and response adaptations.

5/The later learning situation should be considered when choosing a method of instruction.[17]

Drama used as a technique of instruction, therefore, will depend upon the intention of the teacher.

Students learning through creative drama methods are apparently able to approach a transfer situation (which is also free of guidance) with a well-developed method of attacking the problem. They learn such a new task in fewer trials and in less time than that required by students learning under highly structured conditions. Furthermore, the more often spontaneous drama is used, the more effective it is as a form of instruction.

Other Children

But drama instruction is not merely a matter of the teacher-student relationship; drama in schools is a social activity. That is, students constantly work in pairs or in groups in their creative drama explorations. Indeed, unless there is social cohesion within any such group, spontaneous drama in classrooms cannot function at all.

But what precisely is the effect on the individual of other students in a dramatic situation? And what effect does this have upon instructional techniques? Research findings in empirical psychology can throw some light on these questions.

There is little question that children can have a considerable impact upon the learning of each other. Recent studies of various kinds have demonstrated that a child's playmates can bring about desirable educational change. For example, nursery, elementary and retarded children have the ability to shape a peer's performance in a simple game of marbles.[18]

But which children affect the learning of others, and in what ways? Those who most affect the behavior of others are those who are socially highly accepted.[19] The question for the drama teacher, therefore, becomes: in *this* class, and in *this* situation, which children are the most highly accepted, and how do they affect the behavior of others within the drama? Children with a history of peer reinforcement imitate a rewarding model significantly more than a non-rewarding model; a child's socialization history has an important influence on the imitation of peer models.[20] In drama activities, therefore, the child with a history of strong identification with parents and peers is likely to be more influenced by other improvisers than one who has not such a background.

There is much evidence to show the influence for change exerted by children within a group context.[21] Thus the peer group has a profound influence on the acquisition and maintenance of desirable and undesirable behavior.[22] Drama teachers must take care, therefore, that delinquent behavior is not strongly and repeatedly acted by improvisers who are socially acceptable to others. This does *not* mean that trial delinquent behaviors should be banned from drama classrooms. Rather, it means that the teacher must be careful that such necessary traits, particularly important for adolescents, do not become so strong within the drama that they are reinforced. Thus in summary it can be said that children can function effectively as reinforcement agents, that peer groups do differentially reinforce social behaviors, and that a child's social environment strongly influences his behavioral repertoire and, consequently, his social value or desirability.

Do boys influence boys and girls influence girls, or do learning influences in spontaneous drama cross the sexes? It has been said that second grade (7-year-old) children perform better when the agent of change is of the same sex,[23] but there is little evidence that the sex of the peer alters the level of influence in other grades or with other ages. Although students of the opposite sex may affect the *content* of the spontaneous drama of adolescents, and thus affect general social learning,[24] the sex of peers seems to have little relationship to cognitive learning through drama.

But peers do use frequent encouragement, prompting and reminding to assist another child or group to learn. At all ages, any group of students (including those in special education) can consciously work to alter the behavior of others,[25] and the social nature of spontaneous drama would indicate that it is an effective methodology to this end.

This can also be assumed from those studies that have examined the use of peer tutors for learning. Unstructured peer tutoring was found to be superior to control and independent study groups in the performance of spelling.[26] In other instances, when students were given an opportunity to interact with one another on their classwork, their performance improved.[27] The implication is that group interaction, which is a basic requirement in creative drama and improvisation, can improve work on cognitively related tasks.

In another field, it is axiomatic to claim that the therapist benefits at least as much as the client. In a similar vein, what influence does the child tutor receive from the tutee? There is little research in this area; perhaps psychometric and other tests in association with creative drama classes might prove useful.

The research evidence discussed in this section has specifically concerned other children as deliberate agents for change especially in relation to the implications for drama activities. Research evidence in generalized social change has not been reviewed. But it is clear that spontaneous drama can assist learning in this context and also that the drama teacher must take full cognizance of the child as an agent for change when considering methods of instruction.

Intentions

Gavin Bolton has examined the objectives of teachers of spontaneous drama. He considers that there are at least seven direct objectives:

1/*A change in meanings.* In all education, teachers are ultimately concerned with a change in understanding for each child. Drama must meet these same requirements in a special manner that reflects the nature of spontaneous dramatic activity, but in two ways depending on how it is used:
— as a complex art form where there are complex meanings below the dramatic action
— in a more simple, functional use whereby the student has a new self-awareness as a result of the drama.

2/*Group cohesion.* Drama uniquely provides the cementing of group relationships, particularly in small groups and class-size groups, which is important not only for maturation but also for learning.

3/*Trust.* When painting a picture, the student is trusting himself to make it. Working with drama, in contrast, is group-dependent and that same degree of trust is transferred to the group.

4/*Learning about form.* The change of interaction within the improvising group leads to a learning about the ingredients of the art form:

> The teacher may not explicitly be showing how the drama works, but the beginnings of discovery are happening from the inside. Understanding of the rules evolves from within as the needs of the drama are responded to.[28]

5/*Language skills related to levels of thinking.* Children without dramatic activity in schools do not have sufficient chance to draw experientially on different language contexts:

> The language we learn as children is based on experience and new language that we acquire, for many of us, also needs to be experiential. Curiously, this gets missed out. A great deal of work in school expects children to improve their language skills in an abstract way, and we wonder why they don't improve in their language. Drama can give language an experiential base, rather than an abstract one.[29]

6/*Speech skills and* 7/*movement skills.* Improvisation leads to oral and physical skills in an expressive medium which generalize from the other five objectives.

Bolton also discusses the many indirect objectives for drama teachers whereby spontaneous dramatic activity provides a bridge between what it is necessary to learn and experience, such as in reading, writing and number. It is fair to say that recent research in instruction, reviewed above, would give general support to Bolton's objectives for drama teachers.

Yet what is this "drama" from which a change of understanding can result? In the framework of the discussion thus far, the definition given by the Attleboro Conference of 1973 is applicable:

> Drama is the metaphoric representation of concepts and persons in conflict in which each participant is required either to imaginatively project himself into an identity other than his own through enactment, or to empathize with others doing so. This action is structured, occurs in real time and space, and typically demands intellectual, physical and emotional engagement and yields fresh insights into the human condition.[30]

Thus the focus of Bolton's direct and indirect objectives for the teacher must centre upon the impersonatory act.

Unfortunately, research studies on drama instruction are sparse. However, that of Courtney and Park, which examined teachers and administrators responsible for arts programs in elementary schools in Ontario, also studied drama instruction. It showed that spontaneous drama as a methodology had considerable benefits through the following factors of learning:

a/*Perception* was improved through: (i) development of personal resources by the greater use of the senses; and (ii) perception of the self in relation to others, leading to sensitivity to others.

b/ *Awareness* of the environment, relationships and connections was improved through: (i) seeing patterns in life; (ii) realizing the relationship between play and reality; (iii) understanding the self in relation to others; and (iv) assessing feelings and attitudes.

c/*Concentration* was improved through: (i) increased motivation; and (ii) practice in dramatic activity.

d/*Uniqueness of thought style* was improved through: (i) the projection of the self and using various ways to think and respond; (ii) the simultaneous development of cognitive, affective and aesthetic thinking within dramatic action; and (iii) increased understanding of how others think and appropriate ways to respond to them.

e/*Expression* was improved through: (i) the development of a variety of expressive modes in ways that suit the individual; (ii) the opportunity to share work with others; and (iii) the occasional opportunity to see performances of others (the provision of models).

f/*Inventiveness and problem-solving* was improved because students felt that they could choose to direct their own learning.

g/*Confidence and self-worth* was improved through: (i) positive reinforcement, which occurred in multiple ways; and (ii) the students' taking personal responsibility for judgments.

h/*Motivation* for learning was improved through: (i) the students' natural enthusiasm for the activity; (ii) the teachers' enthusiasm for the activity; (iii) the self-discipline of students which carried over to other work, and the special relationship established between teacher and class, leading to easier class management; and (iv) the teacher commencing from the students' own experience and interests.

i/*Transfer* of learning was improved: (i) in learning and learning readiness for other subject areas; and (ii) in life and social learnings generally.

In addition, it was shown that drama improved maturation and development, from primary to junior grades, as follows:

a/Perception developed from free play to structured activities to develop the senses.

b/Awareness developed: (i) from subjective to objective awareness; (ii) from exploration to assessment of feelings; (iii) from general to specific awareness; and (iv) from freedom to "talk and act out" to aesthetic awareness.

c/Concentration developed: (i) from general processes to specific skills; (ii) from inner to outward communication; and (iii) from dramatic play to all areas of learning.

d/Thought styles developed: (i) from concrete to abstract; (ii) from egocentric to alternative learning styles; (iii) from feeling exploration to cognitive, affective and aesthetic styles within "whole" thought; (iv) from thinking what they do is the way everyone does things, to accepting others' ways of thinking and doing; and (v) by teachers challenging students to think ahead, think creatively, and to evaluate their work and that of others.

e/Expression developed: (i) from self-expression as an end, to expression as a tool for other things, and used in a variety of forms; (ii) from sharing for personal growth to sharing to show what they have done and for social learning; and (iii) from dramatic expression in other subjects as well as drama.

f/Inventiveness and problem-solving developed: (i) from within dramatic action to finding and solving problems in general; (ii) from working with stimuli for creative invention to using structures for inventiveness as a tool for problem-solving; (iii) from students determining the "What?" and "How?" to the teacher deciding the "What?" and the students determining the "How?";* (iv) by increasing flexibility of thought; and (v) from dramatic activity to all other subjects.

g/Confidence and self-worth developed: (i) from confidence in self to confidence in self and others; (ii) from self-confident activity to the accomplishment of specific tasks; (iii) from growth of personality potential to growth of aesthetic awareness and judgments; (iv) from self-worth as an objective to self-worth as an outcome; and (v) from self-worth in drama to self-worth in other subjects and social skills.

*This curious finding may be more related to the specific forms of instruction in Ontario than to factors that can be generalized.

h/Motivation developed from solely intrinsic to both intrinsic and extrinsic motivation.

These findings clearly relate to the recent research in instruction per se, shown above, as well as to the objectives given by Bolton.

Conclusion

We have examined recent research in instruction with specific reference to its use within spontaneous drama techniques. In doing so, we have considered error, retention, strategies and the place of other children within drama teaching. The objectives given by Bolton, and the research findings of Courtney and Park, would indicate that spontaneous drama is an effective technique within discovery methods of learning.

Chapter 5

Drama and the Different: Creativity and Giftedness

> "Drama is the only form in which we can fully use man in the exploration of himself in the living situation. Whether the living experience is recorded in a text or is set in motion by one or more ideas, its fullest discovery as personal experience must be realized through improvisation."
> —*John Hodgson* and *Ernest Richards*

"Just what is creative about creative drama?" is a common question. Moreover, it is one which the experienced teacher must face squarely otherwise the rationale for the activity is insufficient.

Much depends on what is meant by "creative." It is the unwary teacher who begins by defining creativity from the research literature with "high creatives." None of us have a classful of creative geniuses every day. Moreover, there are confusions between the terms "gifted" and "creative" students (as we shall see below). Furthermore, tests and measures for creative ability are in their infancy, and any attempts to extrapolate from them in great detail smacks of pseudo-science.

Students who achieve high marks on creativity tests are often characterized as "different." It has been said that they are loners, they think up bizarre answers, and that they are disliked by teachers, peers and their own parents.[1] If this is the case, does creative drama attempt to lead all students towards such behaviors? It would be a poor world if this were achieved.

It is more likely, it seems to me, that one of the aims of the creative drama teacher is to encourage the student to develop his own potential. This would include the development of his *creative* potential. Yet isn't what is creative to me different from what it is to you? Are we not encouraging the student to develop his own aptitudes and abilities so that how he thinks, feels and acts is a unique expression of himself? In this sense, we are indeed leading students to be different. Yet, at the same time, are we not also aiming to have them cooperate as fully as possible with their fellows? And just what is creative about that?

These are genuine problems for the experienced drama teacher. This chapter will not attempt to give glib answers to them, nor to provide "how to do it" solutions. Rather, it will examine specific aspects of the problems, hoping to illumuniate rather than solve them.

Creativity

There is much confusion about the nature of creativity. But it is clear that creativity can take innumerable forms, and that it does not respond well to precise definitions or instruments of measurement. Moreover, most research is concerned with the "high creatives," those exceptional young people whose thinking is far beyond the norm. It has only tangential relationship to the creative processes of children with average abilities.

The tests for creativity are innumerable—far too many to review here.[2] We can, however, consider the most influential. Torrance reports validities for his tests; yet they are lengthy to administer, and some of the instructional materials can influence some scores in divergent thinking. Guilford's batteries have been shown to lack validity;[3] and, while the test of Wallach and Kagan has both predictive validity and independence from IQ,[4] it is also very lengthy to administer. The Remote Associates Test is short but relies heavily on verbal intelligence and, in addition, punishes imaginative answers.[5] The Barron and Welsh test has excellent validity,[6] but misses so many traits that Barron has had to add supplementary measures.

More fruitful than tests and measures is the use of personality and biographical information about high creatives. Davis has reviewed this literature and indicates:[7]

1/There are attitudes, motivations, interests, values and other personality traits that predispose a person to think and behave more creatively.

2/Biographical reports of past creative interests, habits and activities are excellent predictors of future creative interests, habits and activities.

3/There are, in addition, some very subtle indicators from biographical information. For example, highly creative students are likely to have:
— parents who play musical instruments and read magazines of the cultural-intellectual-foreign affairs variety;
— friends who are older or younger than themselves;
— moved house more frequently than the norm;
— had an imaginary companion when young.[8]

Clearly such information is of help for predictions of creative behavior, including within drama, but is of less value for teacher implementation.

More practical assistance to the drama teacher from research in personality and biographical research is the use of adjectives to describe common forms of creativity. Davis indicates that for the Gough Adjective Check List[9] there are nineteen common adjectives among the various scoring keys that have been devised:

artistic	impulsive	quick
assertive	ingenious	reflective
clever	insightful	resourceful
complicated	intelligent	sharp-witted
cynical	inventive	spontaneous
idealistic	original	unconventional
imaginative		

The drama teacher might consider that class activities that encourage such traits might well increase creativeness. Certainly Davis, using similar adjectives as the basis for his own How Do You Think (HDYT) inventory[10] achieved a remarkably high correlation between personality factors and creativity. However, research studies based on high creatives alone are limiting. They predispose the drama teacher towards behaviors of the few rather than the many.

Giftedness

There are many kinds of giftedness, including high creativity. Personality and biographical information on the full range of giftedness can provide some rich illumination to the drama teacher.

Elizabeth Drews delineated character profiles of the gifted: four stereotypes which can be used as guides. She strongly emphasized, however, that these types are not pure and stable, there are various combinations of each, and each is subject to change. The types are:

1 / *The high-achieving studious* consider that hard work is good in itself. They tend to conform to what parents and teachers want. Twice as many girls as boys are high achievers. They are not often school leaders and, although they may not be highly creative, they are very productive. They are less interested in the "Why?" of facts than the "What?" They prefer explicit directions from the teacher. Their logic and organization are good; they are liable, therefore, to reject tasks that are directed towards means rather than ends. Reading is important to them, recreation less so.

Teachers respond well to them (understandably) and while many of the girls will become teachers or secretaries, the boys prefer math and science to the humanities and are liable to become engineers. They aim to be conscientious, serious, to live by the rules, to be punctual and not a little punctilious.

2 / *The social leaders* shine in personal or social relationships. They tend to conform more to teenage mores than to teachers' expectations, yet they do well enough academically and sometimes very well indeed. Their social interests come first. Where the studious will be preparing for an examination, the social leader is likely to be getting elected. Yet these students are liable to get better examination results than creative intellectuals. They are fluent and persuasive: teachers, as well as other students, find them hard to resist. They are often physically attractive and are the top athletes.

Although they do not necessarily come from homes with money, they like spending money on themselves—often on clothes. Their parents are likely to be the young middle class. Their basic values are materialistic (even hedonistic) but they have a good-humored togetherness. They are not visionaries, yet they do good works; often they work for the crusade of the moment but rarely for an unpopular cause. They are genuinely popular and tend to become executives, doctors or lawyers.

3 / *The creative intellectuals* comprise at least 20 per cent of gifted students. However, they tend to achieve lower marks than the studious or social leaders. On creativity tests, they are fluent and original, the studious and the social leaders often being as fluent but less original. The creative tend to be prickly people who ask teachers below-the-surface and even below-the-belt questions.

They tend to become future scientists (but not engineers), artists, writers, musicians and scholars-at-large. They are inclined to be sceptical, yet have a deep-seated idealism and a tendency to probe basic issues. They frequently see the discrepancy between people's expressed beliefs and their actions, and this disturbs them. Although they are serious, their humor is impulsive, subtle and, above all, absurd. They are devotees of shaggy-dog stories.

Rather than desiring explicit instructions, they thrive on free choice. They buy books and read them, but are liable to read an exotic variety of things rather than school books. They are an offbeat group: although they care deeply about the human race, they are liable to date late and are more concerned with process than product. Often they do not want or expect rewards, and their eyes are on ultimate goals rather than immediate tasks.

4/*The rebel* is much rarer, and might be termed an individualistic creative non-intellectual. His nonconformity is mainly a means of showing dislike for regimentation at all levels. These students are extremely low achievers, although most are moderately gifted and some are brilliant. They are neither leaders nor followers, yet they can be master-minds in some aspect of the sub-culture (often bordering on delinquency).

Generally teachers reject them, and the students respond in kind. Only a few are active in school activities. If they are, it is usually because a teacher spends much time and effort encouraging them.

Most of the rebels are boys. Their dress is unconventional, and they are generally low in social responsibility. They are more able non-verbally than verbally. As a result, they appear not to be fluent (fluency usually referring to verbal productivity). Yet they are highly original in their ways, and many are clever with their hands.

Most rebels stem from the lower class, and their parents are often outsiders who place little value on social or intellectual things. Sometimes rebels can be responsive to unusual ideas, but they are generally at odds with the school and the community. Only a few will continue their education beyond school, where they are liable to develop technical skills. Others may go into entertainment or sports.

Movement from one type to another is liable to be on a horizontal or vertical basis (see Figure 8 opposite). The rebel is not likely to become a high-achieving studious, nor vice versa; the same is true of the social leader and creative intellectual. This would also apply to overlapping. There are some students who combine characteristics of the high-achieving studious with those of the social leader, but it would be extremely rare to combine the characteristics of the rebel and the high-achieving studious.

The Drews scheme has clearly all the values and difficulties of any stereotype system. If regarded as a series of absolutes it can distort work in schools; however, if treated as an approximate guide it does have certain values. It is more inclusive than personality and biographical information collected only from high creatives because it indicates possibilities for change.

Although Elizabeth Drews' stereotypes are drawn from data given by gifted students, they are clearly generalizable to drama work with students of average ability. How many drama teachers, for example, do not recognize at least most of her profile of the rebel? We all meet up with such a student every now and again. He often has real ability in improvisation (non-verbal skill providing intuitive and non-fluent knowledge), whereas teachers in most other subjects (requiring verbal skills with rational and fluent knowledge) think he is unintelligent.

More importantly, these stereotypes allow us as drama teachers to see in a fairly crude way some basic differences between students. They permit us to have some premises for our work in leading students to develop their own potential. If, as Brian Way says, the purpose of drama in education is to develop people rather than to develop drama, Drews' stereotypes provide us with some basic guidelines ("temporary absolutes," in Louis Arnaud Reid's terminology).

In terms of creativity, they allow us to place the concept in the context of giftedness. Generalized postulations, such as the opposition of the creative with the intellectual student, can be misleading. It is plainly untrue (as drama teachers have known for so long) that the so-called intellectual student is uninterested in drama, while his opposite, the so-called creative student, is more skilled in spontaneous improvisation.

	More Conformity		
Concern with Non-ideas	Social Leader	High-achieving Studious	Concern with Ideas
	Rebel	Creative Intellectual	
	Less Conformity		

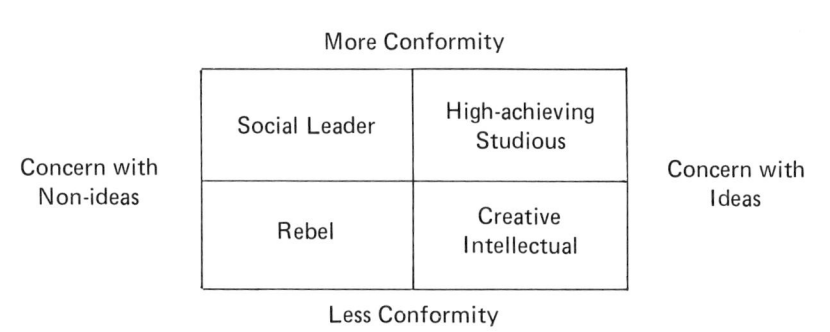

Figure 8: Typology of Giftedness (from Elizabeth Drews).

For example, one drama class of teenage students I taught at Colne Valley High School, Linthwaite, Yorkshire, comprised some thirty-five boys and girls classified as "more able." Specifically this was described as: having an IQ of 140 or more, and being "intellectual" in that they had the highest marks in the total age-year of the area. Yet some of these students demonstrated characteristics parallel to those of Drews' stereotypes: some required specific objectives for an improvisation while others demanded free choice; some were more interested in leading groups while others concentrated on achieving a group product; some had incredible flights of zany imagination while still others were logical and predisposed to common mental patterns. Thus, although classified by the school as "more able," and often treated by teachers as academic or intellectual, this class was in reality made up of a variety of styles of thought. Interestingly, there was no one pure rebel stereotype, though several of those who were predominantly social leaders or creative intellectuals had rebel traits. In improvisation, I quickly discovered that I could not commence from the crude concept of "more able." What I had to do was to evolve a character profile for each, using adjectives and similar methods to that of Drews, in order to "start from where they are."

Creative Learning

But if drama teachers can start from existing individual profiles as a method of determining students' needs, what happens then? How do they teach? What do they expect students will learn? And what will be "creative" about what they learn? In order to discuss these problems adequately, we will examine them in two contexts: first, with *all* students (including the gifted); and second, with the gifted themselves.

Creative Learning of All Students

I have put forward theories of imagination and learning in Chapter 1. These indicate certain basic patterns of mind and maturation which are common to all students. In order for drama teachers to lead students towards creative learning, these patterns must be enhanced.

The basic mental activity of mind is to receive percepts, transmute them, and then to act with the products of the mental activity. This process can be expressed by the paradigm: Percept—Imagining—Act. In the most general terms, drama teachers should lead students to develop their potential in each of these three aspects of existence.

It is assumed that mind is active in an "as if" manner, as we have seen in Chapter 2. It is in constant oscillation: not that polar opposites are constantly created but, like any living organism, the constituent elements are always in a state of tension, creating forms of oscillation. It is no accident, it seems to me, that Witkin can, in terms of creative arts with adolescents, describe these as contrasts, semblances, harmonies, discords, polarities, identities, syntheses and dialectics. Winnicott has shown that the internal world of the baby attempts to relate to the environment by giving it meaning; moreover, he shows that human life is the continual story of relating inner and outer, and that the key factor in doing so is play. This is the basis from which Witkin's qualities can develop in terms of the media used (see Chapters 2 and 6).

In this context, learning becomes the ability to assimilate the levels of substitution, the forms of expression and the types of media *appropriate for the specific student*. Moreover, play is seen as a process that is continuous through life, though its forms develop from the external to the internal. And art is seen as a series of developments on an ontological basis which evolve from play in terms of expression and media.

Thus drama teaching is largely a matter of understanding *representation*. In other words, the primal act is a representation of mental activity, and all other forms of expression are built upon (have within themselves) a dramatic component. This is the reason drama teachers of young children can move with ease from drama to music, dance and painting; or why adolescents revel in light and movement during their improvisations. Each of the substitutes are overlapping yet discrete representations (see Figure 3 in Chapter 1). It matters little to a 4-year-old if he expresses his imaginings in dramatic play or paint or dance. Clearly, however, gifted adolescent students will vary in their forms of representation: the high-achieving studious is likely to use one form at a time, whereas the creative intellectual will probably mix media.

Implementation on the part of the drama teacher, therefore, implies the following:

● acknowledging the personality profile of the student;
● assessing the student's current forms of substitution and expression, together with his or her skill in media;
● providing situations and frameworks within which the student can best develop his or her potential perception, imaginings and forms of action.

For all students the "creative" element in creative drama is the extension of the self to the individual's maximum ability.

Creative Learning of Gifted Students

E. J. Burton has said:

> Drama work undertaken will be no different from dramatic activity elsewhere. The basic experiences and material of living are not affected by the possession of a high IQ, or knowledge gained by reading; nor is the dramatic exploration, assimilation, and re-presentation which are a normal and healthy accompaniment of living. But there may be differences in content; there may be differences in form and aesthetic feeling; there may well be differences in emotional quality and emphasis which seem to stem from the loneliness of the "gifted," who is today subject to "deprivation" more than others because of current trends and social attitudes.[11]

Burton's classic paper on drama work with the gifted examines content, form, affectivity and fantasy, and I shall not rehearse his arguments here. However, it is clear that the basic approach to gifted students is "the same, only more so." Even so, we must acknowledge that gifted students *are* different, and must be treated differently from the norm. In what way is "more so"?

Drews' profiles assist us here. We can create profiles of dramatic stereotypes, somewhat as follows:

1/ *The high-achieving studious* will work hard in drama, though in conventional rather than associative ways. The improvisation may not be very original, but it will be detailed, well structured and thoroughly rehearsed and performed. They work best with explicit directions and do not like open-ended situations to work from.

2/ *The social leaders* will produce good social or group drama, working hard within the group to reach a consensus. They are usually good talkers and are good-humored, and most groups they lead will have a satisfactory product within the time span allotted.

3/ *The creative intellectuals* will have the original ideas, and their dramatic behaviors are best described by the nineteen common adjectives (see p. 100). As they are prickly and sceptical, their group improvisations are not always harmonious. Such students like open-ended situations, respond with enthusiasm to free selection, will tackle situations on their own, and will often produce dramatic humor that is both subtle and absurd.

4/ *The rebel* is as likely to disrupt an improvisation as to support it. Only with considerable patience and encouragement from the teacher can the rebel forego his dislike of socialization and become creative within the drama. He is liable to be better with his body in improvisation than with his voice, better at mime than with scripts. My experience also tells me that the rebel can be a superb slapstick comedian, revelling in his technical proficiency.

The teacher can encourage each of the above stereotypes to change in either or both of two ways: to increase his natural potential within his given mode; and/or to develop his personal characteristics towards other modes. There are, needless to say, moral values implied in the latter.

Thus, for gifted students, what is creative about creative drama is similar to that for average students but, in addition, developments to other modes can occur. Above all, the teacher must always "start from where they are." Where they are, however, is not merely the human base of all students; it also includes certain specific differences. In fact, the same principle applies to all students with differences—the blind, the deaf, the physically handicapped, and so on. In all drama teaching, the teacher must attempt to identify the specific needs of the students in their space, time and age stage, and provide those activities which will lead towards them fulfilling their potentialities.

Conclusion

This chapter has merely attempted to explicate a context for thinking about approaches to creativity. Drama teachers have been much confused by the term "creative." Behavioral scientists have mostly used it to apply to those students we have identified as creative intellectuals; when we wish to apply behavioral findings to the whole field, therefore, we can be led astray.

It is more productive to consider the creative aspects of creative drama in two contexts: as applied to all students; and as applied to those who are gifted (including the creative intellectuals). This approach at least allows us to relate our work to the existence of the individual student. We must assess the needs of his personality, his current forms of expression, and then provide those dramatic situations which will develop his potentiality. In the case of the gifted, and specifically for the creative intellectuals, the teacher may in addition lead him to other modes of personality which will enhance his capacities for learning and for an enriched existence.

Chapter 6

Expression: The Drama of English and Language Learning

> "Look after the sense
> and the sounds will look after themselves."
> —*Lewis Carroll*

Theory

My argument in this chapter will be that dramatic activity is the basis for learning, and particularly for the learning of language (including first language). At first sight, this may seem a little startling. However, it is my intention to show that the increasing rationality of learning, particularly language learning, is set within a holistic context. Moreover, this context, which is both analytic and emotional, is dramatic.

To put it another way, if we expect students to learn how to work with a language (with the increasing complexities of categorization and analysis that are always necessary) then we had better place language activities in a meaningful context. And for a context to be meaningful to the student, it has to be "whole," unified and dramatic.

Now, needless to say, I shall *not* be claiming that students studying English should do nothing else but theatrical performances. Nor shall I be claiming that senior students can only learn to parse, precis or paraphrase by acting *Macbeth* on a stage. Such are not the thrusts of my argument. I am treating the term "drama" in a particular way: as indicating *the process of life whereby we relate to the external world through spontaneous acting.* We can do this either in reality (in life we are improvising every moment of the day); or we can do it in pretence, "as if." Drama is the living process whereby our imaginings (thinking "as if") become externalized (acting "as if"). Dramatic action is the prime method whereby we can express what we imagine, and all other methods are derivative of this.

Thus, while here I will emphasize "play," I am not necessarily including "a play" (a form of literature which may or may not become theatre). And when I insist that drama is the basis of language learning, I do not mean through such performances as the annual nativity presentation of the kindergarten. Rather, I am talking of spontaneous action, creative drama and improvisation. I am asking that speaking, reading and writing should be seen as *partial* representations of thinking. To be learned well, they must include total thought. Creative drama and improvisation are *whole* representations of thought—we act with our total selves. Thus they provide language learning with whole meanings for each student.

Speaking, reading and writing are, like drama, symbolic actions. We have seen in Chapter 1 that we mentally transform the world around us both "in our heads" and in actions. We create a personal world. We create an interior model of the external world. Thus we all have two environments—inner space and outer space. From birth to death, human development is the continuous story of how we relate inner and outer worlds or, as Tagore put it:

> On the seashore of endless worlds
> Children play.

By "as if" thinking, we project ideas into dialogue, or exchange. Once we have imagined, then we can act: we can speak or write, gesture or dance, sing, paint or create in three dimensions. Or we can build homes, make gardens, or create the "miniature worlds" of committees. Thus "we habitually create representations of one kind or another of the things we meet in the actual world in order to use them in making fresh encounters."[1]

Masks and Media

We can look at these actions in two ways: as *forms of expression* (or masks); and as *forms of extension* (or media).

Actions are not merely representations, they are also expressive of our total thought. They are expressive of what we have imagined. Moreover, we combine images in our own particular way: how we combine them relates to the structure of our own inner world. Thus actions are relative:

> Your representation of the world differs from mine, and this is not only in so far as the world has used us differently . . . it is also because your *way of representing* is not the same as mine.[2]

Someone can ask of expressive work in schools, "Expressive of *what*?" Such actions are expressive of both mental work—transforming perception into thought by imagining; and our personality —the particular way in which we mentally work. In this sense, expression is a mask. It is an external expression of our true self—our "face," or our inner world.

But a form of expression can also be seen as an extension. To be effective in the external world, as McLuhan has shown, we use extensions of ourselves. All technological media are extensions of the body: we extend the hand with the pen, the foot with the wheel, and the electrical circuitry of the brain with radio and television. To act effectively, we must use a medium. To express our imaginings in writing, we require the medium of a pen.

Although this is an extension of the body, it is also a projection of the self. The medium is an extension but, *at the same time*, an expressive mask is a projection of our inner felt world. Rembrandt used paint, Thomas Hardy used writing, and Shakespeare used speech. In each instance, they did two simultaneous things: they used a physical medium which was effective for their forms of extension, and they projected a mask which was effective for their forms of expression.

Learning and Expression

The use of effective masks and media is only slowly acquired through maturation. Learning is involved. Teachers must lead children not merely to distinguish between perceptions (through concentration and awareness), to build varieties of images, and connect them into modes of thought; they must also lead students towards appropriate actions—appropriate for them—in *how* they can be expressed in masks, in *how* they can be extended in media, and *which* is most appropriate in each particular instance. Action is conditioned by choice. "Which mask and medium do I use now?" is the permanent sub-text of every student's questions.

Genetic Development and Form

Genetically considered, the baby's first fully successful attempts at expression are dramatic. Our inner world learns how to adapt old masks into new ones, different media out of existing ones, in a continual process of learning to live with others and the external world. Thus different forms evolve. In terms of artistic expression, as indicated in Chapter 1, the primal act becomes displaced on its immediate substitutes: sounding, moving and being. Not only artistic forms but all expressions develop in a similar manner. In other words, each of the displacements of sounding, moving and being can be viewed as forms of expression *and* as forms of extension, and their growth is genetic.

There are four factors in such growth:

1 / *As expressive forms emerge, they increase in discrimination. When we "put on" a new medium, it is more discriminate and accurate than older forms.* The primal act is gross. The medium used when we act is the total self: body, gesture, voice, total being— all existing in time and space. This act (*I am my mother*) is more gross than the refinement of pure sound ("mumumumum . . .") which, in itself, is less accurate than the evolving word ("Mommy").

2 / *Later expressive forms are less rich than earlier ones. Increasing discrimination of evolving media automatically produces a less rich extension than earlier forms.* More sophisticated masks and media are less rich than more gross expressions and extensions. Newer forms are more precise in meaning than earlier ones, but they allow for a less whole expression and extension. What is conveyed may be more sophisticated, but the connotations are less.

Thought is total. It is intuitive and rational, affective and cognitive, unconscious and conscious. Expression represents thought. A mask (which uses a medium) cannot *be* the thought, although it can *represent* it. Thus no expression is as holistic as the thought itself. Moreover, expressions differ in degrees of representation. Initial masks (such as the dramatic) are richer in representation than later ones although they are less discriminating. Thus the dramatic act is richer and less discriminating than speech, which is richer and less discriminating than writing.

3 / *More discriminating expressions have within them the context of earlier masks. Later expressive media contain within themselves the implications of earlier ones.* Advanced expressions may be more sophisticated and less holistic; yet, at the same time, when we use them we *assume* a greater context than they appear to have on the surface. Advanced expressions are more flexible: earlier forms can be incorporated into them by choice. For example, "Hullo" can be said with a variety of emotional overtones, each of which is beyond the simple nature of the word itself. In the same way, we can say that the symbolism of art and religion is richer (if less accurate) than that of mathematics. Yet, as Einstein has said, even the abstraction of mathematics can reveal "the mystery of life"; behind mathematics, there is something greater to be "revealed."

4 / *All forms of expression provide feed-back to the mental activity*

that gave rise to them. Expression produces an act which alters the environment, and this, through perception, affects subsequent mental activity. Further, one form of expression provides feedback which will affect subsequent imaginings in whatever form. That is, initial expression in visual form affects later expression in verbal form; and both visual expression and oral interpretative expression give structure to written expression.

As we shall see below, each of these four factors of growth contains inherent dramatic components.

In terms of expression, thought masked linguistically is liable to be more rational than thought which uses the medium of paint. Yet the feeling expression of visual art has a rational context, and the rational expression of language has an affective context. In contrast, the more gross dramatic expression is holistic: it contains both rational and affective elements, and tends to work from an equivalence of hemispheres. Genetically considered, earlier expressions tend to work equally with both mental hemispheres. With maturation, evolving forms of expression tend to emphasize one hemisphere. Yet it should be remembered that a sophisticated expression has evolved from (and contains within it) the holistic context of earlier masks.

In terms of teaching, this indicates that instruction in the arts must be inclusive of a rational context, and the teaching of language must be inclusive of an affective component. Prior to language, there are many learnings to which language must relate: "A person's behavior may be based upon many interlocking equivalence-difference patterns which are never communicated in symbolic speech."[3] What the mind organizes in creating its inner world is far more than words:

> Woven into its fabric are representations of many kinds: images directly presented by the senses, images that are interiorized experiences of sight, sound, movement, touch, smell and taste; pre-verbal patterns reflecting feeling responses and elementary value judgements; post-verbal patterns, our ideas and reasoned beliefs about the world: images derived from myth, religion and the arts.[4]

Good language teaching, therefore, is built upon learnings which, in themselves, are more holistic. Learning to write follows upon learning both to see and to speak. And learning to see and speak is built upon learning to act dramatically. But it is not merely that dramatic action is genetically earlier—it is assumed by the acts of speaking and writing. Spontaneous dramatic action, therefore, is the very foundation of language learning.

Language and Dramatic Play

Dramatic play is a basic activity for the learning of language at all ages. All functions of consciousness arise from dramatic actions. Piaget says that they are an essential component of all learning: imitative and play actions work on old mental schemas in order for new schemas to grow.

Dramatic play results in two fundamental learnings, *the growth of symbolization,* and *the learning of imaginative intentionality.* These are not diverse learnings, but evolve in a symbiotic relationship.

The elements of symbolization begin in the early sensory-motor period (about 6 months of age) when imitation brings forth the capacity to represent reality. This results in the primal act when imitative actions can take place in the absence of a model. Pretending to be asleep can lead to putting a doll to sleep. Play is the mechanism that permits this to happen. It allows the ego to assimilate the whole of reality, i.e., to integrate it in order to relive it, to dominate it or to compensate for it. The learning of intentionality, on the other hand, permits us to see the possibilities of what we imagine. To do so, we must "feel for" objects or people. That is, we have an empathy for others — we must "get into their shoes," which is a kind of dramatic impersonation. It is this combination of imagination and impersonation which creates the energy (motivation) necessary for action, and upon which learning rests. Dramatic play, therefore, is the life mechanism whereby we learn anything, including language.

There are confusions about the term "play." It is not the opposite of work. As Peter Brook has said: "To play needs much work. But when we experience the work as play, then it is not work any more." Nor is play simply "child's play." It lasts throughout the life span though, with adolescence, it tends to go underground. As Vygotsky observed: "The old adage that child's play is imagination in action can be reversed: we can say that imagination in adolescents and schoolchildren is play without action."[5]

The transition of play from infancy to adolescence is, however, complex. We have already seen that the purpose of play is to relate inner and outer worlds while, at the end of the first year, the baby learns to distinguish the "me" from the "not me." The primal act allows the young child to view the "not me" (the object) as an emotional cue for action; he learns that the "not me" can be replaced by an idea. With maturation, he learns that the "not me" can become an extensional medium (or a mask) whereby he can express his ideas in action. This coincides with advances in speech and language—word meanings replace objects as stimuli for action. Vygotsky's criterion for play is that it is dramatic; it creates an imaginary situation, and "creating an imaginary situation can be regarded as a means of developing abstract thought."[6]

Children's play is dramatic and grounds experience. It provides the "I am" experience that allows for meaningful learning: it results in what Vygotsky calls "renunciation and control." Thus "the child weeps in play as a patient, but revels as a player." In the game of "sorcerer," the child must run away from the sorcerer in order not to get caught. Yet, at the same time, he must help his companion and get him disenchanted. In the game "he acts counter to what he wants." In other words, a rule has become affective—a motivation, an internal rule. Thus, by adolescence, play is undertaken not just for itself but for the meaning it carries: "internal and external action are inseparable: imagination, interpretation and will are the internal processes in external action."[7] In terms of implementation, therefore, the imagined and dramatic situation (the empathized thought expressed in improvisation) is a prime mechanism for learning.

Throughout the life span, the different play forms ground learning in the personality. So much so, indeed, that the paradigm, "I am, I do, I create" becomes the hallmark of good teaching. This paradigm can be viewed in two ways: as the development in infancy—the "I am" and the "I do" must be established before the "I create" can occur in the primal act; and as it applies to all learning whatever the age. The first condition for learning is the "I am" experience: the person must feel he is of worth, and that what is to be learned has an inner significance for him. Then he must be able to "do" those elements of the task that are necessary (the skills of the segments of the task) before he can create.

Dramatic Action as the Basis for Language

The development of play actions is paralleled by those in language. The child first speaks aloud to himself whatever he thinks and feels. This "passes into a whisper and finally becomes internal speech . . . (so) that the child of seven or eight years begins to solve complex problems with the aid of internal verbal connections."[8] Language development is linked with dramatic play, and has been so described by both Bruner and Vygotsky.

Bruner has described the development of language as three stages of representation: the enactive, the iconic, and the symbolic. The enactive is what we have been terming the externally dramatic in which "the infant could thus only 'know' his world by performing his repertoire."[9] In other words, when something is imagined it has to be acted, just as when a word is thought it has to be said. The iconic system occurs when images "stand for" perceptual events. This occurs with the primal act and continues to grow. However, symbolic development can only occur when there is a certain arbitrariness about the symbol. The meaning conveyed becomes specific rather than general. Although the three stages develop in that order, each depends upon the previous one for its development and "yet all of them remain more or less intact throughout life."[10]

That the externally dramatic is contained within symbolic forms of language is implied by Vygotsky's concept of two intersecting circles, the area of overlap being "verbal thought" and the distinct areas being "non-verbal thought" and "non-intellectual speech."[11] Each has relationships with the other and, simultaneously, each can be the predominant mode of operation at any specific time. Non-verbal thought can be exemplified by John Holloway's examples of

> intelligent overt behaviour on the part of ballerinas, sailormen, mountaineers, carpenters, cricketers, and many others. . . . In these fields, it is possible to "think" (in the sense of "solve intelligently") with one's hands, or one's feet, or one's whole body.[12]

Whether we use Bruner's stages or Vygotsky's circles, each demonstrates the factors of growth. Each as it evolves increases in discrimination, decreases in richness, provides implications of earlier forms, and gives feed-back. Feed-back involves what Bruner calls "reciprocal learning," which is particularly important in language. By this he means the way we learn in an interaction. Whatever language mode is used (speaking, reading, writing) within an interaction, we receive from the other person information which enables us to reshape what we do or say even as we are doing it or saying it. The feed-back of dialogue ensures that *we internalize the criteria of the other person*. In other words, we are using the imaginative "as if" process to "put ourselves in someone else's shoes" in order to use their criteria. This shows that even the factors of development, when applied to language learning, inherently contain dramatic components. And, as all language learning is within an interaction of one kind or another, dramatic action is an essential element in all forms of linguistic growth.

Teaching Language Modes

The learning of any language, including English, incorporates more than the language itself. It includes a mass of cultural influences, but learning is directly related to the consciousness of the learner. In other words, it is less effective to teach the modes of listening, speaking, reading and writing *per se* than to teach them in a dramatic and holistic context.

Listening

Good listening is the foundation for the other language modes. Listening and speaking evolve simultaneously: aural perception and oral expression are intertwined. When the child hears what others say, he tries to make sense of it and adapt this to his own sounds. The child takes the initiative to make sense out of sound. Only when he associates a meaning with an utterance can be begin to inquire about the nature of grammatical rules.[13] When parents talk in the child's presence, they expose him to general noise. The child tries to understand this, and the adults provide him with feedback to his own experiments with language. That is, from the child's inherent motivation to listen and to speak he gains the maximum meaning he can by relating his inner world to the outer world of sound.

Speaking

A child learns to speak by speaking *and* comprehending, by being actor *and* audience. His first sounds are more of music than of language: they are creative and spontaneous. Only when he has begun to discriminate sounds from amongst the noise around him does speaking involve language.

The teacher must evaluate the speech development of the student from his viewpoint. The student gives meaning to the external world and, at that specific moment in time, his speech reflects his comprehension of existence. For example:

> Experiments and day-to-day observation clearly show that it is impossible for very young children to separate the field of meaning from the visible field. This is a very important fact. Even a child of two years, when asked to repeat the sentence, "Tanya is standing up," when Tanya is sitting in front of him, will change it to, "Tanya is sitting down".... You say to the child: "Clock." He starts looking and finds the clock; i.e., the first function of the word is to orient spatially, to isolate particular areas of space; the word originally signifies a particular location in a situation.[14]

At any stage of development, speech reflects the individual's world view. With maturation, speech becomes more discriminating—the student will demonstrate his understanding of categories, hierarchies, syntax and the like. Yet it is also a less holistic expression of his thought. That is to say, whatever the nuances of his spoken language, he cannot talk with as much undifferentiated richness as he did in early childhood. Later speech is less of a direct expression of his whole self: on the surface, at least, it does not represent the equivalence of mental hemispheres. Adult speech is predominantly centred in the left hemisphere while the earliest talk is nearer to a hemispherical balance.

At the same time, adult speech has the sub-text of a more holistic representation. That is, dialogue between two speakers has inherently within it some assumptions which, at least on the surface level of mere words, we might hardly expect. A classic example is the dialogue that begins Harold Pinter's *The Birthday Party*:

MEG: Is that you, Petey? (*Pause*) Petey, is that you? (*Pause*) Petey?
PETEY: What?
MEG: Is that you?
PETEY: Yes, it's me.
MEG: What? (*Her face appears at the hatch*) Are you back?
PETEY: Yes.
MEG: I've got your cornflakes ready. (*She disappears and reappears*) Here's your cornflakes. (*He rises and takes the plate from her, sits at the table, props up the paper, and begins to eat. Meg enters by the kitchen door*) Are they nice?
PETEY: Very nice.
MEG: I thought they'd be nice. (*She sits at the table*) You got your paper?
PETEY: Yes.
MEG: Is it good?
PETEY: Not bad.
MEG: What does it say?
PETEY: Nothing much.
MEG: You read me out some nice bits yesterday.
PETEY: Yes, well, I haven't finished reading this one yet.
MEG: Will you tell me when you come to something good?
PETEY: Yes. (*Pause*)

This superbly crafted dialogue is not, of course, a direct imitation of life. Yet it has all the natural rhythms and ordinariness of day-to-day speech. However, as any professional actor knows, the script is only the stimulus for the performance. It is not merely that the actor must understand and learn the lines. On the contrary, the task is a laborious one and has the threefold mechanism involving mind, body and voice. The actor must mold his mind into the thoughts and feelings of the character. Initially, he must increase sensory awareness as a performer in order to react acutely to things and people; the senses have to be trained to respond as fully as possible to real life and, in addition, to imagined situations (which allies the process to play, as viewed by Vygotsky). Then, furthermore, the actor must communicate his sensory awareness to others—to other performers and the audience. Simultaneously, the actor's body must be a finely honed instrument: it has to be fit and skilled so that his physical reactions can be sensitive, intelligent, quick and controlled. Every movement in a performance must have its purpose—not merely the way in which Meg and Petey sit at a table, but the manner in which they walk, gesture, look at each other, raise an eyebrow, sit still—because these and all other movements provide a context of inner meaning for what is said. The process, specially crafted and prepared for in the theatre, is very like that of life. Moreover, it is an exemplar for learning. It is little wonder that, in common parlance, there is a synonymity between "play" and "a play," or that Buber could call the relationship between two people "a dialogue." All the professional actor's skills, and all the human being's abilities, when added together are more than the sum of the parts.

Even in adult life, being accurate and concise with language is not enough. In speech or writing, there is a deeper context of meaning which reflects our inner world, and any representation of that inner world is less than what it is expressive of. A speech expression—such as Petey's first line, "What?"—has a spatial context: his bodily expression of his thought. Willoughby Gray, in the first production of the play, conveyed with his body far more meanings, far more of his inner life, than could possibly be expressed by that single word. In particular, it gave expression to his status relative to Meg (an essential component of genuine dialogue as Johnstone has shown)[15] as well as levels of feeling that are inexpressible in plain words.

Yet the spoken words are the *focus* of meaning. All other meanings in adult life—the thoughts and feelings, the bodily expressions, the level of communication and status—focus on the words that are said. Spoken words may be less than the meaning, but meanings cluster to them according to our own particular way of looking at things—that is, my meanings and yours (even from the same spoken stimuli) may be different. This is clearly seen from the Pinter dialogue. At any moment the words that are said, and even the pregnant pauses between them, have different contexts of meaning to Petey as compared with Meg—and they differ from the meanings given to them by us, the audience.

In speech, the feed-back process affects not merely the words but all levels of thinking and representation. Beatrix Lehmann, as Meg in the first production of *The Birthday Party*, when she asked Petey if he liked his cornflakes, had a look of expectation. When he said "Very nice," she gave a little wriggle of satisfaction before she said "I thought they'd be nice." Her words, her wriggle, together with the whole vocal, bodily and mental context of that moment of delivery were a response to his "Very nice." His words and context gave feed-back to her question and, thereby, enriched her subsequent expression. Further, within any dialogue, expression in one style (voice, body, mind) affects later expressions in whatever style: a word from one can produce a gesture from another, and vice versa, and each later level enriches the earlier.

Thus, although speech can be regarded superficially as spoken expression in language, it is more than this. It assumes more than mere words, and what it assumes is the dramatic and holistic context of all engaged in the dialogue. In order for communication to occur, each person must relate to the other in more than words. For Meg to communicate with Petey—just as a teacher must communicate with a student—she does not merely address words or gestures to him. She must assume, as he speaks, his role: she must *understand what he is saying from his point of view.* From the stimulus (focused on his speech, but inclusive of his body and mind) she must take over his role in order to understand his context. In addition, as she speaks, she must try to *relate her expressions to his context*; she must attempt to make her message meaningful to him, which also implies that her message must assume his role.

Learning to speak, therefore, is not merely learning to say words in an appropriate grammatical structure with accuracy. It is also learning how to provide, and respond to, various sub-texts. Thus when we say that a child learns language by speaking *and* comprehending, this comprehension is seen as a massive intertwining of inner world and forms of expression as related to the inner world and expression of others. If teachers are to evolve effective methods of speech education, therefore, they must be inclusive of the total dialogue of the dramatic relationship between people.

In practical terms, this means talk. With young children, it includes talk with an understanding teacher that arises directly out of shared activity. The personalities of teacher and student must engage in dialogue about activities that really matter to them both. And it means improvisation: the imaginative expression of meaningful activities in terms of spontaneous drama, movement and speech. Talk that arises within, and as a result of, creative drama is meaningful to the student's inner world—probably the most meaningful of all, otherwise it would not be expressed. The same applies at the secondary level, though here it is group talk that is most important. The teacher is no longer the centre of the talk, but the stimulator of talk amongst the group. Talk is improvised vocal language: evaluation of it will be from the criteria of meaning and of length. And talk that is sincere and absorbed always creates a personal context for new experience, or experience that is reworked in improvisation. Language is only meaningful in situations, real or imaginary—and both can be expressed in improvisation. Language cannot be learned in a vacuum; it is a technique for acting with others. Both speaking within the improvisation, and talking about it afterwards, are necessary; speech is learned as both actor and audience, as participant and spectator.

When there are speech difficulties (say, with second language learners) improvisation can be supported by expressions in other forms. Spoken music and "sounding" are prior bases for speech. Thus such activities as playing with words, or using gibberish (nonsense talk), are helpful aids to relate speaking to the "I am" experience. The same type of return to earlier forms is useful elsewhere. For example, senior students studying a play by Shakespeare can relate the script to their inner lives by improvising scenes which they have already acted from the text. In all instances, the form which produces the most spontaneity is the one most likely to result in speech that is most rich and meaningful.

Finally, speech development with older students can be greatly assisted through drama by leading them to an understanding of sub-texts. The dialogue of Pinter (as above), rehearsed in the classroom, is a remarkable exemplar of spoken situations in life. It can lead students to apprehend *and* comprehend the significance of speech. Even more effective is to follow this with improvised situations (based on their own experience) where they can create spoken dialogue with similar qualities. When older students improvise in a form that has the same structure (i.e., in time and space) as the life experience, learnings are fecund. Climax, contrasts, inter-relationships of situations, persons, plot and action— these may be the inherent ingredients of dramatic form, but they are also inherent in the very process of living.

Reading

It is commonly thought that reading is learned by going from sound to shape, either letter or word shape. My argument is that this is not the case. Rather, the student relates shape to sound. Speaking and reading are related, but we do not learn them through the same process. Primarily, we learn speech through *sound* representations and reading through *visual* representations. These are different ways in which our inner world relates to the external world. Smith says:

> For written languges, surface structure is the ink marks or the chalk marks on a contrasting surface. Until interpreted or comprehended in some way, the surface structure of written language is simply visual noise.[16]

In all cultures learning to read is, first, through comprehending visual signs or symbols. It is only when visual discriminations have been made that they can relate to sound, and reading can begin.

But visual discrimination of letters and/or words is brought about by learning in two dimensions. As we have already seen, such learning is dependent upon learnings in drama, movement and three dimensions. These are degrees of discrimination, and one is built upon another. Reading (apprehension of two dimensions) relies upon learnings in three dimensions which, in turn, are built upon apprehensions of movement. Thus teaching young children to read, or instructing older students in remedial reading, must include experience that leads to conceptualization in these modes. To be precise: the two-dimensional learning necessary for reading must be based on rich experience in three dimensions, spontaneous movement and creative drama.

Much of the current literature in reading indicates that the key to language learning is meaning and comprehension. In order to achieve this, two steps are necessary: the student must be able to predict with reasonable certainty what the words on the page mean; and simultaneously, he must be able to make the necessary discriminations in the visual field. These steps are both learnings at the representational level. They do not indicate the total language known by the student. The instructional problem for the teacher is how to relate the language known by the student (in his inner world) to the process of reading.

> A child can only learn to read by reading. Only by reading can a child test his hypothesis about the nature of the reading process, establish

distinctive feature sets for words, learn to identify words and meanings with a minimum of visual information and discover how not to overload the brain's information-processing capacity and to avoid the bottlenecks of memory.[17]

To do this, the student must constantly act "as if" he is reading. He comes across a word he does not know and then acts "as if" he does know it—either by ignoring it until it is recognized, or deciding from the context what it might be. Thus the concept of play is extended into the field of reading. It also bases reading upon the "I am" experience. The teacher must provide the sympathetic climate which allows the student to feel he is of worth: thus instruction means being available when wanted, and asked, and providing such help with warmth and understanding. From the "I am" experience, the student can proceed to the "I do"; he identifies new words by making analogies with similar words, or parts of words, he already knows. "I create" follows. Skipping difficult words, and guessing at the meaning *is* dramatic; it is acting "as if." In creative drama, the student improvising as a policeman is acting "as if" he is the character, and in the spontaneous play he is skipping over the unknown and guessing at the meaning, just like the student learning to read. The student learning to read is fundamentally in the same position vis-a-vis reading-meaning as the improviser is in acting-meaning, speaking-meaning or dancing-meaning.

Reading activities in schools must be set in meaningful situations—and, at best, that means dramatic situations. Reading for a purpose that the student considers valuable is to activate the "I am" experience. That means that he has a need to learn, and the natural self-motivation or imaginative play provides the energy. As to the environment: "They specially need someone who cares about their doings without violating their privacy"[18]—someone who is there to be supportive, not to be on guard; someone they can identify with and who values reading. Reading should be made as easy as possible for students. Swift and easy comprehension is more valuable, even with mistakes, than reading that is slow and accurate. Effective techniques are based on enjoyment.

The use of spontaneous dramatic play for reading is suitable for all ages. And this applies not merely to initial learnings but also to improving reading capacity. The student who needs to read material in order to play (to research a project, to secure content for creative plays, etc.) has a deep-seated motivation to succeed. Moreover, it is the elitist teacher who snubs the so-called popular literature for reading purposes. A good teacher will identify the student's specific interests (and if that be in popular literature, so be it!) and relate reading to these. In recommending material for reading, the teacher's first question becomes: What is the "I am" experience of this student? Learning to read, and the improvement of reading, depends upon its being related to the student's inner world.

Writing

Writing occurs as a need to express the self, using a mask by means of a medium (pencil or pen). It is one means of representation—like acting, speaking, dancing, painting and the like.

Writing is more difficult than reading: "Recognition is easier than reproduction."[19] This is because it is more discriminating, and because the writer is usually concerned that someone else will read what he has written. Speaking first occurs without inner speech, but writing does not: "The act of writing implies a translation from inner speech."[20] There is a natural progression in the first learnings of language expression: drama—speaking—reading—writing. The earlier are progressively built into the later. Young children should have a sound foundation in the earlier forms before moving into later representations, and older students, retarded in a later form, are helped by returning to earlier forms. Drama, speaking and writing are all fundamentally creative activities rather than interpretative; yet they are creative in different ways. In drama, being a spectator comes after being a creator. In speaking, the one balances the other. But in writing, the spectator's learning comes first, through reading. Thus early learnings in drama, speaking and reading help the learning of writing.

Because writing is more precise than speaking, it is easier to say that a mistake is "wrong." However, the method which promotes the most effective learning is similar to that which assists speaking and reading: we learn to write by writing. If we need to write in order to act in the external world (because our inner world needs to express itself) then we are motivated to write and improve our writing. Yet it is a laborious process, both physically and mentally, because it is slower than most other forms of representation. Thus the best way to encourage writing is to make it easy—to make it directly relevant to the needs of the student.

A key teaching method is to encourage the student to put on a role in order to write. This applies at all levels. When first learning to write, the student is encouraged if he is to write something that will be of use in his play. The older student can also be excited by taking on a role in order to write, and the good teacher will extend the idea of play to all teaching situations. In secondary schools, the imaginative projections of dramatic readings and performance can produce rich written expression. Group playwriting, built on previous improvisation, relates to writing about concrete situations. Improvisation stimulated by real objects (e.g., a hat, a ball) which are used imaginatively, can lead to all kinds of writing ("How many uses can you think of for *that* hat?" "What sort of person might you be if you wore *that* hat?"). Play with concrete objects is a good basis in all grades for making descriptive language relate to the word. Simulation games of all kinds assist secondary students in their language development; in particular, they stimulate problem-solving and critical thinking. With all grades "what if" situations are highly productive; they alter real circumstances imaginatively to become inner stimuli for action in writing.

Like speaking and reading, therefore, writing must be related to the student's inner world, and that means the teacher must set all activities within a holistic context. All these modes are more precise than the meanings they express; each is a discrete representation of a total thought (cognitive and affective). The best learnings are those which relate to both mental hemispheres—holistic rather than categorical, affective *and* cognitive, unconscious *and* conscious, intuitive *and* rational, and which are based on an inner identification and empathy with others. Thus we can say that the most significant learnings in all language modes are those which are dramatically based.

Conclusion

Thus far, my argument has been that learnings in English and other languages must be placed in a total dramatic context. However, it is an additional point that methodologies used by those who teach drama as a subject can be useful to teachers of language.

Spontaneous drama has been a fundamental learning method throughout this century. However, it has appeared in a variety of disguises: as "the play way," as "creative drama," as "creative dramatics," or as "improvisation." It has also been related to the discipline of drama/theatre. Each approach has differences—in philosophy, and in techniques of planning, implementation and evaluation. However, they all have one attribute in common which is immensely useful for teachers of language.

The most successful technique of drama teaching is where the instructor provides the "What?" and the students provide the "How?" In other words, the teacher makes a judgment as to what is the most appropriate framework for the students' activity;

how the students pursue this activity is what is spontaneous. Two examples will serve. First, we can illustrate the spontaneous story technique of Slade with Grade 1 students:

    TEACHER: Once upon a time there was a little—
    CHILD 1:   Mouse!
    TEACHER: Good. What was his name?
    CHILD 2:   Peter!
    TEACHER: Yes, it was Peter. Well, one day, Peter was walking down the path. What do you think he saw?[21]

After the story has been completed in words, all the children then act it spontaneously as the teacher tells it again. Second, the teacher may decide that a Grade 10 (15-year-old) class is ready for the topic of job interviews. Through question and answer, he draws out the framework of the exercise: what types of job? what sort of questions? what characters would the interviewers have? and so on. The students then divide into groups of three (interviewer, interviewee and a director) to plan and rehearse the improvisation. Depending on the needs of the students, these improvisations may or may not be performed before the others. The students are always free to create within the framework of the exercise: they provide the "How?" to the teacher's "What?"

The language arts teacher can see the surface value of this type of work for the development of talk. But it has greater values than this: it encourages spontaneity, flexibility and creativity; it teaches the use of masks and media; it grounds symbolization and enhances imaginative intentionality; it internalizes the criteria of the other person and encourages communication and inter-action; and it works through the paradigm of "I am, I do, I create" so that the play/work activity is grounded within the personality. Clearly, the outcomes of such an approach can be dramatic. But that is not all. It is a common approach to social studies and other subjects.

And many learnings are included within those of speaking, reading and writing. This is most obvious in speaking: almost all forms of improvisation (except those of mime and dance) involve speaking. But, in addition, good teachers can easily envisage outcomes in reading and writing. Spontaneous drama convinces secondary students they have something significant to say and do (the personal uses of language). Subsequent expressions allow them through reading and writing (the impersonal uses) to bring forth all the locked up information they have about themselves and their lives.

Chapter 7

Dramatherapy

> "The best in this kind are but shadows;
> and the worst are no worse, if imagination
> amend them."
> —*Shakespeare*, A Midsummer
> Night's Dream, V, 5:215

Dramatherapy is used under a variety of conditions. It can be used both as a treatment for those who are mentally or physically handicapped and as a help for those who are not handicapped. Thus, in the first instance, it can be used in an adjunct capacity to assist psychotherapists and physiotherapists in their work while, in the second instance, it can be used by teachers in schools or by leaders in adult groups in many circumstances—learning, counselling, leisure, recreation and the like.

As a technique it is all-inclusive and not limited to one methodology. A basic assumption is that spontaneous dramatic action is a healthy activity and, within that, a variety of techniques are available, whether these be as propounded by Peter Slade, Brian Way, Dorothy Heathcote, Jacob Moreno, Viola Spolin or others. As an all-encompassing concept, dramatherapy has been responsive to practical approaches from anthropology (Sue Jennings), psychiatry (James Sacks), dance (Judith Koltai), theatre (Richard Schechner), and many others. That it responds so well to diverse approaches demonstrates that dramatherapy is a rewarding concept because it is flexible to life demands.

That it defies brief definition is, in a sense, an advantage. Theoretically it is based upon the dramatic metaphor as a significant way to understand existence. For Cicero, drama was a reflection of truth while Shakespeare and his contemporaries thought that

"All the world's a stage." This metaphor has changed over time and, appropriately for the last quarter of the twentieth century, it has been aptly phrased by Lyman and Scott as "the drama of social reality"—that is, life *is* theatre.

This metaphor is becoming predominant in many theoretic fields. Lyman and Scott's work is merely the most recent in a long line of sociological writings that have taken a dramatic perspective of social existence—Kenneth Burke, Erving Goffman, Peter L. Burger and Hugh Dalziel Duncan amongst them—while Marshall McLuhan's concept of "put on" has enriched communications theory. In anthropology, Victor W. Turner has analysed the dramatic ceremonialism of many cultures; he has shown that these are social dramas which represent the major concerns of people. Theatre scholars, such as James R. Brandon on Southeast Asia and James L. Peacock on Java, have illustrated this in specific instances. In child psychiatry, D. W. Winnicott showed that dramatic play is *mediate* between our inner world and the environment; that is, it is the way in which we attempt to make sense of the world around us, and that this is characteristic of all human beings from birth to death. Specific therapeutic approaches utilize the dramatic metaphor: the gestalt work of Fritz Perls and Janet Lederman who use methods like "the awareness continuum" and "the empty chair" which are inherently dramatic; and Eric Berne's transactional analysis which is shot through with drama.

The diversity of these theoretical approaches, together with the variety of techniques employed, centre around one metaphor, best exemplified by Richard Southern's "the costumed player." Human drama exists in identification and impersonation—in the act of spontaneous performance—whether that be in life itself or in the art form of theatre. Dramatic action of all types is the living analogue of human experience; it is "the double mirror" of existence, reflecting ourselves to others and others to ourselves. Thus its all-inclusiveness is a necessary characteristic of the activity.

But this can raise theoretic problems. It not merely makes definitions difficult but it can raise questions for which there may not be categorical answers. The rest of this chapter will be concerned with several of these theoretical questions.

Dramatic Action

When is an action dramatic and when is it not? In all forms of action we can distinguish two extremes on a continuum: (a) that which is clearly dramatic, such as acting the role of someone who is washing his face; and (b) that which is merely habitual, such as washing one's face in reality. The fact that one may, while really washing one's face, be sometimes imagining that one is somebody else does not negate this point.

However, between these two extremes of action there are a great many actions which it is hard to characterize as purely impersonatory or habitual. At what point does habitual action slip into dramatic action? Clearly the answer to this question lies within the internal activity of the individual. John Seely has illuminated the nature of dramatic action in his book *In Context*. He has shown that there are three models for spontaneous dramatic action: the exploratory, the illustrative and the expressive.

1 / The exploratory model
This is based on the exploratory dramatic play of young children ("Let's be bears") and is characterized by "sincerity and absorption" (Slade) and "concentration" (Way). In play, children's imaginative experience is as real to them as real life, and they are unaware of any audience they may have. This is commonly the type of experience aimed at by creative drama and improvisation in education and in dramatherapy. Yet with normal adolescents this experience is difficult to achieve and, increasingly, teachers are liable to use a darkened studio, emotional lighting and powerful music to induce absorbed dramatic experience. Thus any dramatic action which does not carry a high emotional charge may be undervalued by teachers and dramatherapists.

2 / The illustrative model
Some adolescents enact roles but are well aware of their audience. They use roles to communicate with others in social interaction and so imitate the behavior of others to support some analytic point they wish to make. The acting may stay at the level of mere copying, or it may be full-scale improvisation, even incorporating elements of the exploratory model. The adolescent may be absorbed at one moment and out-of-role the next.

3 / The expressive model
Similar to the illustrative model (indeed, in certain forms it is difficult to distinguish the two) is the expressive model. This is exemplified in Brecht's famous case of an eyewitness at a traffic accident describing the incident to others who have not seen it: at times he describes it in words, at times he uses the illustrative model and he may indeed slip into the exploratory model. The

major distinction between 2/ and 3/ is that the illustrative model analyses aspects of interpersonal behavior while the expressive model communicates both information about an event and comment upon its social significance.

In addition to the three models used in spontaneous drama, there is also:

4 / *The theatrical model*
Unlike the other models, the theatrical is part of a conscious art form. It has similarities with 2/ and 3/ in that its purpose is communicative, but it is contrived and selective, and requires considerable skill to be effective.

Seely's distinctions form a useful base for discussing the nature of dramatic action in therapy. For example, is there a developmental sequence to dramatic action? Do "normal" children and adults progress in age stages? And, if they do, are these sequential through models 1 to 4? If so, such a sequence of age stages would provide diagnostic guidelines for dramatherapists.

With pre-adolescent children there are some clear age stages (see pp. 12-18): (1) up to 10 months the child is identifying but not yet engaged in complete impersonatory acts; (2) prior to approximately 7½ years, children are mainly concerned with their own impersonations; (3) after about 7½ years, they become increasingly involved in planning their improvisations. Throughout pre-adolescence, drama is characterized by the exploratory model.

Adolescent students who have had rich experience in exploratory drama will, thereafter, work equally well with Seely's first three models. Those who have not had rich experience with the exploratory model in pre-adolescence will need to commence with the illustrative and expressive models and may, with the leader's care, return from time to time to the exploratory. There will be some adolescent attempts at the theatrical model but, without adequate experience in the other three, such attempts are liable to be insincere. There is, therefore, no direct hierarchy of dramatic behavior whereby model 1 leads through 2 and 3 to 4. But theoretically we can postulate:

• Model 1 seems to be characteristic of pre-adolescent children. Sara Smilansky has shown the effects of deprivation of dramatic play of this type.
• Models 2 and 3 seem to be characteristic of adolescent students. However, returns to model 1 seem to be necessary from time to time.

- Without adequate experience of model 1 in pre-adolescence, this can be led to in adolescence through models 2 and 3.
- Model 4 may evolve through the other three models though, as it requires considerable skill, it probably remains the domain of the few.

This seems to be borne out by both the literature and experience.

What are the implications of this for dramatherapy? Primarily these postulates provide a framework for assessment of dramatic action. They provide dramatic criteria. Yet, as Wittgenstein would say, the logic of any situation depends on both criteria and context. The dramatherapist will use these criteria within the context of the client group. For example, dramatherapy in the school situation, being a helping activity, must begin with an assessment of the students' needs. Often such children are lacking in self-confidence, and do not have a positive self-image. They like to return to dramatic activities which are characteristic of children whose chronological age is younger. For example, adolescents of this type often like to work with model 1 before 2 and 3. Several groups of less able adolescents (IQs of 72-84) with whom I worked while they were 11-15 years old only rarely moved from model 1. A few, with maturation, slipped into model 2 from time to time. In a number of instances, groups wished to attempt model 4 but, even while doing so, their performances took on the characteristics of model 1.

With psychologically or physiologically handicapped children or adults, the variations between client groups are radical. Many with severe mental retardation, which is so often coupled with emotional retardation, generally stay with model 1. Theoretically, however, one would expect classic patients like Binswanger's Ellen West or Ilse to be happier working in the 2 and 3 dramatic modes. The question for the dramatherapist becomes, therefore, which dramatic model is most suitable for this particular client?

Drama and Other Therapies

While it is theoretically useful to distinguish between types of dramatic action, observation of any dramatherapist at work leads to subsequent questions. He or she, while commencing from dramatic action, will often lead the client or client group into other media—movement and dance, music, poetry, two- and three-dimensional art, for example. Yet there are methodologies known as music therapy, dance therapy, art therapy and poetry therapy. When is an activity properly called dramatherapy, and when is it not?

This is related to a similar question in education *per se*, and an old and thorny question at that: namely, is drama in schools a subject or a method? Given the contexts of therapy on the one side and education on the other, these two questions are part of a key problem in dramatic activity. We have seen that drama is inclusive of many theoretical approaches and methodologies. In addition, however, it can be viewed as generically inclusive of all forms of expressive symbolization. How can this be?

In theoretic terms, this can be approached in at least four ways: sociologically, anthropologically, philosophically and psychologically. We have already briefly described the first two views where the dramatic metaphor is the exemplar of existence. Thus in any society the expression of existence is set within a dramatic context. For example, the Nootka and Southern Kwakiutl of British Columbia do not distinguish art from other elements of life; in fact, their great wooden sculptures, masks, songs, dances and ornamented costumes are conceived as part of their religious performances. Their Winter Ceremonials are a gigantic Mystery Cycle, originally lasting for months, and all artistic elements are an expression of this. For the sociologists and anthropologists cited above, therefore, a people's dramatic expression is the nub of their concerns, and other art forms go to assist this.

In terms of psychology, we have already seen in Chapter 1 that the identification/impersonation process is a key factor in human development. The child's inner world (the domain of psychology) creates meaning out of the external world (the domains of anthropology and sociology) and this occurs in certain well-defined stages. The maturation of the normal child in Western civilizations demonstrates that it is not until socialization has had its real effect (anywhere between 8 and 12 years) that the child conceives "an appropriate medium" for a particular expression. Until that time, he or she will work with any medium to hand in order to express imaginings, even combining them at will. In therapeutic terms, therefore, it is well to view the arts therapies in an integrated context, based upon dramatic action, rather than as therapeutic categories.

A related point is that made by David Best.[1] There is a literary script called *Hamlet*, theatre performances by the same name, as well as ballets, operas, and two-dimensional art forms. However, they cannot each be expressive of the same emotions; in other words, each art form is expressive of a different style of imagining and expressing our emotional life. Any person, therefore, who does not experience *each* of these styles when young is liable to be expressively and emotionally retarded. In terms of schooling, this means that children should experience all of the arts. In terms of therapy, this indicates that there may be a correspondence between forms of emotional retardation and appropriate treatments through the creative arts therapies; even so, however, each of them covertly is based upon dramatic action.

Not only does dramatherapy exist in its own right as an effective methodology but, according to the client's need, it can theoretically utilize any other artistic medium. The fact that there are other creative arts therapies does not negate the point. Just as air is inclusive of hydrogen and people are inclusive of males and females, so dramatherapy is a term for an inclusive style of action.

Drama Assessment

The degrees of substitution we have examined above raise another issue. Is art therapy appropriate for one client and music therapy suitable for another? If so, when is dramatherapy the best treatment and when is it not?

Media at an advanced level of substitution are more discriminate than those which are earlier. Thus we can see that there is a hierarchy of artistic media for therapeutic purposes.

I have shown in Chapter 6 that there are four factors to be taken into account when utilizing the creative arts media:

1/*As expressive forms emerge, they increase in discrimination.*
2/*Later expressive forms are less rich than earlier ones.*
3/*More discriminating expressions have within them the context of earlier media.*
4/*All forms of expression provide feed-back to the mental activity that gave rise to them.*

There is clearly another relationship here between drama in learning as a whole and dramatherapy. The child in school who has reading difficulties is struggling with media at Level 4 (see Figure 3) and his retardation is best tackled through the learnings necessary in previous levels. In such a way, the learnings of two dimensions and of language (both necessary for reading) are grounded in experience at earlier levels. In dramatherapy, too, the question becomes: At what levels are the patient's emotions grounded and at what levels are they not?

For example, Claire was a 12-year-old retarded girl who was referred to me for dramatherapy in 1957. Classroom teachers said she could neither read nor write and that she had great difficulty in saying anything. In her initial work with me she also demonstrated she had little interest in art therapy. In her drama work, moreover, she eventually demonstrated that she was happy not merely in "acting out" but also with the media of movement, dance, generalized sound and created music. In terms of diagnostic theory, therefore, her retardation was centred between Levels 3 and 4.

A second related example was 11-year-old Leonard whose speech was fluent but who could neither read nor write; his teachers said he could not remember anything he was taught even when it was told to him. With me, he demonstrated that he enjoyed drama, movement and dance, sound and creative music. Also, he was a compulsive talker but there was a dichotomy between what he said and what he meant; words were not used for their common meaning but with meanings peculiar to him. Like Claire, but in a different way, his retardation could be diagnosed as lying between Levels 3 and 4.

From such assessments, treatments can begin. In both of the above cases, we commenced all sessions from activities in Levels 1-3, only slowly introducing elements from Level 4 as applicable to each person.

Theatre

What of theatre as a model? Moreno based his psychodrama on it. However, dramatherapy is inclusive of models 1, 2, and 3 as well as theatre. Further, as we have seen, dramatherapy is inclusive of all other media and incorporates many other theoretic views. Thus it uses psychodrama as merely one approach amongst a plethora of others. Moreover, psychodrama uses one particular form of the theatrical model: improvisation before an audience. This has been followed by a variety of other therapeutic techniques, such as Jonathan Fox's Playback Theatre in New York.

But there are other forms beyond improvisational theatre, of which two are important for our discussion. First, and most obviously, is the major form of Western theatre (scripts performed in a playhouse before a witnessing audience) which Aristotle claimed provided catharsis (purgation of terror and pity) for the audience only. Although this mode is not normally used by dramatherapists, perhaps one style should be considered as a possible future helping technique—Theatre-in-Education (TIE).[2] It is possible to conceive, for example, of a group of clients and then, like a TIE team, use this as a stimulus so that each performer then works in spontaneous drama with smaller groups of clients. Such a Theatre-in-Therapy team would require training of its members in theatrical performance, improvisation and dramatherapy.

The second form of theatre which offers opportunity for development is "culture theatre." It is commonplace that, amongst tribal people, dramatic ceremonies provide a social cohesion and give the individual a strong sense of social identity. However, Louis Miller in Israel and Ross Kidd in Botswana have also demonstrated these same values in theatre *per se*. Miller, for example, has worked with communities that have suffered social breakdown, and encouraged them to build from improvisation to performances that make statements about their community; they have then taken these to other towns as performances. This methodology has clear therapeutic values for the original community but also provides other values for the audience-community.

These are simply two theatrical styles which might be developed in the therapeutic field.

Conclusion

I have drawn out only the obvious questions from basic dramatic theory. There are, quite clearly, many other questions that arise from such a statement but space precludes their examination here. It is to be hoped that readers will raise their own questions from this material and, indeed, question the basic theoretic assumptions commonly held by the field. Only in such a way can the combination of theory and practice (the genuine praxis) develop and the field genuinely grow.

Chapter 8
Culture and Curriculum: A Dramatic Context

> "Real education depends on the contact of human living soul with human living soul."
> —*John Stuart Mill*

When I ask taxi drivers, bell hops or bus conductors in various parts of the world about drama in education, they usually think I am talking about the training of professional performers. This kind of misapprehension arose when the world was seen through mechanistic eyes: the machine was the model whereby human beings were understood, deduction provided "truth," and cause-and-effect methods provided strict rules for human beliefs and actions. Mechanism reached its height in the nineteenth century although it has been projected into our own time by behaviorists such as B. F. Skinner. A hundred years ago, Oscar Wilde declared that "all art is useless" because in his mechanistic universe, where all art was object-centred and materialism was rampant, the arts were relegated to "the frills" of education and were only useful for future professionals.

The world has changed somewhat since them—but not as much as we might think. The failure of mechanistic systems is everywhere apparent. In government it progressed to fascism. Hitler's "final solution" to the Jewish question was based on a false cause-and-effect method of thought and resulted in a particular form of dehumanization. The collapse of mechanistic economics occurred in the Depression. Although today it is known that economic trends develop through the dynamic inter-relationship of multiple factors, only a limited amount can be done to control recession and inflation. Yet some politicians bring forward simplistic solutions because they think that cause-and-effect reasoning will produce "truth."

The general public's growing dissatisfaction with education is part of this malaise. During this century, school buildings have grown bigger, teachers have striven for a machine-like efficiency while their administrative duties and attendance at committees have grown in proportion to the demise of the little red schoolhouse. The growth of quantifiable evaluation, or measurement, has influenced the aims and objectives of teachers to such an extent that education has become increasingly abstract and less related to the human concerns of students and teachers. As a result, school education in modern industrial societies appears to the general public to be less effective. In reality, of course, it is no longer possible to set up mechanistic systems in education; nor is it possible to effectively impose abstract objectives on human beings and then numerically evaluate them—as if a school is a factory, manipulating people as if they were Charlie Chaplin in *Modern Times*.

What happens to curriculum is the creation of culture. Educational programs reflect the values of a society or, at least, certain significant elements of that society. Throughout modern industrialized nations, the groundwork of their educational systems was laid in the late nineteenth or early twentieth centuries when scientific mechanism was at its height. But once such systems were established, any alterations to them became mere tinkering with the machine. As a result, our schools reflect the culture of a bygone age.

How can curriculum be related to contemporary culture? To grapple with this question we need, first, to consider the nature of culture itself. In order to do so we shall use some of the concepts of social philosophers such as Paul Tillich, Martin Buber, Alfred Schutz, Maurice Natanson and others. But by placing these ideas within the dramatic metaphor, they are provided with a unique flavor.

What Is Culture?

To begin with, we need to consider what culture is not. First, it is not to be equated with nationalism, nor with the aberrations of a nation. Although it has some tangential concerns with what takes place within national boundaries, it works both inside and outside such boundaries. When Paul Tillich said

> At the time of our emigration it was not so much [Hitler's] tyranny and brutality which shocked us, but the unimaginably low level of his cultural expressions. We suddenly realized that if Hitler can be produced by German culture, something must be wrong with this culture...

he was expressing a common view of many Germans of his time. He went on to say: "If Hitler is the outcome of what we believe to be the true philosophy and the only theology, both must be false."[1]

But the outcropping of fascism in mid-twentieth century Germany was a style of stereotyped thinking that was not, and is not, confined to one country, or even within the confines of a national boundary. In a sense, fascism is merely one example of people becoming alienated from their essential human-ness. This can occur at any time and any place, and must be constantly guarded against. The appeal by Eichmann that, in committing the most inhumane atrocities, he was "merely obeying orders," was an extreme example of a person's estrangement from his human nature. The system, the organization, or (in Eichmann's case) the party, can alienate a person from himself. There is a surface appeal to a kind of objectivity, a non-human and non-feeling collectivity, that brings people to the lowest common denominator. It was this which shocked Tillich.

But such an aberration is not specifically German, nor even the prerogative of fascists. It can happen in any system—including education. Eichmann's defence was designed to appeal to the universal appreciation of the organization man.[2] As a mere link in the machine who passes down orders from above, and with no power to alter their content or influence their ultimate effect, what choice had he? The Nazi party, isolated him from himself. Thus Eichmann lived in an unreality that differed only in density from the schizophrenic.

Modern man is liable to develop schizoid symptoms. The pressures of the organizations to which we all belong, the appeal of the mass man of capitalism or the class man of communism, are not directed to our inner, felt, and unique situation. Rather, they are directed to standards, absolute rules, and objective truths which the organization places at greater value than the human needs of human beings. This trend can lead to an inner dichotomy: an overt recognition of the organization's objective truth, yet a covert need to satisfy our human qualities.[3]

This split between self and role has different effects with different people, and is certainly not confined within national boundaries. Despite what Tillich thought at the time, its outcropping in

Germany under fascism did not invalidate the values inherent in the philosophy of Schopenhauer or Nietzsche, or the theology of Harnack or Karl Barth.

Secondly, culture is not synonymous with high art, although art is a part of culture. Culture is not an elitist term. The Acropolis, a play by Kalidasa, a Zen painting, a symphony by Beethoven, a sonnet of Shakespeare—all are art works of the highest quality. But culture is more than these, and more than all such high art put together. It includes, for example, low art: the artistic activities of ordinary people and the most popular expressions of imagination produced at any given time. In fact, culture has implications far beyond art as such, although art and artifacts are highly significant aspects of cultural expression.

Thirdly, culture is not exactly defined by a linguistic grouping. It is true that those who speak the same language share an aspect of cultural thinking unavailable to others. Yet, at the same time, there are cultural commonalities between some peoples with different languages. For example, certain African peoples with different languages share many cultural traits; and, in Switzerland, people of dissimilar linguistic backgrounds share a common culture. The most common argument for a linguistic basis for culture is made by minority groups within a larger linguistic context: for example, Welsh speakers in Britain, or French speakers in Canada. They have a natural desire to protect their identity from the threat of the larger group's values, and part of their identity is linguistic. However, their argument has similarities with that of minority religious or political groups within larger contexts. Fundamentally, all these arguments are not those of language, religion or politics but of identity. Culture is concerned with identity, yet only one part of this is the language spoken.

Culture, then, is none of these. Nationalism, high art and language are all part of cultural activity, but culture is more than all of them. Culture is a dynamic and should not be confused with the products of cultures.

Culture has similarities with drama and theatre in that it is *a dynamic that exists in time whereby the individuals within it are related dramatically.* Culture is temporal: it is constantly in change, and it exists in the moment-to-moment of flux. Art forms differ as to whether they primarily exist in space, like painting, sculpture and architecture, or whether they are fundamentally within time, like drama and theatre, music and dance. These temporal art forms codify and crystallize existence into moments of significance— music in terms of sound, dance in terms of movement, and theatre in terms of persons who sound and move. In this sense, culture is much like drama and theatre.

Culture exists in a dynamic relationship between people in two ways: first in terms of community and, second, in terms of social life. It is a dynamic created by human beings which has reality for them. Indeed, it is made up of those meanings which have the greatest significance for people: the arts, sciences, religion, politics, therapy and education. These cultural worlds are made up of the significant actions of human beings and constitute significant life. In this sense, culture represents the living theatre of life: it consists of the dynamics between people that are highly significant in representing existence. It has, thus, the deepest importance for questions of curriculum.

Culture and Community

Cultural events can be distinguished from other events. Culture does not refer to habitual actions, to the activities of the mass man or the crowd or, indeed, a collection of individuals that lose their individuality. If he loses his individuality, the mass man loses his human qualities. Yet it is these same human qualities that give significance to cultural life.

Culture has more to do with *community* than *collectivity*. A community struggles for its own reality as a community: the people in it try to retain their individuality. They are human beings with human concerns. They are in touch with others with similar concerns. In contrast, in collectivity people work side by side rather than together. They aim for a unity that will permit the least possible diversity. Collectivity and community both work towards one goal, but community does so through the relation of people as individuals. Community is the working *with* one another by a multitude of persons. As Martin Buber put it, community is based on "its increase and confirmation in life lived towards one another."[4]

How do people in community retain both their unity and individuality? Community is based on love. This is an extension of that love which one person feels for another. In the relation of one person to another, we experience *identification and impersonation, empathy and love*. When we find ourselves in sympathy with others, we identify with them. Then they become models for us. We "put ourselves in their shoes," which is a kind of impersonation. We look at things "from their point of view"—create a drama with them. Empathy results as a kind of inner one-ness with them and, as a result, we can think of them lovingly. Two individuals then become "We."

This love on a one-to-one basis can be extended to others—into community. We move from marriage to community. Buber also said: "Marriage brings one into an essential relation to the 'world'; more precisely, to the body politic . . . the 'community' of marriage is part of the great community."[5] When I love another person, I *acknowledge* them: I accept their existence, fully and completely. In the same way, when I join a community in love, I accept that the community *is*. I share in its existence. I freely join my life to its life. Yet:

> I cannot be answerable for the other as one who is entrusted to me. But thereby a man has decisively entered into relation with otherness; and the basic structure of otherness . . . is the body politic. It is to this, into this, that marriage intends to lead us.[6]

By freely joining the community, I also freely accept your freedom, and the freedom of all others. We have created a dramatic relationship.

Culture is the expression of community. Love is a bond to another person and it leads to a love for the community which demonstrates the rights and legitimacy of others. In both marriage and the body politic, we acknowledge other persons; although they are similar to us as persons, they are in fact different. They are others whom we may help, and who may help us. Within community, we are all entrusted to one another. Yet we are not answerable for them. It is the expression of this state of community that is culture.

In a playhouse, an actor encounters other actors in one way; but he encounters an audience in a different manner. Here is an analogy with community. There are differences between the way we encounter another person and the way we encounter a community. We identify with them both. Yet identification occurs in a qualitatively different way in each instance. With one person, we recognize an actual identity, and this can be extended to those closely akin: for example, spouse, children and near relatives. When we identify with a community, however, love does not occur in such a concrete way. Rather, we understand the others in a community as *types*. Yet they are types who, we assume, exist in similar ways to us and "think like us." In personal love, the model is face-to-face and identification/impersonation happens in a direct way: I have personal empathy with him. Specifically, I do this by excluding my own concreteness. But this does not happen in my relation to community. There, my identification starts from my concreteness and I include others within it.[7]

Love of another, or of a community, is based on *acknowledgment*. We acknowledge that another person, or the community of other people, is of humanity—they are humans with rights like ourselves. Then we can fully realize that we can act in *reciprocity* with them. We acknowledge each other. Each of us has our rights. Yet, at the same time, we can all assist one another. To truly acknowledge another person is to accept a dramatic relationship with him. To truly acknowledge community is to enter into a dramatic relationship with many others.

Politics is one example. There is a considerable difference between a politician and a statesman.[8] The statesman acknowledges community by selecting his actions from the inner reality of individuals[9]—much like a brilliant actor on a stage. But the politician uses only the surface appearances—as does the mediocre actor—because he does not acknowledge others in a dramatic way. Teaching is a second example. A teacher who truly acknowledges the students will "start from where they are."

Culture, then, is an essential part of community. To be cultural, the dynamic of any event must include the acknowledgment of others. If I am interacting with others in a cultural event, I experience my action from the other side, from the viewpoint of the other person or persons. *This is a dramatic event.* It has the characteristics of identification and impersonation. This applies in education:

> It is not enough for [the teacher] to imagine the child's individuality, nor to experience him directly as a spiritual person and then to acknowledge him. Only when he catches himself "from over there," and feels how it affects one, how it affects this other human being, does he realize the real limit.[10]

In a similar way, a great actor inter-relates with his role:

> The great actor does not put on masks. In those formative hours in which he decisively lives his role, he penetrates—transforming himself, surrendering his soul and winning it back again—into the centre of his hero and obtains from him the secret of the personal kineses, the union of meaning and deed peculiar to him.[11]

The theatre provides an analogy with the genuine human exchange characteristic of community.

This dramatic event is not passive. The human drama does not simply reflect a mirror image. The reflection is active. By acknowledging both ourselves and others, we *intend* action. My relationship with you, and my relationship with our community, does not reside in the dominance of one. Rather, it lies in the mutual dynamic between us all. Our intentionalities meet.

Culture and Society

If culture is the expression of community, what of society? What is the relation of culture and society? A cultural event concerns people in a social situation—events where a society (or societies) of persons are involved. Yet we cannot *exactly* characterize a cultural event as a social event. "Society" and "social" are more all-encompassing terms than "cultural." It is true that culture is social, but it is so in a particular kind of way. Social events are of many types. One of these, and one that is highly significant in a society, is the cultural.

We exist in a social world—a stock of previous experience, an existing frame of reference.[12] Human experience varies. Yet it has certain unchanging features: we are born into a world already inhabited by others, into a historical and cultural order. We grow old, and we are all destined to die. We share the same selected aspects of reality: we can appreciate the same poem or the same piece of music. In daily life, we take communication for granted. Society, therefore, is something which is both our own and something handed down to us by our parents and teachers.

The social person has two types of dramatic position: in terms of space and time; and in terms of role—social, moral and ideological. In terms of space, we are aware of social life bodily. Each person occupies some "Here," marked by the place of the body. It is from my "Here" that I assume the shape and organization of the world, that I can perceive what is near or distant as "There." I have learned to do this from birth through the dramatic process of mediation (see pp. 5-9). As an adult, I operate much like a stage performer in a rehearsal: I discover I can move from "Here" to "There" and so I learn I can exchange with others. Thus Natanson can say: "I simply take it for granted that what is true for me is also true for him."[13] But this dramatic exchange also exists in time, just as it does in the playhouse. In the present "Now" of the social encounter, we mutually share a temporal reality with other people.

In terms of society, time means *form* while space means *type*. In everyday experience, we can only understand an object (say, a table) if it is related to things we have already perceived (chairs and the room itself). It is, therefore, grasped in its form. It is the same with people: I perceive another individual with attributes like myself. Thus I understand other persons, spatially, in their typical form through identification and impersonation. This also applies in terms of time. We know predecessors, contemporaries and successors as typifications. As any professional actor knows, this is precisely how one character begins to know the others in a rehearsal—through form and type, in space and time.

We also understand the entire socio-cultural world as aspects of roles. We dramatize ourselves and others in our society in terms of roles, each of which has social, moral and ideological implications. But the meaning of the performance can be understood somewhat differently depending on the viewpoint used: an actor's social actions are understood one way by the actor, and another way by the observer. The actor's meaning lies in his understanding of his acts-in-role—dramatic acts that are created by his inner world. The observer, however, tries to understand these acts-in-role from the viewpoint of the actor. He thinks he has understood another person's action when he determines what it means to the actor. Yet he can never quite *be* the actor. He can never quite "get into the skin" of the actor. Thus the observer's view and understanding of roles is always partial and sometimes faulty.

All these elements are characteristic of society. They are also characteristic of cultural events, culture being part of the larger social scene. What is it, then, that makes a cultural event unique?

Cultural events are primarily active and have a special significance —the meaning contained in the actor's understanding of his performance. It is not that observation is unimportant, however. Rather, *participation more than observation is the proper point of departure for understanding cultural actions.*

Social understandings of the individual's world, the social world and the cultural world are all commonsense frameworks based on typifications. They show that, while time, space and roles activate cultural actions that are meaningful to the actor, partial meanings are also available to the observer. Perhaps the greatest difference between these two levels of meaning—the social and the cultural— lies in the fact that the participant's cultural meanings are specifically those which aim towards the unity of human kind.

Culture and Reality

To be cultural, an event must have significant meaning. We have already seen that culture is a dynamic relationship between people in both community and social life. This provides the structural parameters of a cultural event. But what gives this event significant meaning?

Meaning exists insofar as the actor can view it as having potential *for him* as a human being. For him it is dynamic because, within it, he is coming into Being—he is Becoming. But this leads to its meaning for him *in relation to others*. His personal cultural action affects his own human potential when it also affects the potential of other human beings. A cultural action is, in this way, *reciprocal and dramatic*—and this is its significant meaning.

But how is such meaning "significant"? To understand this, we must distinguish between meanings that are "true" and those that are "real." An abstraction may be objectively "true" but it is not necessarily "real" in the sense that it has real inner meaning for the individual. "Real" meaning must be *felt* meaning, and it is this quality of feeling which makes it significant to the actor.

Plato made a distinction between telling people about many things and teaching them. In this connection, J. M. Heaton has said:

> How do we determine things? What do we do to determine the being of what is? From the age of seven, with ever-increasing complexity and intensity until the child leaves school, we determine what is for him by means of assertions.
>
> We use assertions to characterize things. Thus: the chalk is white. The chalk is stubby. The chalk is small. The chalk is on the desk. The chalk is brand-new. These various assertions determine the chalk. Quality, extension, relation, place and time are categories that are used to determine what a thing is. They are spoken about the thing and pointed out so that it is implied that the thing, in this case the chalk, remains constantly present and underlies the various assertions made about it.
>
> Most teaching creates the thing to be learned—the subject matter—out of a tissue of assertions. The earth is round. 2 x 2 is 4. The French for "boy" is *garçon*. . . .
>
> Assertion becomes the authoritative principle of knowledge. We only know something when it can be pointed out. Knowledge which can't be pointed out is not considered knowledge. Teaching is pointing *out*, learning is taking *in*. The pupil becomes a receptable to be filled by the teacher. . . .
>
> Implicit in this concept of knowledge is the assumption of a split between man and his world. Man is the spectator of things in the world which are pointed out to him. He is viewed as the possessor of consciousness, an empty mind passively open to the reception of deposits of knowledge from the world outside.[14]

An assertion or an abstraction may be "true" but it is not necessarily "real" for the learner. It makes no difference to the assertion 2 x 2 = 4 that we may be concerned with apples, pears, houses or planets. But for the living human being there is a difference between what is abstractly "true" and what is existentially "real." Kierkegaard said:

> When a question of truth is raised in an objective manner, reflection is directed objectively to the truth, as an object to which the knower is related. Reflection is not focused upon the relationship, however, but upon the question of whether it is truth to which the knower is related. If only the object to which he is related is the truth, the subject is accounted to be the truth. When the question is raised subjectively, reflection is directed subjectively to the nature of the individual's relationship; if only the mode of this relationship is in the truth, the individual is in the truth, even if he should happen to be thus related to what is not true.[15]

To look at the matter another way, 2 x 2 = 4 is a statement of mathematical "truth." But supposing it was not? It might, for example, be used as the first line of a modern poem. In a number of workshops with graduate students I have given the following instructions:

> On the piece of paper in front of you write on the first line:
> 2 x 2 = 4.
> That is the first line of a modern poem which you are going to create.
> What is your second line? Please write it down.
> And your third? And others?

Each person writes their own poem, making their own decisions and, in virtually every instance, with different results. I then ask what type of decisions they had to make. They have independently made aesthetic decisions—about rhythm, or association, or color, or emphasis, and the like. But is any one of them "true"? Of course, each poem is "true" in terms of the person who created it. In contrast to mathematical "truth," in aesthetic problems truth is relational. What is significant is, first, its relationship to the participant and, second, the criteria of his choice. That is "real." We give existence meaning, *felt* meaning.

Nor is it, exactly, that what is "real" is subjective and what is "true" is objective. Reality underlies both the subjective and the objective. The meaning of an objective fact is how I relate to it. What is significant is my experience. If I am in the audience when Olivier performs *Oedipus Rex* what is important is the experience

I have; and in the classroom what is significant is the experience of the student. When I am the participant within the experience, I am the one who is doing the experiencing. In the playhouse or the classroom, I am the one who is faced with reality. It is myself who gives it meaning. I acknowledge that it contains my own potential. Then the situation is dynamic for me because I am in relation to others. It is cultural.

When I face a cultural situation I am far from quiescent. I am a genuine participant because I must be newly aware. As it is I who provide the situation with meaning (in the playhouse, for example, or in the classroom), I can hardly rely upon dogma or abstract truth. I am real, and I am in a real event. Thus I am in crisis. I am committed, and I demonstrate this commitment in my action—my appreciation of the performance, or my learning.

Reality, in this sense, is related to self-actualization. Maslow said:

> I could describe the self-actualization as a development of personality which frees the person from the deficiency problems of growth, and from the neurotic (or infantile, or fantasy, or unnecessary or "unreal") problems of life, so that he is able to face, endure and grapple with the "real" problems of life (the intrinsically and ultimately human problems, the unavoidable, the "existential" problems to which there is no perfect solution). That is, it is not an absence of problems but a moving from transitional or unreal problems to a real problem.[16]

Reality, as we know it, is produced by mediation. It is imagining that initiates the dramatic act, but it is our culture which provides the parameters for our choice. Thus being an actor or an audience member in a playhouse is actualizing (in different degrees) the possibilities in the performance; and learning is actualizing all latent possibilities—giving meaning to life.

Reality, therefore, becomes a choice of possibilities. When I engage in a dramatic act, or any act that uses media, my imagining chooses from amongst the alternatives available to me within my culture. This provides the particular temporal quality of reality; the emphasis is upon the future, but within the matrix of the present as informed by the past.

"Truth" only becomes "real" when a person acts with it. But I cannot act with it unless I have commitment to it. Here is the existential paradox: I must commit myself to action before I can see the significant meaning of what I am doing. *Commitment gives cultural meaning.* There is a crisis in potentiality. If, as a participant in any cultural situation (in a playhouse, or in a classroom) I try to activate my potential within it, that means uncertainty. In such a case, there is no abstract "truth"! There is merely the "real." When I give meaning to a cultural situation, therefore, I am on a knife-edge.

Cultural Meaning

What kind of meaning does culture provide? Actions bring forth cultural meanings when they change our reality. Then we activate possibility, self-actualize our human qualities and, through our commitment, create culture.

Cultural meaning is fundamentally moral. Our relationship to cultural life is reciprocal. We create culture when we acknowledge others in community; it is a two-way exchange. Yet through this exchange, culture also identifies our selves with community. This is essentially a dramatization: we identify with it, yet we also view it as part of our selves.

Cultural meaning is related to identity. Without a cultural identity there can be no personal identity. I give meaning to all that I do. My actions are always (at least germinally) social actions. They relate me to others, and others to me.

Cultural meaning is dramatic in character because when I give meaning to community, community gives meaning to me. This is the "I am" experience. This is human identity. But it is not fixed. It is constantly changing and is always in flux.

But what is cultural identity? Cultural identity unifies the subjective and objective in a positive dynamic. When this does not happen, lack of identity can occur in at least two ways: with an over-emphasis on the subjective, personal inner concerns become paramount and the individual lapses into fantasy and unreality;[17] with an over-emphasis on the objective, assertions and external "truth" become paramount and the individual, by denying his feelings, develops schizoid tendencies. But cultural identity, in contrast, produces a healthy body politic because it aims at what is "beyond" individual existence. In this way, culture brings significant meaning to both individual and community identity.

Above all, *culture is the moral meanings we give to life and the actions that bring it to life.* Culture which is "Being-for-others" is highly imaginative, aspirational, even spiritual and, in the final analysis, dramatic. Its meanings are based on an attitude to humanity that is expressed *agape*—altruistic love, charity, brotherhood, community and sharing.[18]

Cultural Worlds

Although culture is a dramatic relationship between people in community which produces significant meaning, some human activities have more significance than others. They can be distinguished because they are produced by actions that are cultural rather than social. Social actions are those which people do in relation to others, whether they be cultural or not. But cultural actions are those which have the special significance we have already outlined.

The most significant human activities can be grouped in cultural worlds. We create such worlds: the cultural unities that express the most significant meanings and intentions of human beings. They include:

the arts
the sciences
religion
politics
therapy
education.

Traditional societies that think "whole" (such as the Amerindian, the Australian aboriginal, the Bushman) consider them as aspects of one entity. Post-Aristotelian societies of the industrial world, thinking in categories, may attempt to distinguish them from one other. But, in reality, all inter-relate and overlap.

Each of these cultural worlds is a way in which people act in the world to give meaning to their lives. Each cultural world creates such meaning in its own way. Each tries to grapple with the central problem of existence—"Who am I, and what am I doing here?"—but it does so in a unique manner.

The arts and religion both work with symbols that mix the affective and the cognitive, the subjective and the objective, in a balanced way. Theoretically, they are the nearest cultural worlds to the living process. They are directly concerned with the moral life and, as a result, are the kernel of a healthy society. In contrast, the sciences attempt as much objectivity as possible. They attempt to provide an objective world to which consciousness can relate. Politics attempts to codify ways in which individuals can work together in a society and, thus, its world incorporates law. It has more of a balance between subjective and objective than the world of science but, because it has to work with order rather than chaos, it is based upon objective truth. Therapy and education are both "helping" worlds of culture as they are based upon working from "another person's point of view." They, too, attempt a balance between inner and outer; however, therapy is more subjective and education is more objective.

In each instance, a cultural world is a paradox. It is a dynamic medium—a bridge between the internal and external—yet it is never completely successful in its intention. Whatever the balance, a cultural world is never quite a unity. Each cultural world, in any given time and space, finds itself emphasizing one or the other. The arts and religion, however, normally achieve the nearest to a balance. As both are essentially moral, they must constantly renew their values and are less bound to rigidity than the other cultural worlds. While both are inherently paradoxical, they are constantly concerned to remake themselves and, therefore, they normally represent the most vital aspects of a society's cultural life. The meanings inherent in the arts and religion of a particular society are sure indicators of its vitality and validity.

In the categorical industrial world, however, it is common to separate art as secular from religion as sacred. This was not always the case—as the instances of ancient Greece and medieval Christianity indicate. Certainly Amerindians, who regard art and religion as parts of the totality of their existence, can find difficulty in relating to the separation of art and religion in the predominantly white society.

Similarly, problems can occur when education is regarded as a distinct category from other cultural worlds. Under these circumstances, education can come to be regarded as exclusively abstract, objective and "true." No longer does a program, nor its design or implementation, provide a bridge between inner and outer. Education is, under these circumstances, not felt as "real." The genuine cultural world of education must be based upon the moral meanings we give to life and the significant actions that result. True curriculum meaning is based upon a love of humanity expressed in "We," and educational actions must be intended towards an aspirational end.

Culture and Pedagogy

The cultural world of education is of vital importance because it is the basis for all the others. The foundations of religion, the arts and sciences, politics and therapy are all laid by education. Education as a cultural world confronts the problem of "reality" and "truth" for all students, and it dramatizes this so that they are prepared to work in the other cultural worlds.

A major curriculum concern is to marry the inner and the outer within the process of learning. Schools must find the appropriate middle ground between the cognitive and affective, and between the logical and the empirical.

This can be provided by the aesthetic which hinges upon *choice*. If the abstract is emphasized at the expense of existence, teaching becomes the transmission of categorical knowledge. As Plato would say, teachers then tell people about things and do not teach them. But merely telling students about things and making assertions about them is diametrically opposed to helping students to their own possibilities. Yet a balance between what is "real" and what is "true" is difficult. Intuitive knowledge of *who* one is requires knowing *what* to do, *how* to do it, and what *can* or *cannot* be done. At the same time, the general and the repeatable, the objective facts and categorizations, are a necessary source in order to know what one can become.

The balance hinges upon the student's choice, and it is best achieved by two key attitudes of the teacher. First, although teacher and student may agree on *what* to do, *how* to do it is a different matter. The *how* is best achieved by indirect rather than direct methods; direct instruction should only occur when the student asks for (or demonstrates that he needs) help. Thus pedagogy should be based on inductive rather than deductive methods. Second, a return to Being must be allowed for in class time. That is, the teacher must provide scope for originality in ways that are the student's own, that will allow him to acquire knowledge in ways that are significant *to him*. It is interesting to note that these two attitudes are fundamental to the teaching of creative drama.

In learning, the feeling world is primordial. Junell indicates that attitudes and feelings provide the matrix for cognition:

> Sometimes it may be dependence on the quality of experience which introduces the element of pleasure or pain. More often it is dependence on specific human models or types, either fictional or real, with which the learner establishes a strong emotional affinity and whose characteristic behaviors he uncritically accepts and makes part of his own way of perceiving the world.[19]

It is essential, Junell considers, to establish an atmosphere that helps identification. This can best be achieved by *the teacher as dramatist*. He places rational processes in an emotional context, he espouses those arguments which favour the attitudes most needed, and he presents himself and his materials in dynamic and dramatic ways. He thus provides a model which will awaken the students to feelings and attitudes that will have an impact upon their own feelings and attitudes. But is this sufficient? Is such a model enough for good learning?

There are dangers in such a proposition. Not the least of these is the improper use of impersonation. Vandenberg indicates[20] that under certain conditions identification can degenerate into pseudo-roles: the individual who surrenders to a role acts according to the image he would like to maintain. He is guided by role expectations rather than the demands of the situation and his own Being. He "pretends" to be a teacher or a student; he gestures and postures. The student pretends to pay attention. The teacher pretends to teach. Then schooling becomes an elaborate game and dramatization has got out of hand. Neither must submit to their roles. Their authentic pedagogic relationship is an encounter where they *acknowledge* each other. That is genuine drama.

A cultural curriculum, as we have seen above, is based upon community and contains the total human experience of identification, impersonation, empathy and love. It is not sufficient, therefore, for the teacher to be a dramatist. If cultural meanings are those which aim towards the unity of humanity through active participation, then *the student must also be a dramatist*. The personal encounter of the classroom is not merely a bond with another. It is "taking his part" and assuming his attitudes and feelings. While Junell provides a sound theoretic base for a teacher's attitude, more is required. A dramatic mutuality implies the dynamic of acknowledgment between the teacher and student. Reciprocity with others requires a dramatic attitude on the part of the student.

In terms of pedagogy, sharing a common meaning indicates identification and impersonation, empathy and love between the child and adult. To fully understand the sub-text of the child, the teacher "becomes" the child and provides answers in such a way that the child can understand. The child, accepting the help of the adult, identifies with the teacher and uses him as a model, either overtly or covertly.

When this happens, adult and child co-exist in a dramatic encounter with play at its centre. Learning then is authentic: it is playful, and sharing one's work with the teacher is to share a joy. Learning that is inauthentic is for the ends of others, and showing one's work becomes an attempt to avoid punishment or to please the teacher. Heaton has contrasted education based on assertion with that based on play:

> The symbolic is known as play.... Cultural experience is in direct continuity with play... play has an essence that is completely independent of the attitude of the player....
>
> In play there is a suspension of belief and non-belief. You cannot really say if a child believes his dolls are babies or not—to him there is no conceptual distinction between playing and being. Hence there is a primacy of play over the consciousness of the player. It happens, as it were, by itself. The game absorbs the player into itself and thus takes from him the burden of initiative—thus the ease of the play when we are playing well. All playing is a being played....
>
> So play does not point to purposes beyond itself, it celebrates itself. It creates a structure in which the identity of the player is lost—the poems of Pindar illustrate this well. The living of play is sheer fulfilment, a bringing forth, the playing of the play.[21]

It is this very independence of play which shows its continuity with the cultural worlds. In play we learn to give ourselves to the activity, to be absorbed in the play world, and it is this giving and absorption in another world that characterizes culture. The dramatic qualities of play and culture ensure our deep motivation, even our devotion to our cultural worlds. Play creates a structure of a type which, under best conditions, develops into the genuine learning of school and the devotion to cultural worlds in adult life.

Good teaching is like an improvised drama. We may prepare for it but, when it occurs, we fall into the drama. We become involved in it. It transcends us. While it is happening, no one knows what the result will be, for it has a spirit of its own, like play. Neither teaching nor play are asserting, but testing:

> And to test is to question, to place the object in the open where it can be seen.
>
> Questioning is not boundless, it is limited by the horizon of the question and the object which is being questioned. A good teacher stands within this horizon. He must have the energy to withstand the tension between the questioner and what is questioned, and so by care to allow the object and his pupil to be seen.[22]

Conclusion

The implications of considering culture and curriculum within a dramatic context are considerable. Curriculum is an important aspect of culture which, like drama and theatre, exists in time, is dynamic, and is created by human beings out of what is "real" to them. Curriculum meanings, like all cultural meanings, are created by people out of those experiences which have most significance for them—those based on identification and impersonation, empathy and love.

The questions of curriculum cannot be considered in isolation. They derive from the persons actively engaged in all aspects of it—they reflect the lives of those engaged within it. The low level of Hitler's cultural expression brought about the curriculum of the schools in Nazi Germany, just as our curriculum today is the expression of our past and current values.

But is the program design and implementation of today sufficient? In my view, it is not. The inherent moral attitudes do not often reflect *agape* which, as we have seen above, directs actions towards aspirational ends.

What is required is a curriculum that places the student, as dramatist, at the centre. Thereafter he should be treated as unique, allowed to encounter conceptual materials so that learning can occur with ease and within a genuine learning encounter with his teacher.

This can only occur when dramatic play is the centre of learning. Human enactment is the basis upon which people build their cultural worlds. It reveals objects as they are, provides the "I do" for the "I am" experience, and it allows the student to incorporate the everyday world into his internal structure. In a dramatic context, the teacher's approach is threefold: (1) the affective, encouraging the feeling world of the student; (2) the practical: the student acts in relation to the material, creating a dramatic relation with it; and (3) the theoretic: the student's own conceptualizations take place. The student's learning is also threefold: he proceeds from the "I am" experience through the "I do" experience to the "I create" through conceptualization. This indicates that school programs should be designed around a dramatic play approach that is multi-disciplinary. When dramatic action becomes the core, all aspects of learning are viewed as genuine inquiry.

When education has such a basis, we will be able to worry less about our cultural experiences than Paul Tillich did about his.

Chapter 9

Axioms and Maxims: A Rationale for the Arts in Education

"The part of the population with artistic talent is assumed, although on no known evidence, to be small. And it is part of the folk attitude towards the arts that the truly inspired artist will excel, whatever the barriers to be overcome. The convenient social virtue thus minimizes the need for expenditure in the arts."
—*John Kenneth Galbraith*

The best guide to a country's culture is the work of its artists. Culture is reflected in, and perpetuated by, the work of its writers, musicians, dramatists, choreographers, film-makers and others. After all, how do most of us remember the ancient Greeks except through their architecture, sculpture and their plays? How will future generations recall us?

The work of artists results from the creative opportunities they had in their childhood and youth. Without experiences in creative writing, a student's potential to become a dramatist or a novelist may well go undetected. Creative potential must be nurtured and developed as early as possible. Schools and educational systems must take responsibility for their country's culture. Programs must offer as many *choices* in the various arts, with the highest degree of *quality* as possible, so that the greatest number of students will have the opportunity to develop their potential.

Artists and arts teachers are to blame for one confusion. They have not made it clear to the general public that there are two kinds of arts programs needed, directed to two kinds of students—the few and the many. The few really talented and gifted students require very special treatment. But it is ludicrous—and grossly wasteful of public funds—to train the rest of us as though we are going to become professional artists. Years ago, children had to learn perspective in junior classrooms, or they had to learn to face the audience in the kindergarten's annual nativity play. But few of them became professional artists, and their teachers should have realized this. Realistically, this kind of arts education is unsuitable for most people.

Arts education for the many—the basis for general education in schools, and most college and university education—should be directed towards those artistic qualities we all need in life. The arts in general education have two goals: to create art to the best of our individual ability; and to appreciate the artistic qualities not merely in works of art but also in every aspect of life. These two goals are learned slowly and steadily over the years. The making of art teaches us to express ourselves: to release and refine our emotions, and to state our values through our choices. Appreciating art teaches us quality: we learn preference and judgment, we understand more about others, and we come to take responsibility for our own choices. The two activities inter-relate: creation balances appreciation; making and liking art together develop the human qualities that are essential to our future life.

Very few students in Western industrialized countries can experience all of the arts in their schools. When the arts are part of classroom work, music and visual art are most likely to be offered. Less likely are drama and, particularly, dance. Very few have the opportunity to work in film, media or puppetry. And the opportunity to experience the arts decreases markedly as the student gets older. This is the result of nineteenth-century mechanistic thinking; in those days, the arts were "the frills" of the curriculum. Those who wish to perpetuate mechanism would have them remain so. But those who have progressed during the last hundred years know that the arts are vital in two ways: for themselves alone—making and appreciating art are valuable in and of themselves; and for mental health and human learning. For these reasons, the arts are the core of the curriculum.

Nothing hampers the development of the arts in schools more than the lack of good teachers. There is no country in the Western world that does not suffer in this way. In Canada and the United States pre-school teacher education is low status and provides virtually no arts experience. Because play and the creative arts are the natural ways for young children to learn, those who are to teach them must have continuous practice in the creative arts.

Although elementary teacher education has more artistic content in Britain, it is still insufficient; in many cases in Australia, Canada and the United States, however, student teachers have no arts training whatsoever. Universally, the major problem in preparing secondary teachers is that most programs are geared towards products (the band concert, the school play, the art exhibition) rather than for the mental health and learning process of the students. Moreover, in a world where children spend more time with television than in classrooms, teacher education programs must not ignore the need for visual literacy. The popular media provide a massive information bank for children and unless they can critically perceive and use this, traditional forms of education must inevitably fail. It is essential that teachers are prepared to use film and other media for both the arts and communication.

If we take one art in one country—drama in Canada—we must take great care when using such an example. There are considerable differences from province to province, between different places in each province, and even from school to school in one community. The following is a generalized profile across the country: ministries of education and administrators give a low priority to drama and many of them confuse it with theatre; there is some dramatic activity in most public elementary schools, but usually not much, while most teachers have no qualifications in drama; drama and theatre courses are taught in a minority of secondary schools and it is rare to find teachers with full majors in the subject (most of these being in cities); only in rare cases do those who are teaching drama report satisfaction with their facilities; most pre-service teacher education institutions do not recognize the necessity for drama training on a sophisticated level; in-service drama programs for existing teachers are few and far between; professional theatre artists-in-schools programs are in isolated pockets throughout the country—rural areas are most badly served while in the province of Quebec there are forty-three companies of which twenty-six are subsidized by the province and sixteen by the federal government (1980); and modern curriculum guides for drama exist in only three out of the ten provinces (British Columbia, Ontario and Quebec). Yet we must put this bleak picture into its context: it is such a radical change in ten years (1969-1979) that it is almost miraculous; in 1969 it was difficult to find any good drama teaching in elementary schools anywhere in the country!

While the situation is better in music and visual art than drama, it is worse in dance, film and media. However much teachers attempt to improve the situation, they are hampered by not having a series of good, logical arguments at hand. Thus the following rationale for the arts in education will be presented in two ways: the ways that the arts can contribute to the general education of every student will be examined axiomatically; subsequently the significance of arts education to particular situations will be considered proverbially.

Axioms

The following axioms apply to the arts in education:

1 / *The arts are conducive to the development of personality.*
2 / *The arts are essential to learning.*
3 / *The arts enhance social growth.*
4 / *The arts are central to contextual education.*

These axioms refer to general education; the arts are integral to the basic education of every student in all school systems, and are integral to lifelong learning of all persons.

Axiom 1: The Arts Are Conducive to the Development of Personality

Each person creates and develops his personality. His mind is active: his imagination creates meaning. By rehearsing the possibilities within a situation, he imaginatively constructs his relationship to the world. This is a dramatic process, based on identification and impersonation. Play initially, and the arts subsequently, develop imaginative constructions whereby people function in the world. The arts are expressions of imagination through which the personality develops, and upon which cognitive and abstract ways of working with the environment are built.

Human beings express their potentiality through creating and appreciating the arts. They are expressive of an awareness of a personal future and so are conducive to psychic health. To create art is to state one's personal identity: it reflects confidence and can work towards integration of the Self. To make an artistic choice is to show one's independence, self-reliance and sense of personal autonomy. The arts increase self-awareness, but they also develop awareness of others: in group arts in particular (such as drama and dance) personal relationships are strengthened and these, in turn, reinforce the sense of the Self.

The arts provide motivation for communication. Music, visual art and design, drama, dance, speaking and writing, film, photography and architecture are intended towards communication with others. This, in turn, is conducive to self-actualization.

The arts help to develop values. The student in the arts experience perceives the relationship of form and content—the specific manner of aesthetic learning (Axiom 2). It is this which distinguishes the aesthetic from the non-aesthetic experience, and results in the individual's value system. Preferences in the arts are expressive of the notion of a person's good. Further, values are constructed by the modelling process, itself a dramatic (artistic) way of working.

The arts develop the ability to make choices; they allow for freedom and responsibility. They provide experiences of exploration and discovery, and permit the choice of lifestyle. Artistic creation in particular, but also appreciation, develops spontaneity.

Creating art starts from imagination but it also relates to society when it results in an art product. In both the process and the product, aesthetic enjoyment occurs through both satisfactions intrinsically desired and the spontaneity of the dynamics of self-actualization.

Axiom 2: The Arts Are Essential to Learning

The arts, being self-motivating, promote learnings that are strongly bonded and permanent. By giving pleasure, they bring self-reward and positive attitudes.

The aesthetic experience gives a specific way of knowing. It starts from perceptual learning and awareness, but builds towards imaginative capacity. It is this which provides the aesthetic way of knowing. It is inclusive of feeling and cognition, yet goes beyond them to an innate "grasping." Aesthetic knowledge is non-discursive; it is an "intuition of an aesthetic gestalt" rather than "knowing about" something.[1] Through it we are increasingly able to understand existence metaphorically—that is, symbolically. Symbols provide a double meaning and are a particularly rich way of thinking. Through aesthetic choices we perceive qualities in the environment and express them. We develop our own aesthetic criteria and learn informed aesthetic choices. Thus we come to the sub-learnings of preference, judgment and justification.

The arts are essential to all school learning. They are basic components of speaking and writing, reading and mathematics, and all other content areas. Aesthetic learnings such as sound and movement, time and space, color and mass, energy and line, shape and symbolization, are constituent and prior factors within all forms of learning.[2] They provide the logical and rational bases for all methods of learning,[3] as well as the feeling upon which they are grounded.

Reading, for example, is essentially a matter of making sense of patterns. But understanding patterns is itself based upon the creation of patterns in play which become meaningful codes. Play and art create patterns and regularities which make predictability possible. We get to know others by "reading" their body language, voice styles and life styles—by predicting them through making sense of patterns. Similarly, learning to read is to make sense of two kinds of pattern: visual discrimination and the ability to "read between the lines."[4]

The arts affect all the creative ways in which we know. There is a unity to creativity. It transfers between modes and generalizes to all fields, and it works through imagining, which is the fundamental operation of the aesthetic. And our modern world is in desperate need of creative thinkers.

I have shown elsewhere that drama and aesthetic education help recall.[5] A fact must be meaningful if it is to be memorized. Play and artistic activities have direct relevance to us: these are things we really *want* to do. Use of the arts, therefore, considerably helps the development of memory.

Yet, at the same time, there is a specific quality to the symbols of aesthetic learning. This is qualitatively different from the symbolization in other fields, such as mathematics, which use signs. Through the arts, we become aware of the particularity and perceptual richness of things that can lead to discrimination.

In summary, we can see that the arts provide students with knowledge that is not only relevant to their inner selves but also to their general education. The arts provide learnings that are unique to the individual. Artistic experience allows each person to learn in his own style. Thus it allows for lifelong learning through the development of unique value systems within each person.

Axiom 3: The Arts Enhance Social Growth

Arts learnings can occur in two circumstances: when we are participant and when we are observer. Aesthetic meaning occurs not only by creating art but also in witnessing others create art. We learn both as actor and audience. Thus the arts lead to *acknowledgment* of others; their witnessing of our artistic acts, and our witnessing of theirs, provides meaning beyond that for which we alone are responsible. Thus the arts enhance social growth and, specifically, cultural growth.

Although arts activities are generated by individuals, they are shaped by interaction with society. We extend our perceptions and awareness of the arts into a cultural context; the immediate group, the local environment, community and culture as a whole. This leads to our understanding of others in their similarities and differences with ourselves. Further, it provides human beings with a cultural context for community.

The arts are a major instrument of cultural transmission, and have been throughout the history of the human race. Creation and appreciation of the arts allow us to become aware of our cultural heritage. Further, they have a particular social relevance; artistic concepts learned in the environment have a considerable significance to real life and our living of it.

The traditional humanist argument for the arts is that they enrich the quality of our experience. The arts as a whole, their interrelationship, and each arts field on its own, permit a growth of human awareness and discrimination. Thus they provide important values in both formal and informal education.

Axiom 4: The Arts Are Central to Contextual Education

The symbolization of the arts provides each person with his way of living in the world. Arts creation gives each individual his own way of existing, realizing his potential, acknowledging others, and coping with the language systems and role performances he meets. Creation also gives him his own time structure—his imaginative way of expressing his possible futures, as related to past and present. Appreciation of the arts is concerned with many elements: sensuous and affective qualities, formal modes such as design, technical elements like skills, and the expressive levels of meaning and import. Both creation and appreciation have their own contextual logic; each individual develops his own criteria, as well as sharing criteria with others.[6] It is this context that is the basis of all human education.

The context of the arts is the future. The artist expresses his own time structure, his own imaginative sense of his potential and the potentialities of existence. To appreciate the arts is to imaginatively project possibilities into sensuous, affective, formal, technical and expressive modes. Arts education, therefore, leads the student in learning to cope with his potentiality and all human futures.

All meaningful education is contextual. It is grounded upon the uniqueness of the individual. It begins from his inner reality, as imaginatively expressed, and develops through the media available to him. The most significant of these media are the arts, both because they are inherently meaningful to the personality, and because they are self-motivating and self-actualizing.

Maxims

The following maxims apply to the arts in education:

1 / *Young children learn to play and play to learn.*
2 / *Those who are slow to learn are quick to learn the arts.*
3 / *Able students achieve the arts of the possible.*
4 / *The deaf man paints and the blind man sings.*
5 / *Keep your skills and your skills will keep you.*
6 / *Arts learning brings a life in the arts.*
7 / *A man's culture is his art.*

These maxims refer to specific educational contexts, whereas the axioms refer to all educational situations.

Maxim 1: Young Children Learn to Play and Play to Learn

Babies, infants and young children grow through play. Inner imaginative activity is initially expressed through play activities. Steadily, however, play becomes a method of learning, as well as evolving into the arts. There is an intimate relationship between play, learning and the arts.

Play is a universal phenomenon. Its aim is to relate the deep needs of the inner life (Axiom 1) with the external world through others (Axiom 3). Its inner motivation provides significant learning (Axiom 2) which, in due course, becomes extended to the arts. With young children, therefore, contextual education (Axiom 4) is based upon play.

However, play and the arts are not mere play. Rather, they afford freedom from everyday concerns without simply being escape. The individual provides the experience with importance: it has value for its own sake, and not as a symptom or portent of something else. Yet, at the same time, it generalizes from itself to all activities that relate to that modality. Initially, play appears to be innate. Within the first weeks of life, however, other aspects seem to be learned and become generalizable to all modalities. Initially, the thinking within play is not oriented to the external world; it is for inner purposes. But it is expressed in action. This is then heightened by the awareness of the external experience which is assimilated to the inner world. The process thus becomes circular and dynamic. It is the human context not only for play and the arts but also for all meanings we give to activities.

Play experiences enrich the child. Within play, there is an interrelation of all kinds of experience: visual, auditory, oral, emotional, kinesthetic, cognitive. This totality of experience gives a wider expression of personality than the merely rational and linguistic, yet these latter are deeply affected by the play experience. Education that is purely rational can limit the mental development of children. The expression of the total personality is more easily manifest in play and the arts. This particularly affects the learning of communication. Communication is holistic: it is dramatic in that it involves gesture, sound and personality in one total and unified act. Communication in language *per se* is a subsequent mode. Communication learnings, therefore, must be based upon play for young children.

A further implication is that students at all levels should have the opportunity to return to the modalities of play and the arts. Disorientation and dissociation can occur at any time in life. Play and arts activities can then provide the grounding needed by the personality to achieve the required learnings.

Maxim 2: Those Who Are Slow to Learn Are Quick to Learn the Arts.

Maxim 3: Able Students Achieve the Arts of the Possible.

Maxim 4: The Deaf Man Paints and the Blind Man Sings.

All students progress best when learning is directly related to the needs of their personality. For every person, meaningfulness is the context of learning. Unfortunately, too many educational programs are absolutist. They assume that all students, whatever their ability, should aim for standardized achievements. Such programs are not contextual (Axiom 4).

While this axiom applies to the education of "normal" students, it applies with equal force to those who are categorized as "special": the slow learners, the highly able, the handicapped and the disturbed. For these students, an absolutist program is particularly denigrating; they can never achieve the categoric standard. In contrast, an arts program which is based upon the four axioms can provide such students with a meaningful education. Thus:

> Educators are now recognizing that the arts can provide new modalities for general learning for the handicapped. They are discovering that the arts can play a role in the education of all children, not just a talented few. They are recognizing that the arts can be a vehicle to improve perceptual skills, to increase the quality and quantity of responses to stimuli, and to develop the ability to generalize from perceptions and res-

ponses. Arts programs can improve creative abilities and the abilities to evaluate and develop manipulative skills. In fact, the arts process is really a process for general learning. Recognition of these needs and potentials has motivated a new effort that is rapidly becoming a national direction.[7]

Needless to say, education of the handicapped must emphasize what have been called "survival skills" (how to keep house, and the like). These very activities should be approached contextually and aesthetically. But, in addition, education must provide for life-enrichment: there is little point in learning "survival skills" in order to leave an institution and, thereafter, live in a lonely room which becomes a kind of private institution. For both the handicapped[8] and the disturbed,[9] a contextual education in the arts provides both meaningful learning and a quality to their lives which ensures significant existence.

Perceptually handicapped persons must also be educated in their own context. Those who are blind can orient themselves to the world through other perceptions: music, for example. On the other hand the deaf can create and appreciate the visual and plastic arts. The teacher's expectations of the handicapped must be related to the abilities of the individual.

It is similar with slow learners. Little is achieved through standardized expectations for such students. Many retarded children have perceptual difficulties, or appear to have gaps in their early learning stages that prevent subsequent development. If such students can return to earlier perceptual learning in the arts, and they can be led to many intuitive aesthetic gestalts, much of their learning can be grounded. Once this has happened, further arts experience can be taken at the student's own rate of achievement within his genuine context.

The educational problems of the most able students are very particular. We must distinguish between the gifted and talented on the one hand, and the process of creativity which is possessed by most people. The gifted student may be an isolate. The arts, particularly those which involve groups (e.g. music, drama and dance) help to break down this isolation (Axiom 3). Gifted modes of thinking are often unique but are based on what Arthur Koestler has called "bi-sociation." Not only do these have resemblances to the metaphoric and allegoric connections of the arts, but activity in the arts can generate further bi-sociations (Axiom 2). The most able students have unique personality requirements which arts experience (being diverse and metaphorical, non-categorical and non-discursive) can satisfy through generating possibility. Arts expectations include the absurd, the different and the symbolic, each of which relates closely to the personality needs of the gifted (Axiom 1).

For all "special" students, therefore, contextual education can be based upon the arts. By doing so, educators are placing the existence of such students in a context that is inherently meaningful to them. This is necessary for all students:

> only in aesthetic education is the whole child implicated in the educative process, as only in informed aesthetic perception are the centers of sense, affectivity, conceptualization, and imagination brought to focus in a single experience. Nowhere else, indeed, can one have such a clear notion of the experiencing self.[10]

Maxim 5: Keep Your Skills and Your Skills Will Keep You

For a small percentage of students, the arts offer career possibilities. However, in the past most programs were directed to acquiring professional skills; as a result, they were directed to the few rather than the many, and were conspicuously unsuccessful. The arts in general education should specifically not be directed towards career possibilities.

But, for those students who have genuine career needs in the arts, programs based on the highest arts skills should be available:

> The various fields of the arts offer a wide range of career choices to young people. Arts-in-education programs provide opportunities for a student to explore the possibility of becoming a professional actor, dancer, musician, painter, photographer, architect, or teacher. There are also many lesser known opportunities in arts related technical areas, such as lighting engineer, costumer in a theater, or specialist in designing and installing exhibitions in museums. Other opportunities lie in administrative and educational work in arts organizations, such as museums, performing arts groups, and arts councils.[11]

Maxim 6: Arts Learning Brings a Life in the Arts

Arts learning is pleasant and rewarding and so can encourage positive attitudes towards education. As we have seen (Axiom 2), play and the arts are self-motivating; through them a wide variety of activities are given meaning and significance. This can generalize to most aspects of everyday living, so that the arts can become a valuable component of lifelong learning.

Further, leisure education is becoming increasingly significant. There are now needs in the field of recreation which indicate that the arts are a necessary component in many aspects of adult education.

Maxim 7: A Man's Culture Is His Art

Creation and appreciation in the arts are the centre of a person's cultural existence. Who we are, and how we relate to others, commence from our imagination and the ways in which this is artistically expressed in relation to other people. The arts are the basis for the communication process that bonds people together—as one-to-one in marriage, or as one-to-many in community. The arts are central to our cultural life, and are the kernel of contextual education (Axiom 4).

Specific ethnic or other cultures within a society have their own contexts. Urban groups, minorities, linguistic sub-groups and the like, establish and develop their individual identities most strongly through their arts. Established or emerging countries need to ground educational programs upon their cultural identity which is essentially aesthetic.

Conclusion

The arts are an essential element of the total education process. They are so in two ways. First, in general education:

●/The education of children, students and adults is not complete unless the arts are part of the daily learning process. Programs can be designed so that each of the arts is integral to basic education.

●/Lifelong learning is based upon aesthetic experience. Arts programs, commencing from the context of the human personality and its needs, provide experiences that are self-actualizing and culturally binding.

Second, the arts are valuable in specific educational contexts:

●/Aesthetic experience is invaluable in "special" education because it commences from individual human need, and not from standardized expectations. Arts programs relate to each human difference and encourage contextual growth.

●/For those who are specially skilled, education programs can be designed to satisfy a wide range of career choices.

●/Play and the arts are particularly relevant to the education of young children. Programs based on play assist the growth of the individual personality and enhance social development.

●/Arts-in-education programs are highly significant for ethnic and other sub-groups in society. They also give a cultural grounding for the education of emerging countries and cultures.

Appendix A

Drama and the Field of Curriculum

The theory of Curriculum has a long history, particularly in North America. It is only in recent years, however, that there have been attempts to relate the central metaphors of the arts to it. One reason for this is that previous mechanistic models have been less than satisfactory. Behavioral objectives that determine the nature of outcomes based on the input/output model, or preordinate methods that measure programs in quantifiable ways, have been shown to be neither inclusive nor particularly human ways of approaching the acts of teaching and learning. Models drawn from the sciences are liable to distort the multiple facets of human existence: they are usually impersonal, numerical, abstract and as far as possible divorced from the observer's feelings and personal understandings.

In contrast, models drawn from the arts and humanities are as much affective as cognitive. They are essentially qualitative rather than quantitative. They are liable to be inclusive rather than exclusive, and to catch the totality of existence rather than mere elements of it. This approach is exemplified by Eisner and others who have used the metaphors of literary and aesthetic criticism to illuminate the nature of Curriculum.[1]

The following is a theoretic attempt to describe the field of Curriculum through the dramatic metaphor. Life, spontaneous drama and theatre share certain commonalities with the teaching-learning process. They all exist in time and never, at any particular moment, are static like a painting, a sculpture or a building. They are on-going events which exist in the *now* of the present moment. These events exist *between* people, *between* objects. Thus *reality lies in interactions*. It is verbal and not nominal. It is dynamic not static.

Within all of these events, what activates the dynamic is the human person. Human performance is the focus of life, spontaneous drama, theatre and education. Within each, we present ourselves whole and complete. Our Being, supported by our voice and movements, is placed in a dynamic context with other Selves. The persona we assume is our "mask." Our clothes are our costumes, and we position ourselves in space as if we are within "a scene."

The interaction of human performers is the essential dynamic of social life. This dynamic is in itself spontaneous. Although I may plan, or rehearse, what I will say and do when we meet, what actually happens may only be tangentially related to that plan. The event of our meeting may follow the rehearsal more closely in the art form of theatre (though, even there, spontaneity is an essential element of the form), but the "as if" thinking and action inherent in all interactions ensure that in both life and classrooms we meet in the temporal flux.

We must distinguish between two images: the dramatic metaphor and the theatrical metaphor. The theatre metaphor (the *Theatrum Mundi* of the classical world) is exemplified in Shakespeare's "All the world's a stage." Although this has been related to Curriculum with profit,[2] it is limited by the fact that modern theatrical performers in a playhouse communicate to a relatively passive audience. To relate the theatre metaphor to the teaching-learning process, where the students are hardly passive like an audience in a playhouse, is therefore somewhat difficult.

However this is not the case with the dramatic metaphor, the classic example of which is also by Shakespeare:

> We are such stuff
> As dreams are made on; and our little life
> Is rounded with a sleep.

By the end of his days, Shakespeare had moved from the simple image that life is *like* a stage to the metaphor that life *is* a drama.

Internal imagination (thinking "as if") becomes externalized in action that is symbolic of our inner world (acting "as if"), and we work with this process, overtly or covertly, between birth and death. Once we view the spontaneous dramatic actions in life and classroom situations in terms of this metaphor, the results can be remarkably rewarding.

1: The Nature of Curriculum

1.1 CURRICULUM CONSISTS OF EVENTS THAT TAKE PLACE IN TIME.

1.1.1 Within a specific moment of time, teachers teach and learners learn. Curriculum can be said to occur at such moments.

1.2 *The major characteristic of Curriculum is the encounter of teacher(s) and learner(s).* This encounter is a dynamic—a living relationship between teacher and learner.

1.2.1 Although many other factors impinge upon this characteristic (such as the physical environment, the emotional climate of the school, the administration, the parents, the community, curriculum documents and materials, and the like) and each can provide differing qualities to Curriculum, they do not alter its nature as a dynamic event.

1.2.2 In this sense, Curriculum is to be theoretically distinguished from:
a/curriculum guides, programs of study, syllabuses, and other forms of curriculum documents that inform Curriculum proper;
b/curriculum materials that are used by teacher(s) and/or learner(s) within the dynamic event;
c/curriculum processes which are experiential events engaged in by teachers and others to design, implement or evaluate particular approaches to Curriculum proper;
d/foundation and applied studies in education which also inform Curriculum proper.
Each of these can affect what occurs in Curriculum proper but they are not, in and of themselves, the dynamic event.

1.3 *In the Curriculum event, the teacher is present or his presence is assumed.*

1.3.1 There are three styles of Curriculum event: direct, indirect, and non-direct. Curriculum is direct when the teacher is present, an active part of the exchange. Curriculum is indirect or non-direct when the presence of the teacher is merely assumed.

1.3.2 Indirect Curriculum occurs when the student encounters materials that have been purposely prepared for learning. In these circumstances, the student encounters the teacher-as-writer (for print materials), the teacher-as-director (for video materials), the teacher-as-mechanist (for teaching machines).

1.3.3 Non-direct Curriculum occurs when the student independently uses materials that have *not* been purposely prepared for learning and creates a learning encounter with them. In this context, virtually any materials or experience can be independently intended by the student; yet the assumed teacher might well judge that some non-direct events are valuable in Curriculum terms while others are not valuable.

1.4 *The proper intention of Curriculum is to bring about a learning experience for the student.*

1.4.1 A theoretical distinction can be made between Curriculum as an event and learning as a student experience. The learning experience is not properly speaking Curriculum. Any program is designed and implemented in such a way as to bring about a Curriculum event and that, in itself, is intended to provide the student with the maximum opportunity to learn. Whether he does so or not depends on many variables, not the least of which is the student's choice. The Curriculum encounter is usually effective or ineffective depending on how well it activates the student's Being towards learning choice.

1.4.2 Restated in terms of mind, a Curriculum action is a mediate event between the inner learning of the student and the external world. That is, it is a temporal unit that actively relates the subjective and the objective, and so brings about meaning (see 2.4 below).

2: The Field of Curriculum

2.1 THE FIELD OF CURRICULUM CONSISTS OF:
a/Temporal *events;*
b/The *applied study* of those events (see 3.1 below);
c/The *academic study* of those events (see 4.1 below).

2.2 *The field of Curriculum encompasses the reality of time and "maps" of that reality.* It is characterized by a series of diverse approaches toward the educational moments of encounter—that is, those sequences of time when it is expected that the learner learns and the teacher teaches. As in any field in which the subject of study is primarily temporal (e.g., music, drama/theatre, dance), there is a fundamental distinction between the reality within time and the relative understandings of that reality.

2.2.1 As Korzybski said, "The map is not the territory." In this sense, what occurs in time within the learning/teaching situation is the territory while diverse understandings (definitions/descriptions/analyses, etc.) are relative maps that inform the territory.

2.3 *This way of apprehending the field of Curriculum has the support of both modern science and modern art.*

2.3.1 In science, Heisenberg indicated that a particle may be said to have position (e.g., it can be examined in terms of space) or to have velocity (e.g., it can be examined in terms of time) but it cannot, *in any exact sense*, be said to have both. Or as P. W. Bridgman has put it:

> Nature does not present us with frames of reference ready made and labeled as such. We construct them for our own purposes out of the objects we find. To the naive, primitive intuition, which is satisfied with mere recognition of the objects of its experience as they occur and recur, a frame of reference is not necessary. The necessity for a frame does not arise until one attempts to analyse one's experience to the extent of at least describing it.[3]

In other words, our personal frame of reference (based on our assumptions or "world view") provides us with the parameters for a particular map. This map allows us one particular understanding of the temporal territory.

2.3.2 In art, forms exist on a continuum between two poles: from those that exist in space (e.g., visual art and architecture) to those that exist in time (e.g., music, drama/theatre, dance). The latter temporal arts parallel the field of Curriculum.

Modern "performance theory" regards the performance event as the territory, and the frames of reference which provide diverse understandings of this event as maps. These have been described in a variety of ways. Thus Bernard Beckerman has said:

> Theatre occurs when one or more human beings, isolated in time and/or space, present themselves to another or others. . . . The elements of analysis, therefore, are not plot and character but units of time: what occurs within these units and how they relate to one another. Units of time are, in fact, the contextual frames within which the drama evolves. . . .[4]

Or, As Richard Schechner puts it:

> The drama is, by definition, that which can be passed on through successive socio-cultural transformations. The original version is

tied to the original matrix, and decays with it. I don't think that even the first production of a drama is privileged in this regard—unless the author stages the play himself.[5]

On this view, the temporal events of performance and Curriculum are similar: they are unrepeatable except insofar as they are successive socio-cultural transformations.

2.3.3 In this sense, the events (the velocity of a particle, an artistic performance, or a Curriculum moment) are all territories and each can be studied through maps.

2.4 *The study of Curriculum is most appropriately a dramatic perspective.*

2.4.1 The study of territories has been accurately described by Husserl as "cultural anthropology." That is, such studies are of events that we "live through."

We have seen (at 1.4.2 above) that Curriculum is a mediate event in time that oscillates between the inner subjective world and the environment in which we live. Thus it cannot be accurately described as either subjective or objective but as a temporal unit uniting the two. Human performance (including that of Curriculum) creates inner meaning above and beyond the event itself. By living through the Curriculum encounter, the student discovers meaning and creates his own learning. Similarly the teacher, having lived through such a dynamic event, discovers meaning about program plans and methods of implementation, and can more easily create improved Curriculum designs. Meaning and learning are conceptually distinguishable from Curriculum events, and result from them.

2.4.2 Studies in cultural anthropology do not exactly parallel ethnoscience or ethnomethodology.

Ethnoscience[6] attempts componential analyses of cognitive systems: the relationship between the way a person talks about the world through his use of terms, and the way he understands the world. This approach creates specific problems: it narrows study to the linguistic categories used; emotional and related behaviors are ignored, and human experience is equated with cognition; the techniques used can determine what is studied; human significance can be ignored for the sake of precision; and, for holists, the method can be seen as cumbersome or even inappropriate.

Ethnomethodology[7] is concerned not merely with language, like ethnoscience, but also with the practical activities of human beings. The ethnomethodologist accepts that people create a cultural world and, thereby, interpret their own activities. Yet, like ethnoscience, it can be riddled with cultural relativism. Where it is of value, however, is in its use of cultural phenomenology.

2.4.3 Cultural phenomenology relies on the universal human condition within temporal events:

> ... men assume, and assume that others assume, that "if I change places with the other, so that his "here" becomes mine, I shall be at the same distance from things and see them with the same typicality that he does; moreover, the same things would be in my reach which are actually in his (and that the reverse is also true)"; that the world is taken for granted to be an intersubjective world; that the world existed yesterday and will exist tomorrow; that my actions are based on my believing that others can interpret those actions as intelligible, given their understanding of what we know in our culture, etc.[8]

When it asks that we aim to "see the world through another person's eyes" and that we consider the "whole frame of reference which the other occupies," cultural phenomenology assumes a dramatic posture. It uses dramatic models like cooperative exploration, the patient-therapist relationship and participant observation. Max Weber has shown that sociological action can only be considered *as action* when the acting person attaches meaning to it, and when it is directed towards others—when, in other words, it is inherently dramatic. Subjective meanings, intentions and interpretations are brought into the social situation by the actors.

Alfred Schutz's paper, "The Stranger,"[9] helps us to relate this to Curriculum. A new arrival from one ethnic group enters a classroom made up of students from a different cultural community. He comes with a fixed (outside) picture of the host community which is largely useless. His orientation forces him, first, to become an observer and, second, to reconstruct the rules for practical conduct whereby he can operate. He has to reconstruct his view of the world, and he does so with the help of raw materials offered to him by the others in the group. How does he achieve this? Through *his dramatic actions within time*. Action is conscious conduct: it has within it a plan, says Schutz. But that implies an imaginative "as if" which becomes externalized in dramatic action (the external "as if"). The processes of transformation (from perception to thought) and mediation (from thought to action in the world) indicate that we all have, as Schutz would say, "a dramatic rehearsal of future action." The plan may be different from the result of the action; in the same way that a school program may be different from what happens in the classroom, actions always modify plans. Yet the plan itself is always future-oriented. Typifications play a role in all anticipations: they are based on expectations generated from the past, yet they are altered within the temporal action. In such ways, Curriculum events and the dramatic process of life are similar in structure.

2.4.4 Schutz' work has direct relevance to Kenneth Burke's "dramaturgical perspective"[10] and subsequent developments in that field.

Burke distinguished action from motion: things move, men act—and the human quality is symbolic activity. We create a symbolic universe and live in that as well as in the physical one. Human action means behavior structured through symbols (which implies choice, conflict and co-operation) which people communicate to one another. Society (and by extension Curriculum) is a drama in which actions are the crucial events. Both society and Curriculum, therefore, are explicable within a dramatic paradigm: they each have their temporal Scene, Act, Agency and Purpose.

This dramatism has been followed by many in psychology and social psychology. In their differing ways, Erving Goffman, Eric Berne, Ray Birdwhistell and Edward T. Hall have attempted to describe the temporal nature of life as being *like* theatre. This view has been extended by Peter L. Berger and, in particular, by Lyman and Scott's *The Drama of Social Reality* which indicates not merely that "All the world's a stage," but that life *is* theatre and should be studied in those terms (see also "performance theory" as at 2.3.2 above).

From this perspective, life, drama and theatre as well as Curriculum are *representations* of the "world views" of the participants. The intentions of the participants create meaning from the dynamism of their actions within specific contexts.

2.4.5 This view is paralleled by studies in ceremonialism and ritual. For example, anthropologist Victor W. Turner views cultures from "the root paradigm" of "social dramas." For Turner, these are *processual*: they are about Becoming—and that implies genetic continuity, telic growth, cumulative development and progress. Such dramatic rituals bring the conflicting elements of a culture or a situation into frightening prominence. They are disharmonic processes arising in conflict situations, and highlight the key elements in any culture.

Turning the relationship of ritual and society on its head, theatre scholars can view theatrical ceremonialism as reflecting the social dynamics of a culture. Thus James R. Brandon in Southeast Asian drama, and James L. Peacock with the specific drama form of *ludruk* in Java, can both view theatrical forms as reflections of cultural dynamics.

I have related these two approaches towards ceremonialism and culture in a study of Pacific Northwest Coast Indians to demonstrate that the dramatic event (as ceremonial ritual, or as Curriculum) is the key way in which persons create meaning from the environment through dramatic actions.[11]

2.4.6 Studies of the temporal event (the territory) within the context of cultural anthropology can be from a variety of maps —such as ethnoscience, ethnomethodology, cultural phenomenology, dramatism, theatre and anthropological ceremonialism, amongst others. Clearly, no one map is sufficient, although some have more relationship to the territory than others. A plurality of maps is required in order for study to approximate to reality.

3: The Applied Study of Curriculum

3.1 THE APPLIED STUDY OF CURRICULUM CONCERNS DISCOURSE ABOUT THE PROCESSES INVOLVED WITHIN CURRICULUM EVENTS FROM MULTIPLE FRAMES OF REFERENCE
(see figure 9).

3.2 *Applied discourse about Curriculum processes can occur at different levels of abstraction*, as follows:

3.2.1 Level 1: the Curriculum Moment
This language is assumed. It takes place during the Curriculum encounter between teacher and student. The language used is always in the *present* tense with such assumed questions as, "What am I to do now?"

3.2.2 Level 2: Instruction
This is language of the *immediate future* and it has two styles:
(a) *Classroom design*
The teacher asks, "What will happen on Friday?" What is happening in the present, while he/she is teaching, provides

```
LEVELS OF          ┌─────────────────────────────┐
APPLIED            │ 1. THE CURRICULUM MOMENT    │
DISCOURSE          └─────────────────────────────┘
              ┌──────────────────────────────────────────┐
              │ 2. INSTRUCTION                           │
              │ Classroom Design, Short-Term Planning    │
              └──────────────────────────────────────────┘
        ┌─────────────────────────────────────────────────────────┐
        │ 3. GENERAL PLANNING                                     │
        │ General Program, Institution, Subject Matters, Community│
        └─────────────────────────────────────────────────────────┘
```

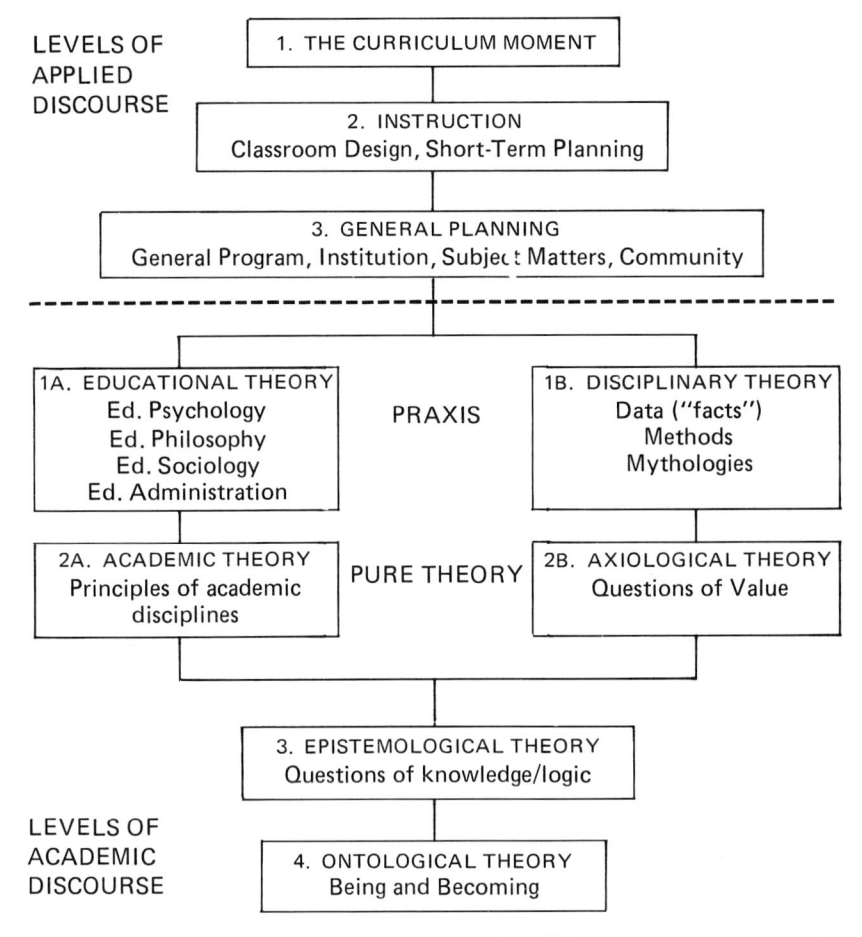

┌─────────────────────────┐   ┌─────────────────────────┐
│ 1A. EDUCATIONAL THEORY │   │ 1B. DISCIPLINARY THEORY │
│   Ed. Psychology   │   PRAXIS   │   Data ("facts")   │
│   Ed. Philosophy   │   │   Methods   │
│   Ed. Sociology   │   │   Mythologies   │
│   Ed. Administration   │   │   │
└─────────────────────────┘   └─────────────────────────┘

┌─────────────────────────┐   ┌─────────────────────────┐
│ 2A. ACADEMIC THEORY   │   PURE THEORY   │ 2B. AXIOLOGICAL THEORY │
│ Principles of academic │   │ Questions of Value   │
│   disciplines   │   │   │
└─────────────────────────┘   └─────────────────────────┘

                    ┌──────────────────────────────────┐
                    │ 3. EPISTEMOLOGICAL THEORY   │
                    │ Questions of knowledge/logic   │
                    └──────────────────────────────────┘
LEVELS OF
ACADEMIC   ┌──────────────────────────────────┐
DISCOURSE   │ 4. ONTOLOGICAL THEORY   │
                    │ Being and Becoming   │
                    └──────────────────────────────────┘

Figure 9: Levels of Curriculum Discourse.

information for use in the immediate future: what is happening with this class, at this moment, informs what will happen next time.

(b) *Short-term planning*

From questions in classroom design, the teacher asks how he/she will implement what is to happen next time. "How can I best approach the next lesson? What will be the aims, content, methods and style of assessment for the next lesson? How will I implement the classroom design?"

3.2.3 Level 3: General planning

This is the language of the *generalized future*. It is particularly affected by the variety of contexts in which education takes place. For example, it is affected by the cultural context: what is suitable for an urban classroom may not be effective in a rural area, and what is appropriate in Toronto may not be in Nairobi.

(a) *General program of the school*

"How will my classroom work fit into the context of the total school program?" Clearly this is affected by the general program of studies undertaken by the class as well as the school as a whole. It is also affected by the curriculum documents that refer (guides, syllabuses, etc.).

(b) *Institution*

Talk within this context has many variables, such as: "Will the teaching milieu be highly structured or free? What are the limitations of space, equipment, finance?"

(c) *Principles of subject matters*

"What content should I be teaching, and through which methods? Why this one, rather than that?"

(d) *Community*

The community affects discourse about general planning in a variety of ways: for example, from individual parents to small sub-groups, and through the larger community as a whole to the over-riding views of society at large.

3.3 *Applied discourse at all levels has its own inner logic of aims (or objectives), content, methods and assessment (or evaluation).*

3.3.1 None of these four logical elements has a cause-and-effect relationship to one another (see 6.5 below). The nature of their relationship is rational rather than causal and each interacts with the other.

3.4 *Applied discourse about Curriculum can take place at a variety of levels of educational administration*, thus:

Classroom	Teachers
School	Teachers, administrators, elected representatives
Area	Boards/local authorities, directors, supervisors/consultants, elected representatives
Region	Regions/provinces/states, administrators, elected representatives
Nation	National/federal, administrators, elected representatives

Conversely, this discourse can be conceived in terms of the roles the individuals fulfil within the administrative structure.

In either case, discourse is liable to be at its most concrete at the classroom level and, at the subsequent levels, increasingly abstract.

3.5 *Applied discourse about Curriculum can occur within Curriculum Development processes*, thus:
(a) *Policy implementation*
Once a policy has been promulgated at an administrative level, activity can be generated and discourse occur whereby this policy is implemented at lower levels.
(b) *Role implementation*
Discourse can occur at each level of administration (as at 3.4 above) so that individuals fulfilling roles can become more efficient in the planning and implementation of programs.

4: The Academic Study of Curriculum

4.1 THE ACADEMIC STUDY OF CURRICULUM CONCERNS DISCOURSE PROPER FROM MULTIPLE MAPS.

4.2 *Academic discourse about Curriculum occurs at different levels with increasing degrees of abstraction*, as follows:

4.2.1 Level 1: Praxis (practical/theoretic mix)
(a) *Educational theory*
This is discourse about types of educational theory which directly concerns practical decisions. From educational psychology, teachers may consider theories of learning, motivation, transfer, development and the like. From educational philosophy, teachers may consider principles or concepts, engage in philosophical analysis, and so on. From educational sociology, teachers may consider social structures, interactions and roles. From educational administration, teachers can ask questions about statistics, structures, sequences, themes and similar problems.
(b) *Disciplinary theory*
This is discourse about the discipline that lies behind particular school subject matters: (i) the data—the "facts" of the subject matters; (ii) the methodologies appropriate; and (iii) the theories and assumptions (mythologies) that lie behind the subject matters—each in terms of Curriculum.

4.2.2 Level 2: Pure theory
Unlike the discourse from praxis, it is possible to have talk about Curriculum that is entirely theoretic, thus:

(a) *Academic theory*
Here questions are raised in pure philosophy, aesthetics, the humanities, the social sciences and the sciences, such as: "What are the philosophical principles behind what I do?" and so on.

(b) *Axiological theory*
Here questions are raised about value, such as: "Is what I am doing valuable? What is value?"

4.2.3 Level 3: Epistemological theory
Behind the level of pure theory, lie questions of epistemology, such as: "What is knowledge? What type of knowledge is involved in different types of experience? In what ways can this knowledge be acquired?" These also imply questions of logic, such as: "What type of logic is involved in securing knowledge? What criteria are to be used?"

4.2.4 Level 4: Ontological theory
Behind the previous three levels of theory lie questions of ontology. We answer all questions that arise in these three levels from our viewpoint about Being and Becoming, where we ask: "Who are we? How do students understand who they are?"

5: The Use of Curriculum Levels

5.1 THE MODEL FOR THE LEVELS OF DISCOURSE IN APPLIED AND ACADEMIC STUDY OF CURRICULUM WORKS IN A SPIRAL FASHION.

5.1.1 What is happening in the Curriculum Moment feeds directly into ontological theory, and vice versa. The crux of education lies in what happens between teacher and student; but that also depends upon who they are and how they view themselves.

5.2 *Talk about Curriculum must be on the same level.*

5.2.1 Many of the confusions in the planning and implementation of programs arise because people will talk about different kinds of things at the same time. As it is confusing to talk about apples in terms of butter, so it is confusing to talk about evaluation in terms of axiology. Discussion that takes place at the level of pure theory should not be confused, in particular, with applied discourse, though one can inform the other.

6: The Logic of Curriculum

6.1 THE STUDY OF CURRICULUM (BOTH APPLIED AND ACADEMIC) IS CHARACTERIZED BY LOGIC.

6.1.1 Just as confusions arise because people will use different levels of discourse about Curriculum, so other confusions arise when such talk is not logical.

6.2 *Modern logic is based upon the use of criteria in contexts and not upon "natural laws."*

6.2.1 Aristotelian logic resulted in later "natural laws" (rules and absolutes) and, even later, in mechanistic methodologies and extremes of categorization. Subsequent upon Einstein's theory of relativity, and Russell's denial of Aristotelian logic, Wittgenstein developed his form of modern logic. When he said that "philosophy is not a science" he was advocating "demonstrating, but not telling; going through the moves, but not compiling a manual of them; teaching a skill, not dictating a doctrine" (Gilbert Ryle). For Wittgenstein, the "skill" or inner logic of any study of temporal events (and including, therefore, Curriculum) must be demonstrating, but not telling. The essential quality of such demonstrating is by the use of particular criteria within specific contexts.

6.3 *The criteria to be used will depend upon our frame of reference.*

6.3.1 In Heisenberg's terms (see 2.3.1 above), either we can use criteria of time or we can use criteria of space.

6.3.2 In Schechner's terms (see 2.3.2 above) the criteria we use will depend upon the particular socio-cultural transformation with which we are working.

6.3.3 Possible criteria to be used within a specific situation are, therefore, many but they are not limitless.

6.3.4 The scholarly study of Curriculum includes the examination of the particular criteria used within individual frames of reference (see also 6.8.7 below).

6.4 *Four examples of frames of reference used within the study of Curriculum are:*
- A. Language of subject field
- B. Language about subject field
- C. Language about Curriculum in general

(Connelly and Roberts)[12]

- Education occurs through self-learning and not through teaching towards goals which the individual can only dimly define as he tries to understand at least the current meaning of that experience.

(Rogers) [13]

- Comrade Stalin has called our writers engineers of human souls. What does this mean? ... It means knowing life so as to be able to depict it truthfully ... to depict it not in a dead, scholastic way, not simply as "objective reality" but to depict reality in its revolutionary development.

(Zhdanov) [14]

- The four commonplaces of Curriculum;
    teacher;
    milieu;
    subject matter; and
    learner.

(Schwab)[15]

These and other frames of reference may be at different levels of abstraction and deliberation, yet they have been (and are) used as maps of the Curriculum territory.

6.4.1 In terms of the scholarly study of Curriculum, each of such frames of reference will or will not evolve criteria that are valid in terms of that framework.

6.4.2 Further, the criteria that evolve from one framework may be similar to or different from the criteria used in other frames. For example, the criteria of the Connelly and Roberts framework are in terms of degrees of abstraction in "talking *about*" Curriculum (see 7.2 below). In contrast, Schwab's four commonplaces have no hierarchy and, thus, the character of his criteria are different.

6.5 *Criteria are to be contrasted with evidence.* David Best has shown that criteria are clearly distinguishable from evidence, and that this distinction has considerable logical significance. The appearance of raincoats and umbrellas used by people in the street is evidence that it is raining. In contrast, my sensations of wet drops are criteria of rain. Evidence and criteria are to be distinguished as indirect and direct ways of knowing. Thus the statement, "It is raining," does not necessarily imply that people are carrying umbrellas, but it does indicate that wet drops are falling.

Behavioral investigation deals with indirect evidence. Sometimes, however, behaviorists take behavior as evidence but, strictly speaking, this is a form of dualism—it is evidence and, also, *that for which* it is evidence. At other times, an unsophisticated form of behaviorism can assume the position of monism; that is, it can assume that behavior *just is* the emotion or sensation. But, clearly, I can feel pain or sadness without behavioral manifestation, and vice versa.

In contrast, criteria provide logical connections between behavioral statements and mental-experience statements. The behaviorist would be right if he said that the actions of other people are criteria of their mental experience; instead, he can mistakenly view their behavior as evidence. Thus Best can say:

> Expressive movements in dance are criteria of the emotions which are being expressed. . . . If we take the movement to be evidence for, or to be standing for, the emotion which is being expressed, we thereby create a gap between the . . . movement and the emotion. . . . Expressive movements do not stand for anything, they are not evidence of anything. They are *criteria* of the emotions which they express. And this is true not only of expression in the art of movement, but also of expression in the arts generally.[16]

6.5.1 There are two familiar methods of substantiation: the empirical and the logical.

Empirical substantiation is provided by "going and seeing."[17] That is, it is obtained by the gathering of information, or by investigation. It is in this way that we would answer such questions as: "How many textbooks are required for this school? How many students in this class can read?" In contrast, logical substantiation is provided by means of argument or reasoning. An example of this is the proof of the Pythagorean theorem by steps of deductive reasoning from the axioms and rules of inference. An empirical investigation of various right-angled triangles is unnecessary to substantiate the theorem; it follows as a matter of logic.

To put the matter another way, scientific study proposes or considers a hypothesis which is subjected to rigorous empirical tests—in effect, it tries to refute the hypothesis by seeing if all examples obey it. But logical study attempts to refute or confirm an argument by reasoning.

6.5.2 Human behavior is capable of two quite different modes of explanation:

(a) in terms of reasons; and

(b) in terms of causes.

Reasons are confirmed in terms of logical criteria. Causes are confirmed in terms of empirical evidence.

6.5.3 It is often falsely assumed that causal (scientific) explanations are the only objective kinds of explanations of human actions and experience. Yet there is an important sense in which *action* is primary, since it has to be presupposed for a scientific examination. For example, if a physiologist wants to examine a tennis service action, or if a psychologist wants to examine a student's writing, he has to know *that* it is that action; and he cannot discover what *action* it is by scientific means.

To put the matter another way, empirical evidence is always subject to presuppositions which are given by understanding the character and meaning of the information one already has.

Both the logical (explained by reasons) and the empirical (explained by causes) are objective in that substantiation is given by what actually occurs or exists. But the logical is not empirical, since no additional investigation or information is required. Because scientific explanation is assumed to be causal, it is tempting to believe that it is the only genuine sort of explanation.

6.5.4 Reasons should not be confused with causes.

In a causal account, a cause and its effect can be identified separately. They do not require comprehension of the context in which they occur. Yet, as Best shows, it is difficult to apply the rules of cause-and-effect to the reason for a move in chess. Such a move is given its reason from the context of the total positions of the pieces on the board together with the conventions of the game. A causal account is external rather than internal.

This is not to deny the possibility of causal explanations. Such explanations are satisfactory in some circumstances but not in others. They cannot, for example, capture the notion of chess as a game. A movement in chess might be explained in terms of nerve impulses or muscle contractions but it would be irrelevant. In a similar way, a causal account cannot capture the notion of Curriculum; it would be external rather than internal.

6.5.5 Reasons, not causes, are the foundations of logic within the study of Curriculum.

Curriculum is an event, and an event can only be understood in terms of a context: one has to take into account the total circumstances (see 6.8 below). To explain an action is to explain the *relationship* of the contextual factors—the dynamics of the interchange. This can only be done by reasons, not by causes. It is unintelligible to regard the context as external to the action, which is what a causal explanation would ask. Reasons, on the other hand, take into account the context of Curriculum and knowledge of the agent(s).

6.5.6 Reasons indicate the meaning of Curriculum events—that is, what they *are* rather than what caused them—and they are examined through criteria.

6.6 *The prime language of Curriculum is that of logic and reasoning.*

The most important contribution of Curriculum study, in either its applied or academic aspects, is the ability to question perceptively, to think critically and objectively, and make decisions accordingly.

While empirical study can support logical statements about Curriculum, it is at a second level of discourse.

6.6.1 The criteria used within any particular Curriculum frame of reference should be logical. That is, they should be statements of reason and of direct experience. Empirical statements are of a second order for Curriculum, but they are valid insofar as they support or refute logical statements.

6.7 *There are a variety of logical reasons that can be used in Curriculum discourse.*

6.7.1 The notion is still prevalent that genuine reasoning must either be inductive (as, characteristically, in science) or deductive (as, characteristically, in mathematics). But there is more scope for reasoning than these two forms. For example, inductive or deductive reasoning is not characteristically (or, at least, exclusively) employed for an emotional reaction, for a view of life, or for an aesthetic judgment, as David Best shows. At the same time, all reasoning must be answerable, at least in principle, to what could be perceived.

6.7.2 Within the study of Curriculum, reasons can be given which are:
inductive
deductive
moral
interpretative

Statements of direct experience are commonly accounted for by moral and interpretative reasons.

6.7.3 In moral reasons, it is not the character of the direct experience which is primarily in question but the moral justification for it.

Justifying, commending and explaining direct experiences by reference to moral attitudes are common. The strength of these reasons is derived from the fundamental attitudes of the person who gives them.

Two sets of opposing moral reasons may be equally sound and internally consistent. But the less the overlap of fundamental belief, the less the possibility of reaching agreement.

6.7.4 Interpretative reasons are different. They attempt to discern or convey the salient features of patterns of behavior in relation to their moral character.

Thus, for example, a group of children in a classroom may not be learning what the teacher expects them to learn. The teacher might interpret this in terms of the disturbances wrought by the entry of a senior administrator into the room. The senior administrator might interpret it, however, as a lack of ability on the part of the teacher. Both might be right.

Although interpretative reasons do not necessarily lead to definite conclusions, this does not mean that any conclusion is as good as any other. Each person may be able to give good reasons for his conclusion, but not just any conclusion can be put forward. There must be a logical relationship between the event (or work, or situation) and our interpretation of it. To explain my interpretation of the event (or work, or situation) is to give adequate reasons, rather than causes, for my particular way of looking at it. Or, as Best puts it: "It is true of objectivity in any sphere as it is in the arts that it has to allow for the indefinite but not unlimited possibilities of valid or intelligible interpretation."

6.7.5 In both moral and interpretative reasons, the fact that good reasons can be given does not imply that there is only one correct solution. An opposing view may be supported by equally good reasons.

6.8 *The criteria of a particular frame of reference must be placed within a specific context in order to be logical.*

6.8.1 A temporal event (such as life, a dramatic action, or Curriculum) when examined in isolation from its normal, perceivable context, is unintelligible. As Wittgenstein put it: "The very fact that we should so much like to say: "This is the important thing"—while we point privately to the sensation —is enough to show how much we are inclined to say something which gives no information."[18]

6.8.2 There is a peculiarly intimate connection between the *character* of a unique Curriculum event and *the relative balance of its inherent logical structure* (see 3.2.2 above). That is to say, each Curriculum event will be different according to the inter-relationship of *aims, content, method* and *assessment*. These internal elements can only be examined within the context of the unique event. The end cannot be identified apart from the manner of achieving it.

Analyses of Curriculum, therefore, consist largely in giving reasons why specific features contribute effectively to, or detract from, this particular program. Every feature of Curriculum is relevant to an analysis of it: reasons must exist in the total context.

6.8.3 A specific logical element within the Curriculum event (that is, aims, content, method or assessment) can only be considered satisfactory if, within the context of that unique event, it is seen as contributing towards the achievement of the required end.

6.8.4 There is a logical relation between meaning and the medium in which it is expressed—in this instance, Curriculum.

In the case of language, the meaning of a word is given by the various sentences in which it is used. Those sentences derive their meaning from the whole activity of language of which they are a part.

The same is true of meaning within Curriculum. Meaning requires a context. In Curriculum, meaning is given by the context of the action, or the complex of actions, of which it is a part. Precisely the same movement may have different meanings (i.e., it might *be* different actions) in different contexts.

6.8.5 An assessment made from one framework within one context may well be different from an assessment made from the same framework within a different context. For example, an assessment made from Schwab's framework about a program in an Ontario school may well have different qualities from a similar assessment made about a program in a Nigerian school.

6.8.6 The influence of contexts upon the logic of Curriculum is particularly related to moral and interpretative reasoning.

Not everyone can see the same thing in a work of art. One person may interpret Picasso's *Guernica* in one way and another person can interpret it quite differently. In the same way, the facts about an *action*, as opposed to the physical movement, depend upon how the incident is seen. That is, it depends upon one's attitude towards it. We have to take into account not just an isolated physical event but, implicitly, wide factors such as the circumstances in which it occurred, and our knowledge of the person concerned.

In this sense, the study of Curriculum is bound to a whole cultural tradition and the life of a society. The imposition of a colonial program and values upon a subjugated culture, or the imposition of middle-class values upon working-class students, is the result of using either a form of Aristotelian logic or *only* causal reasons.

Further, individual differences of sensitivity and understanding affect the possibility of seeing and responding to what takes place in schools. To fully appreciate Curriculum, one needs to have developed the capacity to imaginatively grasp and respond to complex interactions. To paraphrase Wittgenstein, when a student asked why his landlady liked particular pictures on her walls and he did not: "Very well, then—that's that!" We all have our own frames of reference. Yet individual differences only make sense against a background of objective meanings; and objectivity is relative to cultural, not individual, differences. The meaning of Curriculum, therefore, depends upon a *social* conception given by our mutual dramatic life.

6.8.7 The scholarly study of Curriculum includes the examination of the effect of social contexts upon criteria and meaning.

6.9 *The internal logical structure of programs (aims, content, method and assessment) is essentially rational and not causal.* This structure, therefore, will be determined by criteria within contexts and will be subject to logical substantiation.

7: Definitions

7.1 WITHIN THE FIELD OF CURRICULUM, THE CHARACTER OF

KNOWLEDGE VARIES ACCORDING TO THE STYLE OF ACTIVITY, AND THIS AFFECTS FORMS OF DEFINITION.

7.2 *Knowledge occurs in two inter-related ways.* According to Bertrand Russell, we secure knowledge in two conjoint ways: knowledge by acquaintance, or direct empirical evidence; and knowledge by description, or thinking and talking about direct experience.

In terms of activity (such as performance or Curriculum) the primary emphasis will vary:
- within the temporal events, we secure *knowledge in* the activity;
- within the study of those events, we secure *knowledge about* the activity.

7.2.1 This theory of knowledge is to be distinguished from that given by A. O. Lovejoy who pointed out a difference between:
- the memory of an object, which provides direct or immediate knowledge only of certain subjective states of mind; and
- the direct sensation of an existing object which duplicates these states of mind, and it is by virtue of this that we know what we do about the rest of the world.[19]

Lovejoy's theory of knowledge is, in fact, an amplification of Russell's knowledge by acquaintance.

7.2.2 The "critical realism" of such thinkers as Lovejoy and Santayana was opposed by the "new realists" who considered that "nothing intervenes between the knower and the world external to him. Objects are not presented to consciousness by ideas; they are directly presented."[20]

7.2.3 In contrast, Dewey said that perceiving does *not* consist of inspecting sensible appearances, reading off their characteristics, and then attributing these characteristics to physical things. He quoted with approval a passage from Rousseau's *Emile* and then said:

> This passage . . . indicates how far ahead he was of the psychology of his own day in his conception of the relation of the senses to knowledge. The current idea (and one that prevails too much even in our time) was that the senses were a sort of gateway and avenue through which impressions traveled and then built up knowledge pictures of the world. Rousseau said that they were part of the apparatus of action by which we adjust ourselves to our environment, and that instead of being passive receptacles they are directly connected with motor activities—with the use of hands and legs. In this respect he was more advanced than some of his successors who emphasized the importance of sense

contact with objects, for the latter thought of the senses simply as purveyors of information about objects instead of instruments of the necessary adjustments of human beings to the world around them.[21]

Although his critique of Rousseau is penetrating, it is more difficult to understand Dewey's own positive account of perception and epistemology. His clearest statement is:

> That a perception is cognitive means, accordingly, that it is used; it is treated as a sign of conditions that implicate other as yet unperceived consequences in addition to the perception itself. That a perception is *truly* cognitive means that its active use or treatment is followed by other consequences which follow independently of its being perceived. To discover that a perception or idea is cognitively invalid is to find that the consequences which follow from acting upon it entangle and confuse the other consequences which follow from the causes of the perception, instead of integrating or coordinating harmoniously with them.[22]

As I understand what Dewey meant, a teacher perceives that the particular classroom situation is appropriate for his/her plan to be implemented; a "transaction" occurs with the result that the teacher acts, or becomes prepared to act, upon the belief that the plan may now be implemented. If, however, the situation was not appropriate, there would be a state of "inbalance"—and this would precipitate further inquiry.

Quite clearly, the "cognitive validity" of any perception or form of knowledge is, for Dewey, in terms of deliberating and acting.

7.2.4 In the most general terms, therefore, there is a form of agreement between Russell and Dewey about the bi-polar nature of knowledge: *knowledge in* and *knowledge about*. (This does not obviate their considerable differences in detailed epistemology.)

Knowledge in would be inclusive of Dewey's acting and Russell's "knowledge by acquaintance." *Knowledge about* would be inclusive of Dewey's deliberation and Russell's "knowledge by description."

7.2.5 Yet, because knowledge is bi-polar and is created within a dynamic does not mean that it falls into the dualistic trap. Rather, these aspects of knowledge co-exist and oscillate in their emphases according to the style of activity.

In fact, the tendency is for *knowledge in* to be primarily characteristic of Curriculum events, while *knowledge about* is characteristic of the study of Curriculum.

7.3 *Within the field of Curriculum, the types of definition used will vary the style of knowledge emphasized.*

7.3.1 There are two types of definition:
- *the denotative*, which denotes, is usually used in dictionaries, and describes the unique qualities of things and action; and
- *the connotative*, which provides the various personal understandings of things and actions—their special associations to the individual and the culture—usually by example.

Korzybski called the denotative the *intentional* definition, and the connotative the *extensional* in that it provides examples of the denotative. Denotative and intentional definitions are more abstract than connotative and extensional definitions. The former are likely to be more objective than the latter.

7.3.2 In terms of epistemology, denotative and intentional definitions are more likely to be used in *knowledge about* while connotative and extensional definitions are more likely to be used in *knowledge in*.

7.3.3 In terms of education, a denotative and intentional definition of a program will likely describe the particular qualities that make it different from other programs. A connotative or extensional definition, on the other hand, will likely provide specific examples of what takes place in particular programs.

7.3.4 In terms of Curriculum, connotative and extensional definitions are more likely to be used in descriptions of the Curriculum Moment and, to a lesser extent, within applied discourse. Denotative and intentional definitions, on the other hand, are most likely to be used in academic discourse.

Precision within the study of Curriculum will depend upon using the style of definition appropriate to the type of knowledge and level of discourse currently in operation. Just as talk about Curriculum must be on the same level, so epistemological frameworks and forms of definition must be of similar kinds if Curriculum discourse is to have sense.

Summary

In attempting to describe the field of Curriculum through the dramatic metaphor, it has been shown that Curriculum consists of events that take place in time (1.1), that is, those moments when teachers teach and learners learn. This encounter is temporal and dynamic and must be distinguished from programs, materials, curriculum design, and similar elements which exist at a different level of operation.

The field of Curriculum consists of temporal events and the study of these events (2.1). Such study represents a plurality of "maps" whereby we can understand the "territory" of Curriculum. This way of apprehending the field has the support of modern science and modern performance theory. It has been characterized as "cultural anthroplogy": studies of events we "live through" whereby we "see the world through another person's eyes." This is a dramatic perspective upon a symbolic universe which we have created.

The study of Curriculum is both applied and academic. The applied study of Curriculum (3.1) describes the processes involved with increasing degrees of abstraction: that of the Curriculum Moment is in the present tense; that of instruction is of the immediate future; and that of general planning is of the generalized future. The academic study of Curriculum (4.1) concerns discourse proper. It, also, is in increasing degrees of abstraction: praxis, pure theory, epistemology and ontology. The applied and academic levels of discourse work in a spiral fashion: what happens in the Curriculum Moment feeds directly into ontology, and vice versa (5.1). Talk about Curriculum must be on the same level, otherwise confusions arise (5.2).

The study of Curriculum is characterized by logic (6.1) whereby particular criteria are used within specific contexts. The criteria we use depend upon our frame of reference. Criteria are not evidence: they are gained by reason and not by gathering information. Nor do they provide a causal account. Rather, they relate to the total context of Curriculum events—what they *are* rather than what caused them. The most important contribution of Curriculum study is the ability to question perceptively, to think critically and objectively, and to make decisions accordingly (6.6). Logical reasons can be inductive, deductive, moral and interpretative, but these reasons must always be related to a context. Thus an assessment made from one framework within one context may well be different from a similar assessment within a different context. The facts about any action (including both performance and Curriculum) depend on how the incident is seen.

Curriculum knowledge varies in character according to the style of the activity, and this affects forms of definition (7.1). Primarily, *knowledge in* takes place at the Curriculum Moment while *knowledge about* occurs in academic discourse; applied discourse mingles the two. Thus connotative definitions are liable to occur in descriptions of Curriculum events, and denotative definitions will be used in academic study.

This analysis of Curriculum can equally well be applied to dramatic action where a distinction can be drawn between dramatic events which exist in time and dramatic theory which is the study of those events. Needless to say, the implications seen in what is stated here will depend upon the criteria used by the reader, the method of reasoning used, and the context within which it is read.

Appendix B
Drama and Research

There are many confusions about Developmental Drama research. It may be useful to sort out the major issues in brief. The following would apply to research studies in the field and to dissertation methods. In the latter instance, however, there are some differences of emphasis according to the discipline within which the dissertation is presented: social science (including education), the arts and humanities, or the fine arts (including drama/theatre).

Modes of Research

There are two prime modes of Developmental Drama research: experiential and reflective. Experiential research is practical. It consists of human beings acting and role-playing in a specific situation. This is a common mode for professional actors; they are practically engaged in a workshop and that experience *of itself* is considered research in the medium. A variant of experiential research is for records (written, taped, filmed) to be made of the experience by non-actors while it is taking place, or for the performers to deliberate about it afterwards. In both cases, once this occurs the research mode has become reflective. In some instances, dissertations in the fine arts (including drama/theatre) can be primarily in the experiential mode, leading to the degrees of MFA and DFA, but they are usually accompanied by records of the events.

Reflective research is inquiry *about* enactment. The researcher is not normally engaged within the dramatic action but, in some way, inquires into its nature and function from outside the event. Most research studies in Developmental Drama are within this mode and the rest of this appendix will be devoted to it.

Subjectivity and Objectivity

Despite popular beliefs to the contrary, there is no such thing as a "pure" subjective or objective approach to research. Rather, some research can be more subjective and some can be more objective. It is a question of emphasis. Although the sciences are often regarded as using the most objective modes of research, we have seen (Appendix A: 2.3.1) that the perspective of the scientist gives him a view (a frame of reference) from which he examines phenomena. In the social sciences, it is often assumed that the phenomenological method (Appendix A: 2.4.3) is the most subjective; yet, even in this case, a selection must be made from the data.

The Developmental Drama researcher, however objective or subjective he wishes to be, must make some choices. He is making a map of the territory, yet no map can *be* the territory. He will have his own dramatic perspective on the phenomena concerned. Yet he will have to make his own choices according to logic and reason. Needless to say, there are extremes amongst such choices: from using pre-specified categories to examine the information (more objective) to searching for emergents from the data (more subjective).

Research Design

Views of what constitutes valid research design have altered over the years. In 1963 the standard view was that there were two types of educational research; the descriptive and the causal.[1]

The Descriptive Method attempts to describe rather than explain phenomena in the following styles:

- Survey Research. Instruments of data collection (e.g., questionnaires and interviews) are linked to statistics for analysis. The Gallup Poll is probably the best-known survey to sample public opinion. One instance in drama education is the survey of Victorian Post Primary Schools (Australia).[2]
- Observational Research. This involves direct observation by persons, audiotape, videotape, etc. It is limited because of the complexity of human behavior, the degree to which the presence of the observer changes the situation, and the considerable time needed. This was the basis (but only one method) used in the British Schools Council, Drama Teaching Project (10-16).[3]
- Historical Research. This systematically locates, evaluates and synthesizes evidence in order to draw conclusions about past events. This was the method used in *Theatre for Children in the United States: A History*, by Nellie McCaslin.

The Causal Method attempts to deduce causes for phenomena in the following styles:
- Causal-Comparative Research. This deduces causes for a behavior pattern by comparing subjects in whom this pattern is present with similar subjects in whom it is absent. Thus reading achievement might be compared between two groups: one where the teacher frequently uses drama for reading, and the other where he does not.
- Correlation Research. This discovers or clarifies relationships through the use of correlation coefficients—a statistical tool measuring scores of school achievement where the relationship can be negative (-1.00 to zero), unrelated (zero), or positive (zero to 1.00). This method was used in Huntsman's research on the effect of improvisation upon self-actualization.
- Experimental Research. This is the most rigorous causal method, the other two methods often being part(s) of an experimental design. This method manipulates one variable and observes its effect upon another variable. Thus if the same group of teachers use drama for reading with one group of students but not another, then, if drama has an effect upon reading, the first group should exceed the second on a measure of this variable. This method was used in D. B. Cook's study of infant identification with the mother, and others are reported in the journal *Empirical Research in Theater*.

Such an arbitrary categorization of what constitutes "proper" research has, however, broken down in the subsequent twenty years. Much has been due to the fact that researchers have discovered that there are many phenomena requiring research which cannot be adequately examined within such limited methodologies. As a result, other styles of research have been developed, from those that still remain empirical, such as the laboratory approach,[4] to those that revalue the whole conceptual basis of research, such as those which are based upon models.[5]

Thus, by 1980, the following ways of categorizing research designs were put forward:[6]

By Kind:
- Analytical: Frameworks, classification and categorical systems are developed to help analyse the phenomena.
- Empirical: A hypothetical relationship between selected variables is statistically investigated.
- Historical: Events, developments and past experiences are investigated through a critical analysis of evidence; there is usually

an interpretation of the evidence.
- Narrative/Descriptive: The phenomena are addressed and observed as they exist or operate.
- Application of Theory: A theory is selected, explicated and then applied to phenomena.

By Function:
- Confirmative: This usually refers to empirical research which seeks to verify previously researched and published results.
- Exploratory: This usually refers to empirical research which investigates a hypothetical relationship between two or more variables.
- Methodology Development: This refers to the development of a methodology for research.
- Theory/Concept Development: This refers to the development of theoretical and/or conceptual notions related to phenomena.
- New Perspective: This refers to the examination of a previously researched, familiar problem from the viewpoint of a new discipline or with a new "set of lenses."
- Descriptive: This refers to a study which describes phenomena; there is usually some element of analysis in the description.

By Methodology:
- Case Study: In this instance there is only a sample of one unit (e.g., one event, one school, one person).
- Survey: In this instance data are collected from a sample; tests, questionnaires or interviews are used, and sets of scores are examined.
- Field Study: In this instance the phenomena are observed either with or without a framework for viewing; the sample is greater than one.

Clearly there are far more research designs possible than there were twenty years ago.

Dramatic Methods

Within such research designs, a variety of dramatic methods can be used. I have described these elsewhere[7] and will, therefore, refer to them only briefly in this Appendix:

- *Categoric and Analytic:* attempts to analyse enactments into their categorical parts. Examples:
    Ann Shaw's taxonomy of creative dramatics.
    Lazier and Karioth's *Inventory of Dramatic Behavior,* which is

designed to analyse one-person improvisations in terms of time, space traversed, number of stops, dramatic incidents, novel dramatic incidents, dramatic acts, repeated scenes and characters created.

- *Extrinsic:* methods from other disciplines particularly useful to drama. Examples:
    Sociometry.[8]
    Proxemics.[9]
    Creativity (see pp. 98-107 above).

- *Descriptive:* methods that attempt to describe events and discover emergents from the data. These are of two types. The first acknowledge the subjective view of the researcher and amongst those recommended for drama by Hoetker and Brossell[10] are:
    The model of the psychoanalyst whereby intensive case studies of a few individuals are made and significant issues are teased out of the data.
    Various anthropological models using participant-observation methods (one model being micro-ethnography).
    Self-actualization models whereby the researcher participates in the drama activity, stepping back from time to time to review events and refine his ideas about the emerging patterns.
The second type includes methods of collecting value-free data. Examples:
    Phenomenological.[11]
    Check lists.[12]

- *Dramatic:* methods from the field of drama/theatre. These include those of dramatic and theatrical criticism (specific analytic and categorical forms), history of drama and theatre, and those of spontaneous drama of which examples are:
    Sutton-Smith and Lazier's *Assessment of Dramatic Involvement Scale* which examines focus, completion, use of imaginary objects, elaboration, use of space, facial expression, body movements, vocal expressions and social relationships.[13]
    Dorothy Heathcote's "eight rules of drama."[14]

- *Developmental:* methods derived from the developments of dramatic action. Examples:
    Gavin Bolton's three levels of dramatic symbolism.[15]
    Dramatic age stages (see pp. 12-18 above).
    Personal dynamic developments (see pp. 7-18 above).
    Cultural dynamic developments (see pp. 18-40 above).

Conclusion

These notes are not an attempt to deny the validity of experiential research, particularly that carried out by theatre practitioners. Peter Brook's *The Empty Space* and Richard Schechner's *Environmental Theater* are exemplars of records and descriptions of such valid experiments. Rather, this appendix simply provides some indicators of the possibilities within reflective research of human dramatic action.

Notes

All entries refer to publications itemized in detail in the bibliography.

CHAPTER 1: DEVELOPMENTAL DRAMA (pages 5-42)
1. Polanyi, 1964: 64-65.
2. Ibid.: 320-21.
3. Piaget, 1951.
4. Slade, 1954.
5. Piaget, 1951; Erikson, 1965; Kohlberg, 1978; Hoffman, 1976.
6. Winnicott, 1974.
7. Eliade, 1959: 358.
8. Matthews, 1895: 418.
9. Eliade, 1965: 6.
10. Kramer, 1969: 63.
11. Eliade, 1963.
12. Ibid.
13. Ibid: 33.
14. Strehlow, 1947: 56-57.
15. *John*, 13-15.
16. Eliade, 1969: 172.
17. Van Gennep, 1960.
18. Titiev, 1960.
19. Coon, 1976.
20. Eliade, 1965.
21. Ibid.: 87.
22. Williams, 1923.
23. LaBarre, 1970.
24. Brody, 1969; Cawte, 1978.
25. Opie, 1948; Gomme, 1964.
26. Peacock, 1968: 6.
27. E.g., Eliade, 1963; Van Gennep, 1960, etc.
28. Brody, 1956; Brody, 1964; Sears et al., 1965; Whiting and Child, 1953.
29. Winnicott, 1974; for cross-cultural references see, Mead and Wolfenstein, 1955.
30. Courtney, forthcoming
31. Southern, 1962.
32. Henry, 1972; Kneller, 1965; Roberts and Akinsanya, 1976; Shinn, 1972; Spindler, 1963; Whiting and Whiting, 1975.

CHAPTER 2: HUMAN DYNAMICS: DRAMA AND MOTIVATION (pages 43-68)
1. For instincts as motives, see McDougall, 1908. For animal psychology, see Lorenz, 1950, and Tinbergen, 1951. For motivation and the nervous system, see Woodworth, 1918, and Hebb, 1955. For drive and

drive manipulations, see Hull, 1943.
2. Thorndike, 1911; Troland, 1932; Young, 1959.
3. Gaier, 1952.
4. Woodworth and Schlosberg, 1954; Warden and Aylesworth, 1927.
5. Montgomery, 1954; Olds, 1958; Valenstein and Valenstein, 1964; Berlyne, 1960.
6. Carlow, 1976a, 1976b.
7. Pfaffman, 1960.
8. Mowrer, 1960.
9. Anna Freud, 1950; Hartmann, 1950.
10. For curiosity, see Berlyne, 1950. For exploration, see Myers and Miller, 1954. For activity, see Kagan and Berken, 1954; Hill, 1956. For manipulation, see Harlow, 1953. For mastery, see Hendrick, 1942, 1943a, 1943b. For success, see Kardiner, 1947. For motility, see Mittelmann, 1954. For initiative and industry, see Erikson, 1953, 1972. For novelty, stimulation and excitement, see Hebb, 1949; Leuba, 1955; McClelland, 1953; McReynolds, 1956. For the visceral, see Murphy, 1947. For hedonism, see Young, 1949, 1955. For relations with the environment, see Diamond, 1939; Skinner, 1953; Woodworth, 1958; Piaget, 1962; Winnicott, 1974.
11. Sutton-Smith, 1973: 289.
12. Winterbottom, 1958.
13. Crandall, 1963.
14. Hollenberg and Sperry, 1950; Kagan and Moss, 1960.
15. Bruner, 1963.
16. Jones, 1968.
17. Maslow, 1976: 67.
18. Von Bertalanffy, 1960: 103.
19. Nuttin, 1968: 4-5.
20. Sherrington, 1951: 247-48.
21. For the directions of action, see Suchman, 1971. For spontaneity, see Moreno, 1966.
22. For biological adaptation, see Nuttin, 1968: 9. For obstacles, see Pieron, 1959: 45; Fauville, 1955: 114-20.
23. Witkin, 1974: 113.
24. Nuttin, 1968: 47.
25. Hampden-Turner, 1971: 79.
26. Ornstein, 1975: 77.
27. MacLean, 1979.
28. See article by Perkins, in Eisner, 1978.
29. For frustration, see Dollard, 1939. For catharsis, see French, 1944. For arbitrary acts, see Pastore, 1952. For punishment, see Chasdi and Lawrence, 1951. For punishment and imaginary activity, see Sears, 1951.
30. Mahler, 1933.
31. Phenix, 1974.
32. Stake, 1974.
33. Bühler and Hetzer, 1928.
34. Eysenck and Himmelweit, 1946; Himmelweit, 1947.
35. Abbagnano, 1969; 214.
36. Witkin, 1974: 113.
37. Morris, 1966: 138-39.
38. Ibid.: 138.
39. Witkin, 1974: 78-79.
40. Morris, 1966: 140.

CHAPTER 3: DRAMA AND THE TRANSFER OF LEARNING
(pages 69-85)

1. Allen, 1968.
2. N.A.D.I.E., 1977.
3. Way, 1968.
4. Cook, 1917.
5. For "the basics," see Madeja, n.d.; Eisner, 1978. For language arts, see Burton, 1974; Britton,

1970; Cornwall, 1970; Stewig, 1973. For social studies, see Birt and Nichol, 1975; Fines and Verrier, 1974; Craig, 1976. For second language, see Turkewych and DiVito, 1978. For politics and economics, see Hunt, 1976.
6. Adland, 1964.
7. Ellis, 1965: 7.
8. Thorndike and Woodworth, 1901.
9. Judd, 1908.
10. Ellis, 1965: 3.
11. Harlow, 1949, 1959.
12. Vygotsky, 1962.
13. Harlow, 1959.
14. Stevenson, 1978.
15. Hamilton, 1950.
16. Russell and Storms, 1955.
17. Sutton-Smith and Lazier, 1971: 37.
18. E.g., Gibson, 1941.
19. Osgood, 1949.
20. Witkin, 1974: 172.
21. Miller and Dollard, 1941; Ellis and Muller, 1964; Vanderplas, Sanderson and Vanderplas, 1964.
22. Gibson and Gibson, 1955.
23. Bunch, 1936.
24. Ellis and Burnstein, 1960; Ellis and Hunger, 1960, 1961a, 1961b.
25. Mandler, 1962.
26. Postman, 1962.
27. Harlow, 1949; Duncan, 1958.
28. Craig, 1953; Werner, 1930.
29. Spence, 1964.
30. Gaier, 1952.
31. Schultz, 1960, in contrast to Duncan, 1959.
32. Heathcote, 1967; Ward, 1957.
33. Hilgard, Irvine and Whipple, 1953.
34. McGregor, Tate and Robinson, 1977: 59.
35. Ellis, 1965: 70.
36. Ibid.: 71.
37. McGregor, Tate and Robinson, 1977:59.
38. Ibid.: 93.
39. Witkin, 1974: 88-89.
40. McGregor, Tate and Robinson, 1977: 80-81.

CHAPTER 4: DRAMA AND INSTRUCTION (pages 86-97)
1. Singer and Dick, 1974.
2. Heathcote, 1971b.
3. Terrence, 1963a, 1963b.
4. Holding, 1970b.
5. Taylor, 1970.
6. Kay, 1951.
7. Aiken and Lau, 1967.
8. Craig, 1953, 1956; Kittell, 1957.
9. Kersh, 1958, 1962; Worthen, 1968.
10. Anthony, 1973.
11. Macrae and Holding, 1965a, 1965b, 1966a.
12. Berry, Prather and Bermudez, 1973; Prather and Berry, 1970.
13. Prather, 1969; Prather and Berry, 1970; Prather, 1971.
14. Macrae and Holding, 1966b.
15. Singer and Pease, 1976.
16. Hartnett, 1975; Malle and Duthie, 1975.
17. Singer, 1977.
18. For elementary students, see Patterson and Anderson, 1965. For nursery children, see Hartup, 1964. For retarded children, see Terrel and Stevenson, 1965.
19. Hartup, Glazer and Charlesworth, 1967.
20. Hartup and Coates, 1967.
21. Patterson, Shaw and Ebner, 1969.
22. Solloman and Wahler, 1973.
23. Blinn and Jacobsen, 1973.
24. McGregor, Tate and Robinson, 1977.
25. Rosenbaum *et al.*, 1976.
26. Harris, *et al.*, 1972.
27. Harris and Sherman, 1973.

28. Bolton, 1979: 29.
29. Ibid.: 30.
30. Shaw, 1975: 84.

CHAPTER 5: DRAMA AND THE DIFFERENT: CREATIVITY AND GIFTEDNESS (pages 98-107)

1. Getzels and Jackson, 1962.
2. Davis, 1971, 1973; Kaltsounis, 1971, 1972.
3. Taylor *et al.*, 1971; Mackinnon, 1971.
4. Bartlett and Davis, 1974; Wallach and Wing, 1969.
5. Mednick, 1967. For criticism, see Davis, 1975.
6. Barron, 1965.
7. Davis, 1975.
8. Schaefer and Anastasi, 1968.
9. Gough, 1952.
10. Available from Professor Gary Davis, Educational Psychology, University of Wisconsin, 1025 West Johnson Street, Madison, Wisconsin 53706.
11. Burton, 1970: 3.

CHAPTER 6: EXPRESSION: THE DRAMA OF ENGLISH AND LANGUAGE LEARNING (pages 108-125)

1. Britton, 1970: 12-13.
2. Ibid.: 14.
3. Kelly, 1963.
4. Britton, 1970: 29.
5. Vygotsky, 1966.
6. Ibid.
7. Ibid.
8. Luria, 1971.
9. Britton, 1970: 192.
10. Bruner, 1974.
11. Vygotsky, 1966.
12. Holloway, 1951.
13. Smith, 1971: 175-76.
14. Vygotsky, 1966: 70.
15. Johnstone, 1975.
16. Smith, 1971: 21.
17. Ibid.: 195.
18. Mackay and Simo, 1976: 19-20.
19. Smith, 1971: 189.
20. Vygotsky, 1962: 99-100
21. Slade, 1954.

CHAPTER 7: DRAMATHERAPY (pages 126-134)

1. Best, 1974.
2. O'Toole, 1976.

CHAPTER 8: CULTURE AND CURRICULUM: A DRAMATIC CONTEXT (pages 135-153)

1. Tillich, 1959: 163-64.
2. Rosenberg, 1972: 191-92.
3. May, 1969.
4. Buber, 1973: 51.
5. Ibid.
6. Ibid.: 83.
7. Ibid.: 124-25.
8. Jaspers, 1961.
9. Buber, 1973: 127.
10. Ibid., 128.
11. Ibid.: 68.
12. Schutz, 1964.
13. Natanson, 1970.
14. Heaton, 1978: 120-21.
15. Kierkegaard, 1951: 210-11.
16. Maslow, 1959: 24.
17. Sarbin, 1954.
18. Assagioli, 1976; Fromm, 1956; Lewis, 1960; Sorokin, 1954.
19. Junell, 1974: 110.
20. Vandenberg, 1971.

21. Heaton, 1978: 124-25.
22. Ibid.: 130-31.

CHAPTER 9: AXIOMS AND MAXIMS: A RATIONALE FOR THE ARTS IN EDUCATION (pages 154-165)

1. Reid, 1968.
2. Witkin, 1974.
3. Best, 1974.
4. Eisner, 1978.
5. Courtney, 1974.
6. Best, 1974.
7. Kukuk and Sjolund, 1976.
8. Ibid.; E.F.L., 1975.
9. Courtney and Schattner, 1982; Lowenfeld and Brittain, 1970.
10. Kaelin and Ecker, 1976: 7.
11. Bloom and Remer, 1976.

APPENDIX A: THE FIELD OF CURRICULUM (pages 166-191)

1. Black, 1973.
2. Grumet, 1978.
3. Bridgman, 1963: 13-14.
4. Beckerman, 1970: 10, 37.
5. Schechner, 1977: 42.
6. Sturtevant, 1964.
7. Garfinkel, 1964.
8. Psathas, 1968.
9. Schutz, 1944.
10. Burke, 1968: 445-51.
11. Courtney, forthcoming.
12. Connelly and Roberts, 1974: A-9.
13. Rogers, 1961: 275.
14. Zhdanov, 1950.
15. Schwab, 1969, 1971, 1973.
16. Best, 1974: 92-93.
17. Emmett, 1968.
18. Wittgenstein, 1953.

19. Lovejoy, 1930.
20. Holt *et al.*, 1912.
21. Dewey, 1915: 11-12.
22. Dewey, 1929: 323-24.

APPENDIX B: DRAMA AND RESEARCH (pages 192-197)

1. Borg and Gall, 1963.
2. McLeod, 1978.
3. McGregor *et al.*, 1977.
4. Golembiewski and Blumberg, 1970.
5. Brodeck, 1973; Black, 1973.
6. Connelly and students, 1980.
7. Courtney and Schattner, 1982: Vol. 1: Chapter 1.
8. Moreno, 1934.
9. Hall, 1956, 1966.
10. In Stephenson and Vincent, 1975.
11. Courtney, 1973.
12. Courtney and Schattner, 1982: Vol. 1: Chapter 1, Appendix.
13. Sutton-Smith and Lazier, 1971.
14. Fiala, 1977.
15. Bolton, 1977.

References

Abbagnano, Nicola. *Critical Existentialism.* New York: Doubleday, 1969.

Adland, David. *Group Drama.* London: Longman, 1964.

Adler, Alfred. *Studie über Minderwertigkeit von Organen.* Berlin: Urban und Schwarzenberg, 1907.

———. "Der Aggressionstrieb im Leben und in der Neurose," *Fortschritte der Medezin*, 26 (1908): 577-84.

Allen, John. *Education Survey 2—Drama.* London: HMSO, 1968.

———. *Drama in Schools: Its Theory and Practice.* London: Heinemann, 1979.

Ayllon, M., and S. Snyder. "Behavioral Objectives in Creative Dramatics," *Journal of Educational Research*, 62, 8 (1969): 355.

Aiken, E., and A. Lau. "Response Prompting and Response Confirmation: A Review of Recent Literature," *Psychological Bulletin*, 5 (1967): 330-41.

Ansbacher, H. L. and R. R. Ansbacher, eds. *The Individual Psychology of Alfred Adler.* New York: Basic Books, 1956.

Anthony, W. S. "Learning to Discover Rules by Discovery," *Journal of Educational Psychology*, 64 (1973): 325-28.

Arnheim, Rudolf. *Art and Visual Perception: The Psychology of the Creative Eye.* Berkeley, Calif.: University of California Press, 1964.

Assagioli, Roberto. *The Act of Will.* Harmondsworth: Penguin, 1974.

———. *Psychosynthesis.* Harmondsworth: Penguin, 1976.

Ausubel, David P. *The Psychology of Meaningful Verbal Learning.* New York: Grune and Stratton, 1963.

Barker, Clive. *Theatre Games.* London: Eyre Methuen, 1977; New York: Drama Books Specialists, 1978.

Barron, Frank. "The Psychology of Creativity," in F. Barron, *et al. New Directions in Psychology*, II. New York: Holt, 1965: 1-134.

——— and Welsh, G. S. *Barron-Welsh Art Scale.* Palo Alto, Calif.: Consulting Psychologists Press, 1963.

Bartlett, M. M., and G. A. Davis. "Do the Wallach and Kogan Tests predict real Creative Behavior?" *Perceptual and Motor Skills*, 39 (1974): 730.

Beckerman, Bernard. *Dynamics of*

Drama. New York: Knopf, 1970.
Berlyne, D. E. *Conflict, Arousal and Curiosity.* New York: McGraw-Hill, 1960.
Berne, Eric. *Transactional Analysis in Psychotherapy.* New York: Grove, 1961.
Berry, G. A., D. C. Prather, and J. M. Bermudez. "Effect of Verbalization on Trial-and-Error and Prompted Learning of a Perceptual Skill," *Proceedings*, 81st Annual Convention of the American Psychological Association, 8 (1973): 481-82.
Best, David. *Expression in Movement and the Arts.* London: Lepus, 1974.
———. *Philosophy and Human Movement.* London: Allen and Unwin, 1978.
Binswanger, Ludwig. "The Case of Ellen West," and "The Case of Ilse," in Rollo May, *et al.*, eds. *Existence: A New Dimension in Psychiatry and Psychology.* New York: Basic Books, 1958.
Birt, David, and Jon Nichol. *Games and Simulations in History.* London: Longman, 1975.
Black, Max. "Models and Archetypes," in H. S. Broudy, *et al. Philosophy of Educational Research.* New York: Wiley, 1973: 483-501.
Blinn, R. H., and L. I. Jacobsen. "The Effectiveness of Peers and Adults as Social Reinforcement and Information Feedback Agents in Conceptual Learning," *Proceedings*, 81st Annual Convention of the American Psychological Association, 8 (1973): 73-74.
Bloom, Kathryn, and Jane Remer. "A Rationale for the Arts in Education," *National Elementary Principal*, 55, 3 (January/February, 1976): 45.

Bolton, Gavin. "The Process of Symbolization in Improvised Drama as an Art Form," paper privately circulated, 1977.
———. "The Aims of Educational Drama." *Journal*, National Association for Drama in Education (Australia), 4 (December 1979): 28-31.
———. *Towards a Theory of Drama in Education.* London: Longman, 1980.
Borg, W., and M. D. Gall. *Educational Research: An Introduction.* New York: David McKay, 1963.
Brandon, James R. *Theatre in Southeast Asia.* Cambridge, Mass.: Harvard University Press, 1967.
Bridgman, P. W. *A Sophisticate's Primer of Relativity.* London: Routledge, 1963.
Britton, James. *Language and Learning.* London: Allen Lane, 1970.
Brodeck, M. "Models," in H. S. Broudy, *et al. Philosophy of Educational Research.* New York: Wiley, 1973: 475-82.
Brody, Alan. *The English Mummers and their Plays.* London: Routledge, 1969.
Brody, Sylvia. *Patterns of Mothering.* New York: International Universities Press, 1956.
———. *Passivity.* New York: International Universities Press, 1964.
Bruner, Jerome S. "Needed: A Theory of Instruction," *Education Leadership*, 20 (May 1963): 523-32.
———. *Towards a Theory of Instruction.* Cambridge, Mass.: Harvard University Press, 1966.
———. "Child Play," *New Scientist* (April 1974).
Buber, Martin. *I and Thou.* New York: Scribner's, 1958.
———. *Martin Buber on Theater*, ed.

M. Friedman. New York: Funk and Wagnall, 1969.

———. *Between Man and Man*. New York: Macmillan, 1973.

Bunch, M. E. "The Amount of Transfer in Rational Learning as a Function of Time," *Journal of Comp. Psychology*, 22 (1936): 325-37.

Bühler, Charlotte, and H. Hetzker. "Das erste Verstandnis von Ausdruck im ersten Lebensjahr," *Z. Psychol.*, 107 (1928): 50-61.

Burger, Peter L. *Invitation to Sociology: A Humanistic Perspective*. New York: Doubleday, 1963.

———, and Thomas Luckman. *The Social Construction of Reality*. New York: Doubleday, 1966.

Burke, Kenneth. *A Grammar of Motives* and *A Rhetoric of Motives*. Cleveland: World Pub. Co., 1961.

———. *Language as Symbolic Action*. Berkeley, Calif.: University of California Press, 1965.

———. "Dramatism," in *International Encyclopedia of the Social Sciences*, 7. New York: Macmillan, 1968.

Burton, E. J. *Teaching English Through Self-Expression*. London: Evans, 1949.

———. *Drama in Schools*. London: Jenkins, 1952.

———. "Aspects of Dramatic Work with Gifted Children," *Speech and Drama*, 19, 1 (Spring 1970): 2-6.

Carlow, Chester D. "The Application of Psychological Theories to a Curriculum Development Project: An Example," *Educational Psychology*, 12, 1 (1976a): 36-48.

———. "Theories of Motivation with Applications to School Problems at the Junior and Intermediate Levels," paper privately circulated, 1976b.

Cawte, E. C. *Ritual Animal Disguise*. London: Folk-lore Society, 1978.

Chasdi, E. H., and M. S. Lawrence. "Some Antecedents of Aggression and Effects of Frustration in Doll Play," in W. Wolff, ed. *Personality*, 1951: 32-43. Also published in: D. C. McClelland, ed. *Studies in Motivation*. New York: Appleton, 1955: 517-29.

Connelly, F. M., and D. A. Roberts. *Graduate Studies in Curriculum: A Data Base and Issues for Deliberation in Program Planning*. Toronto: Curriculum Department, Ontario Institute for Studies in Education, 1974.

——— and students. Paper privately circulated, 1980.

Cook, Caldwell. *The Play Way*. London: Heinemann, 1917.

Cook, D. B. "An Exploratory Study of the Effects of Maternal Personality and Language Style upon Mother-Infant Interaction." Ph.D. dissertation, University of Toronto, 1980.

Coon, Carlton S. *The Hunting Peoples*. Harmondsworth: Penguin, 1976.

Cornwall, Paul. *Creative Playmaking in the Elementary School*. London: Chatto and Windus, 1970.

Courtney, Richard. "Drama and Aesthetics," *British Journal of Aesthetics*, 8, 4 (1968): 378-86.

———. "On Langer's Dramatic Illusion," *Journal of Aesthetics and Art Criticism*, 29, 1 (Fall 1970a): 11-20.

———. "Drama and Pedagogy," *The Stage in Canada*, 6, 5a (1970b): 56-67.

———. "A Dramatic Theory of Imagination," *New Literary History*, 2, 3 (Spring 1971a): 445-60.

———. "Imagination and the Dramatic Act: Some Comments on Sartre, Ryle and Furlong," *Journal of Aesthetics and Art Criticism*, 30, 2 (Winter 1971b): 163-70.

———. "Theatre and Spontaneity," *Journal of Aesthetics and Art Criticism*, 32, 1 (Fall 1973a): 79-88.

———. "Drama and the Phenomenological Description," *Discussions in Developmental Drama*, 3 (Feb. 1973b): 12-25.

———. *Play, Drama and Thought: The Intellectual Background to Dramatic Education*. London: Cassell; New York: Drama Book Specialists, 3rd ed., 1974.

———. "Imagination and Substitution: The Personal Origins of Art," *Connecticut Review*, 9, 2 (May 1976a): 67-73.

———. "Dramatic Action: A Genetic Ontology of the Dramatic Learning of the Very Young Child," *Journal of the Canadian Association for the Very Young Child* (November 1976b): 32-42.

———. "The Discipline of Drama," *Queen's Quarterly*, 84, 2 (Summer 1977a): 231-43.

———. "Goals in Drama Teaching," *Drama Contact*, 1, 1 (May 1977b): 5-8.

———. *Teaching and the Arts: Arts Education in Australia, with specific reference to Drama Education in Victoria*. Melbourne: Melbourne State College, 1979.

——— and Paul Park. *Learning in the Arts: The Arts in Primary and Junior Education in Ontario — Roles and Relationships in the General Program of Studies*, 1980. A research project funded under contract by the Ministry of Education, Ontario.

———. *The Dramatic Curriculum*. London, Ontario: University of Western Ontario, Faculty of Education; London, England: Heinemann; New York: Drama Book Specialists, 1981.

——— and Gertrud Schattner, eds. *Drama in Therapy*, 2 vols. New York: Drama Book Specialists, 1982.

———. *Secret Spirits: Performance and Possession of Canadian Indians on Vancouver Island*. Downsview: Ont.: CTR, York University, forthcoming.

Craig, R. C. *The Transfer Value of Learning*. New York: Teachers' College, Columbia University, 1953.

———. "Directed Versus Independent Discovery of Established Relations," *Journal of Educational Psychology*, 47 (1956): 223-34.

Craig, Therese. "Drama as a Tool in the Social Studies Curriculum," *Elements: Translating Theory into Practice* (University of Alberta), 8, 4 (December 1976): 5-6.

Crandall, V. J. "Achievement," in H. W. Stevenson, ed. *Child Psychology*. Chicago: University of Chicago Press, 1963.

Davis, G. A. "Instruments Useful in Studying Creative Behavior and Creative Talent," *Journal of Creative Behavior*, 5, 3 (1971): 162-65.

———. *Psychology of Problem Solving*. New York: Basic Books, 1973.

———. "In Frumious Pursuit of the Creative Person," *Journal of Creative Behavior*, 9, 2 (1975): 75-87.

Dewey, John. *The Schools of Tomorrow*. New York: Dutton, 1915.

———. *Experience and Nature*. New York: Norton, 1929.

Diamond, D. "A Neglected Aspect of

Motivation," *Sociometry*, 2 (1939): 77-85.

Dollard, J., et al. *Frustration and Aggression.* London: Kegan Paul, 1944.

Drews, Elizabeth. "The Four Faces of Able Adolescents," *School Record* (January 19, 1963): 68-71.

———. *The Creative Intellectual Style in Gifted Adolescents.* Washington, D. C.: U. S. Department of Health, Education and Welfare, 1966.

Duncan, C. P. "Transfer after Training with Single versus Multiple Tasks," *Journal of Exp. Psychology*, 1, 55 (1958): 63-72.

———. "Recent Research on Human Problem-Solving," *Psychology Bulletin*, 56 (1959): 397-429.

Duncan, Hugh Dalziel. *Symbols in Society.* New York: Oxford University Press, 1968.

Eberle, Bob. "Does Creative Dramatics Really Square with the Research Evidence?" *Journal of Creative Behavior*, 8, 3 (1974): 177-82.

Education Facilities Laboratories. *Arts and the Handicapped: An Issue of Access.* New York, 1975.

Eisner, Elliot W., ed. *The Arts, Human Development and Education.* Berkeley, Calif.: McCutchan, 1976.

———, ed. *Reading, the Arts, and the Creation of Meaning.* Reston, Va.: NAEA, 1978.

Eliade, Mircea. *The Sacred and the Profane.* New York: Harcourt Brace, 1959.

———. *Myth and Reality.* New York: Harper and Row, 1963.

———. *Rites and Symbols of Initiation.* New York: Harper and Row, 1965.

———. *Images and Symbols: Studies in Religious Symbolism.* New York: Sheed and Ward, 1969.

Ellis, H. C. *Transfer of Learning.* New York: Macmillan, 1965.

———. *Fundamentals of Human Learning and Cognition.* Dubuque, Iowa: Wm. C. Brown, 1972.

——— and D. D. Burnstein. "The Effect of Stimulus Similarity and Temporal Factors in Perceptual Transfer of Training," *Technical Report No. 1*, Albuquerque, New Mexico: Sandia Corporation, 1960.

——— and J. E. Hunter. "Response Meaningfulness and the Temporal Course of Transfer," *Technical Report No. 2*, Albuquerque, New Mexico: Sandia Corporation, 1960.

———. "The Effect of Response Familiarization on the Temporal Course of Transfer," *Technical Report No. 3*, Albuquerque, New Mexico: Sandia Corporation, 1961a.

———. "A Comparison of the Temporal Course of Retention and Non-Specific Transfer," *Technical Report No. 4*, Albuquerque, New Mexico: Sandia Corporation, 1961b.

——— and D. G. Muller. "Transfer of Perceptual Learning following Stimulus Predifferential Training," *Journal of Experimental Psychology*, 68 (1964): 388-95.

Emmett, E. R. *Learning to Philosophize.* Harmondsworth: Penguin, 1968.

Empirical Research in Theater, journal. Bowling Green, Ohio: Bowling Green State University, in series.

Erikson, Erik H. *Childhood and Society.* New York: Norton, 1952; Penguin, repr. 1965.

———. "Growth and Crisis of the

Healthy Personality," in C. Kluckhorn, *et al.*, eds. *Personality in Nature, Society and Culture.* New York: Knopf, 2nd ed., 1953: 185-225.

———. "Play and Actuality," in Maria W. Piers, ed. *Play and Development.* New York: Norton, 1972.

Eysenck, H. J., and H. T. Himmelweit. "An Experimental Study of the Reactions of Neurotics to Experiences of Success and Failure," *Journal of General Psychology*, 35 (1946): 59-75.

Fauville, A. "Les premières réponses de l'enfant et leurs excitante," in A. Michotte, *et al.*, eds. *La Perception.* Paris: PUF, 1955: 111-20.

Fiala, Oliver. "An Artistic Affinity: Some Notes on Dorothy Heathcote's and Bertolt Brecht's Modes of Work," *Journal*, National Association for Drama in Education (Australia), 2, 1 (June 1977): 29-32.

Fines, John, and Raymond Verrier. *The Drama of History: An Experiment in Co-operative Teaching.* London: New University Education, 1974.

Fox, Jonathan. "Playback Theater: The Community Sees Itself," in Courtney and Schattner, *op. cit.*: II: 295-306.

French, J. R. P. "Organized and Unorganized Groups under Fear and Frustration," in E. Lewin, ed. *Authority and Frustration: Studies in Topological and Vector Psychology*, III. Iowa City: University of Iowa, 1944: 231-308.

Freud, Anna. "The Mutual Influences in the Development of the Ego and the Id: Introduction to the Discussion," *Psychoanalytic Studies of the Child*, 5 (1950): 74-95.

Freud, Sigmund. "Mourning and Melancholia," *Collected Papers*, IV. London: Hogarth Press, 1925.

———. *An Outline of Psychoanalysis.* New York: Norton, 1949.

———. "The Relation of the Poet to Day-Dreaming," *Collected Papers*, V. London: Hogarth Press, 1950.

Fromm, Erik. *The Sane Society.* New York: Rinehart, 1956.

Gagne, R. *The Conditions of Learning*, 3rd ed. New York: Holt, Rinehart and Winston, 1977.

Gaier, E. L. "The Relationship Between Selected Personality Variables and the Thinking of Students in Discussion Classes," *School Review*, 40 (1952): 404-11.

Garfinkel, H. "Studies of the Routine Grounds of Everyday Activities," *Social Problems*, 11 (1964): 225-50.

———. *Studies in Ethnomethodology.* Englewood Cliffs, N. J.: Prentice-Hall, 1967.

Getzels, J. W., and P. W. Jackson. *Creativity and Intelligence.* New York, Wiley, 1962.

Gibson, E. J. "Retroactive Inhibition as a Function of the Degree of Generalization Between Tasks," *Journal of Experimental Psychology*, 28 (1941): 93-115.

Gibson, J. J. and E. J. Gibson, "Perceptual Learning: Differentiation or Enrichment?" *Psychology Review*, 62 (1955): 32-41.

Goffman, Erving. *The Presentation of Self in Everyday Life.* New York: Doubleday, 1959.

———. *Encounters.* Indianapolis: Bobbs-Merrill, 1961.

Goldstein, K. *The Organism.* New York: American Book, 1939.

———. *Human Nature in the Light of*

Psychopathology. Cambridge, Mass.: Harvard University Press, 1940.

Golembiewski, R. T., and A. Blumberg, eds. *Sensitivity Training and the Laboratory Approach.* Itasca, Ill.: F. E. Peacock, 1970.

Gombrich, E. H. *Meditations on a Hobby Horse,* 3rd ed. London: Phaidon, 1978.

Gomme, Lady Alice. *Traditional Games in England and Wales,* 2 vols. New York: Doubleday, repr. 1961.

Gough, H. B. *Adjective Check List.* Palo Alto, Calif.: Consulting Psychologists Press, 1952.

Greer, V. J., and J. M. Sacks, eds. *Bibliography of Psychodrama.* Paper privately printed, 1973.

Grumet, M. R. "Curriculum as Theater: Merely Players," *Curriculum Inquiry,* 8, 1 (Spring 1978): 37-64.

Guilford, J. P. *The Nature of Human Intelligence.* New York: McGraw-Hill, 1967.

Hadamard, J. *The Psychology of Invention in the Mathematical Field.* New York: Dover, 1954.

Hadfield, J. A. *Dreams and Nightmares.* Harmondsworth: Penguin, 1954.

Hall, Edward T. *The Silent Language.* New York: Doubleday, 1956.

———. *The Hidden Dimension.* New York: Doubleday, 1966.

Hamilton, C. E. "The Relationship between Length of Interval Separating Two Learning Tasks and Performance on the Second Task," *Journal of Experimental Psychology,* 40 (1950): 613-21.

Hampden-Turner, Charles. *Radical Man: The Process of Psycho-Social Development.* New York: Doubleday, 1971.

Harlow, H. F. "The Formation of Learning Sets," *Psychology Review,* 56 (1949): 51-65.

———. "Mice, Monkeys, Men and Motives," *Psychological Review,* 60 (1953): 23-32.

———. "Learning Set and Error Factor Theory," in S. Koch, ed. *Psychology: A Study of Science,* 2. New York: McGraw-Hill, 1959: 492-537.

Harris, V. W., and J. A. Sherman. "Effects of Peer Tutoring and Consequences on Math Performance of Elementary Classroom Students," *Journal of Applied Behavior Analysis,* 6 (1973): 587-97.

———, J. A. Sherman, D. G. Henderson, and M. S. Harris, "Effects of Peer Tutoring on the Spelling Performance of Elementary Classroom Students," in G. Senb, ed. *Behavior Analysis in Education—1972.* 1972.

Hartnett, O. M. "Error in Response to Infrequent Signals," *Ergonomics,* 18 (1975): 213-23.

Hartup, W. W. "Friendship Status and Effectiveness of Peers as Reinforcing Agents," *Journal of Experimental Child Psychology,* 1 (1964): 154-62.

———, and B. Coates. "Imitation of a Peer as a Function of Reinforcement from the Peer Group and Rewardingness of the Model," *Child Development,* 38 (1967): 1003-16.

———, J. Glaser, and R. Charlesworth. "Peer Reinforcement and Sociometric Status," *Child Development,* 38 (1967): 1017-24.

Heathcote, Dorothy. "Improvisation," *English in Education,* 1, 3 (Autumn 1967): 27-30.

———. "Drama and Education: Subject or System?" in Nigel Dodd

and Winifred Hickson, eds. *Drama and Theatre in Education.* London: Heinemann, 1971a.
——. *Three Looms Waiting.* Motion Picture. London: BBC, 1971b.
Heaton, J. M. "Ontology and Play," in Bernard Curtis and Wolf Mays, eds. *Phenomenology and Education: Self-consciousness and its Development.* London: Methuen, 1978: 119-30.
Hebb, D. O. *The Organization of Behavior: A Neuropsychological Theory.* New York: Wiley, 1949.
Henry, Jules. *On Education.* New York: Vintage, 1972.
Holding, D. H. "Repeated Errors in Motor Learning," *Ergonomics*, 13 (1970): 727-34.
Hollenburg, E., and M. Sperry. "Some Antecedents of Aggression and Effect on Doll Play," *Personality*, 1 (1950): 32-43.
Holloway, John. *Language and Intelligence.* London: Macmillan, 1951.
Holt, E. B., *et al. The New Realism.* New York: Macmillan, 1912.
Hoppe, F. "Erfolg und Misserfolg," *Psychol. Forsch.*, 14 (1930): 1-62.
Hudgins, B. B. "Effects of Group Experience on Individual Problem Solving," *Journal of Educational Psychology*, 51, 1 (1960): 37-42.
Hull, C. L. *Principles of Behavior.* New York: Appleton, 1943.
Hunt, Albert. *Hopes for Great Happenings.* London: Eyre Methuen, 1976.
Huntsman, K. H. "Improvisational Dramatic Activities: Their Effect upon the Self-Actualization of College-Age Students." Ph.D. dissertation. Brigham Young University, 1979.
Husserl, Edmund. *Ideas.* New York: Collier Macmillan, repr. 1975.

Jaspers, Karl. *The Future of Mankind.* Chicago: University of Chicago Press, 1961.
Jennings, Sue. *Remedial Drama.* London: Pitman, 1973.
Johnstone, Keith. "Status Transactions and Theatre," *Queen's Quarterly*, 82, 1 (1975): 22-40.
——. *Impro.* London: Methuen; New York: Theatre Arts Books, 1979.
Jones, G. T. *Simulation and Business Decisions.* Harmondsworth: Penguin, 1972.
Jones, Richard M. *Fantasy and Feeling in Education.* New York: New York University Press, 1968.
Judd, C. H. "The Relation of Special Training and General Intelligence," *Education Review*, 36 (1908): 42-48.
Junell, Joseph S. "Is Rational Man Our First Priority?" in E. W. Eisner, and E. Vallance, eds. *Conflicting Conceptions of Curriculum.* Berkeley, Calif.: McCutchan, 1974.
Jung, Carl. *Memories, Dreams, Reflections.* New York: Pantheon, 1963.
Kaelin, Eugene, and David Ecker. "The Institutional Prospects of Aesthetic Education," in *The Arts and Aesthetics: An Agenda for the Future.* St. Louis: CEMREL, 1976: 1-15.
Kagan, J., and M. Berken. "The Reward Value of Running Activity," *Journal of Comp. Physiol. Psychol.*, 47 (1954): 108.
—— and H. A. Moss. "The Stability of Passive and Dependent Behavior from Childhood through Adulthood," *Child Development*, 31 (1960): 577-91.
Kaltsounis, B. "Instruments Useful in Studying Creative Behavior and Creative Talent," *Journal of Creative Behavior*, 5, 2 (1971): 117-26.

———. "Additional Instruments useful in studying Creative Behavior and Creative Talent," *Journal of Creative Behavior*, 6, 4 (1972): 268-74.
Kardiner, Abraham, and H. Spiegel. *War Stress and Neurotic Illness*. New York: Hoeber, 1947.
Kay, H. "Learning of a Serial Task by Different Age Groups," *Quarterly Journal of Experimental Psychology*, 3 (1951): 166-83.
Kelly, G. A. *The Psychology of Personal Constructs*, 2 vols. New York: Norton, 1955.
———. *A Theory of Personality*. New York: Norton, 1963.
Kersh, B. Y. "The Adequacy of 'Meaning' as an Explanation of the Superiority of Learning by Independent Discovery," *Journal of Educational Psychology*, 49 (1958): 282-92.
Kidd, Ross, and Martin Byram. "Popular Theatre: A Technique for Participatory Research," *Participation Research Project*, Toronto, 1978.
Kierkegaard, Søren. *Concluding Unscientific Postscript*. Princeton: Princeton University Press, 1951.
Kittell, J. E. "An Experimental Study of the Effect of External Direction during Learning on Transfer and Retention of Principles," *Journal of Educational Psychology*, 48 (1957): 391-405.
Klein, Melanie. *The Psychoanalysis of Children*. London: Hogarth Press, 1930.
Kneller, George F. *Existentialism and Education*. New York: Philosophical Library, 1958.
———. *Educational Anthropology*. New York: Wiley, 1965.
Koestler, Arthur. *The Act of Creation*. London: Pan Books, 1964.
Kohlberg, Laurence. *Recent Research in Moral Education*. New York: Holt, Rinehart and Winston, 1978.
Koltai, Judith. "Movement, Dance and Therapy," in Courtney and Schattner, *op. cit.*: II: 197-211.
Korzybski, Alfred. *Science and Sanity*, 4th ed. Lakefield, Conn.: International Society for General Semantics, 1958.
Kramer, Samuel Noah. *The Sacred Marriage Rite: Aspects of Faith, Myth, and Ritual in Ancient Sumer*. Bloomington: Indiana University Press, 1969.
Kukuk, Jack W., and James A. Sjolund. "Arts for the Handicapped," *National Elementary Principal*, 55, 3 (January/February 1976): 86-88.
Laban, Rudolf. *Modern Educational Dance*. London: Macdonald and Evans, 1948.
LaBarre, Weston. *The Ghost Dance*. London: Allen and Unwin, 1970.
Landy, Robert. "Dramatic Education." Ph.D. dissertation. Santa Barbara: UCLA, 1975.
Langer, Suzanne K. *Feeling and Form*. New York: Scribners', 1953.
Lazier, Gil, and E. J. Karioth. "The Inventory of Dramatic Behavior: A Content Analysis Technique for Creative Dramatics," Theater Science Laboratory, Tallahassee, Florida, 1972.
Lederman, Janet. *Anger and the Rocking Chair*. Palo Alto: Esalen, 1970.
Lett, Warren. "Thinking About Multi-Arts?" Paper privately circulated, 1978.
Lewis, C. S. *The Four Loves*. New York: Harcourt, Brace, 1960.
Ledson, Sidney. *Teach Your Child*

to Read in 60 Days. New York: Norton, 1975.

Leuba, C. "Towards Some Integration of Learning Theories: The Concept of Optimal Stimulation," *Psychol. Rep.*, 1 (1955): 27-33.

Lorenz, Konrad. "The Comparative Method in Studying Innate Behavior Patterns," *Symb. Soc. Exp. Biol.*, 4 (1950): 221-68.

Lovejoy, A. O. *The Revolt Against Dualism*. New York: Norton, 1930.

Lowen, Alexander. *Bioenergetics*. Harmondsworth: Penguin, 1976.

Lowenfeld, Viktor, and W. Lambert Brittain. *Creative and Mental Growth*, 5th ed. New York: Macmillan, 1970.

Luria, A. R. *Speech and the Development of Mental Processes in the Child*. Harmondsworth: Penguin, 1971.

Lyman, Stanford M., and Marvin B. Scott. *The Drama of Social Reality*. New York: Oxford University Press, 1975.

Mackay, David, and Joseph Simo. *Help Your Child to Read and Write*. Harmondsworth: Penguin, 1976.

MacKinnon, D. "Education for Creativity: A Modern Myth?" in G. A. Davis and J. A. Scott, eds. *Training Creative Thinking*. New York: Holt, 1971: 194-207.

MacLean, P. D. "Psychosomatic Disease and the 'Visceral Brain': Recent Developments bearing on the Papez Theory of Emotion," *Psychosom. Med.*, 11 (1949): 338-53.

———. Cited in Arthur Koestler, *Janus: A Summing Up*. London: Hutchinson, 1979. See, *American Journal of Medicine*, 25, 4 (October, 1958): 611-26.

Macrae, A. W., and D. H. Holding. "Guided Practice in Direct and Reversed Serial Tracking," *Ergonomics*, 8 (1965a): 487-92.

———. "Method and Task in Motor Guidance," *Ergonomics*, 8 (1965b): 315-20.

———. "Rate and Force of Guidance in Perceptual-Motor Tasks with Reversed or Random Spatial Correspondence," *Ergonomics*, 9 (1966a): 289-96.

———. "Transfer of Training after Guidance or Practice," *Quarterly Journal of Experimental Psychology*, 18 (1966b): 327-33.

Madeja, Stanley S. *All the Arts for Every Child*. Washington, D. C.: JDR 3rd Fund, n.d.

Mahler, W. "Ersatzhandlungen verschiedenen Realitätsgrades," *Psychol. Forsch.*, 18 (1933): 27-89.

Mandler, G. "From Association to Structure," *Psychology Review*, 69 (1962): 415-27.

Mannell, R. C. and J. H. Duthie. "Habit Lag: When 'Automation' is Dysfunctional," *The Journal of Experimental Psychology*, 89 (1975): 73-80.

Maslow, Abraham H. *Motivation and Personality*. New York: Harper and Row, 1954.

———. "Critique of Self-actualization," *Journal of Individual Psychology*, 15 (1959): 24-32.

———. *Towards a Psychology of Being*. New York: Van Nostrand, 1962.

———. *The Farther Reaches of Human Nature*. Harmondsworth: Penguin, 1976.

Matthews, R. H. "The Bora or Initiation Ceremonies of the Kamilaroi

Tribe," *Journal of the Royal Anthropological Institute*, 24 (1895): 411-27; 25 (1896): 318-39.

May, Rollo. *Love and Will*. New York: Norton, 1964.

McCaslin, N. *Theatre for Children in the United States: A History*. Norman: University of Oklahoma Press, 1971.

McClelland, D. A., et al. *The Achievement Motive*. New York: Appleton, 1953.

McDougall, A. *An Introduction to Social Psychology*. London: Methuen, 1908.

McGee, C. S., J. M. Kauffman and J. L. Nussen. "Children's Therapeutic Change Agents: Reinforcement Intervention Paradigms," *Review of Educational Research*, 47 (1977): 451-77.

McGregor, L., M. Tate, and K. Robinson. *Learning Through Drama*. London: Heinemann, 1977.

McLeod, John N. *A Survey of Drama in Post Primary Schools*. Melbourne, Australia: Education Department, Victoria, 1978.

McLuhan, Marshall. *Understanding Media*. London: Routledge, 1964.

——— and Quentin Fiore. *The Medium is the Massage*. New York: Bantam, 1967.

———. *War and Peace in the Global Village*. New York: Bantam, 1968.

McReynolds, P. "A Restricted Conceptualization of Human Anxiety and Motivation," *Psychol. Rep.*, 2 (1956): 293-312. Monograph Supplement 6.

Mead, G. H. *Mind, Self and Society*. Chicago: University of Chicago Press, 1934.

Mead, Margaret and Martha Wolfenstein, eds. *Childhood in Contemporary Cultures*. Chicago: University of Chicago Press, 1955.

Mednick, S. A. *Remote Associates Test*. Boston: Houghton Mifflin, 1967.

Meyers, K., R. Travers and M. Sanford. "Learning and Reinforcement in Student Pairs," *Journal of Educational Psychology*, 56 (1965): 67-72.

Miller, Louis. "Creativity and Identity: Social Drama and Social Action," in Courtney and Schattner, *op. cit.*: II: 327-37.

Miller, N. E. and J. Dollard. *Social Learning and Imitation*. New Haven: Yale University Press, 1941.

Mittelmann, B. "Motility in Infants, Children and Adults," *Psychoanalytic Studies of the Child*, 9 (1954): 142-77.

Montgomery, K. C. "The Role of Exploratory Drive in Learning," *Journal of Comp. Physiol. Psychol.*, 47 (1954): 60-64.

Moreno, Jacob L. *Psychodrama*, 2 vols. New York: Beacon House, 1946, 1959.

———. "The Creativity of Personality," *New York University Bulletin, Arts and Sciences*, 46, 4 (January 1966): 19-24.

Morris, Van Cleve. *Existentialism in Education*. New York: Harper and Row, 1966.

Mosston, M. *Teaching: From Command to Discovery*. Belmont, Calif.: Wadsworth Publishing Co., 1972.

Mowrer, O. H. *Learning Theory and Personality Dynamics*. New York: Ronald, 1950.

Murphy, Gardner. *Personality: A Bisocial Approach to Origins and Structure*. New York: Harper, 1947.

Myers, A. K. and N. E. Miller. "Failure to Find a Learned Drive based on Hunger: Evidence for Learning Motivated by 'Exploration'," *Journal of Comp. Physiol. Psychol.*, 47 (1954): 428-36.

Natanson, Maurice. *The Journeying Self*. Reading, Mass.: Addison-Wesley, 1970.

National Association for Drama in Education. "Proposed New Drama Course," *Journal*, NADIE (Australia), 2, 1 (June 1977): 77-80.

Nissen, H. W. "Phylogenic Comparison," in S. S. Stevens, ed. *Handbook of Experimental Psychology*. New York: Wiley, 1951: 347-86.

Nuttin, Joseph. "Motivation," in Paul Fraisse and Jean Piaget, eds. *Experimental Psychology: Its Scope and Method*, V. London: Routledge and Kegan Paul, 1968: 1-101.

Olds, J. "Self-stimulation Experiments and Differentiated Reward Systems," in H. H. Jasper et al., eds. *Rectiular Formation of the Brain*. Boston: Little, Brown, 1958: 671-87.

Opie, Iona and Peter. *The Lore and Language of School-Children*. Oxford: The Clarendon Press, 1948.

Ornstein, Robert E. *The Psychology of Consciousness*. Harmondsworth: Penguin, 1975.

Osgood, C. E. "The Similarity Paradox in Human Learning: A Resolution," *Psychology Review*, 56 (1949): 132-43.

O'Toole, John. *Theatre in Education*. London: Hodder and Stoughton, 1976.

Parres, B. "The Dynamics of Aesthetic Learning with Specific Reference to Gallery Education." M.A. thesis. University of Toronto, 1980.

Pastore, N. "The Role of Arbitrariness in the Frustration-Aggression Hypothesis," *J. Abnorm. Soc. Psychol.*, 47 (1952): 728-31.

Patterson, G. R. and D. Anderson. "Peers as Social Reinforcers," *Child Development*, 35 (1965): 951-60.

Patterson, G. R., D. A. Shaw and J. J. Ebner. "Teachers, Peers and Parents as Agents of Change in the Classroom," in A. M. Benson, ed. *Modifying Deviant Social Behaviors in Various Classroom Settings, Monograph No. 1*. Eugene, Or.: Department of Special Education, University of Oregon, 1969.

Peacock, James L. *Rites of Modernization: Symbolic and Social Aspects of Indonesian Proletarian Drama*. Chicago: University of Chicago Press, 1968.

Perls, Frederick S. *Gestalt Therapy Verbatim*. Moab, Utah: Real People Press, 1969a.

———. *Ego, Hunger and Aggression*. New York: Random House, 1969b.

Pfaffman, C. "The Pleasures of Sensation," *Psychological Review*, 67 (1960).

Phenix, Philip H. "Transcendence and the Curriculum," in E. W. Eisner and Elizabeth Vallance, eds. *Conflicting Conceptions of Curriculum*. Berkeley, Calif.: McCutchan, 1974: 117-33.

Piaget, Jean. *The Origins of Intelligence in Children*. New York: International University Press, 1952.

———. *Play, Dreams and Imitation in Childhood*. London: Routledge, 1962.

Piéron, H. "Les bases physiologiques de la motivation," in L. Ancona et al., eds. *La Motivation.* Paris: PUF, (1959): 35-54.

Polanyi, Michael. *Personal Knowledge: Towards a Post-Critical Philosophy.* New York: Harper and Row, 1964.

Postman, L. "Transfer of Training as a Function of Experimental Paradigm and Degree of First-List Learning," *Journal of Verbal Behavior,* 1 (1962): 109-18.

Prather, D. C. "The Effects of Trial-and-Error or Errorless Training on the Efficiency of Learning a Perceptual-Motor Skill and Performance Under Transfer and Stress." (Doctoral Dissertation, Arizona State University, 1969). *Dissertation Abstracts International,* No. 69-20, 790 (1969): 2385-A.

———. "Trial-and-Error Versus Errorless Learning: Training, Transfer and Stress," *American Journal of Psychology,* 84 (1971): 377-86.

———. and G. A. Berry. "Comparison of Trial-and-Error Versus Highly Prompted Learning of a Perceptual Skill," *Proceedings of the 78th Annual Convention of the American Psychological Association,* 5 (1970): 677-78.

Psathas, George. "Ethnomethods and Phenomenology," *Social Research,* 35 (1968): 500-20.

Reid, Louis Arnaud. "Knowledge and Aesthetic Education," *Journal of Aesthetic Education,* 2, 3 (July 1968): 41-49.

Reisman, David. *The Lonely Crowd.* New Haven: Yale University Press, 1954.

Roberts, J., and S. Akinsanya, eds. *Schooling in the Cultural Context.* New York: David McKay, 1976.

Robertson, S. M. *Rosegarden and Labyrinth: A Study in Art Education.* London: Routledge, 1963.

Rogers, Carl R. *On Becoming a Person.* Boston: Houghton Mifflin, 1961.

Rosenbaum, A., A. D. O'Leary and R. G. Jacob. "Behavioral Intervention with Hyperactive Children: Group Consequences as a Supplement to Individual Contingencies." *Behavior Therapy,* 6 (1975): 315-23.

Rosenberg, Harold. *Act and the Actor: Making the Self.* New York: Meridian, 1972.

Russell, Bertrand. *Human Knowledge.* London: Allen and Unwin, 1948.

Russell, W. A. and L. H. Storms. "Implicit Verbal Chaining in Paired-Associate Learning," *Journal of Experimental Psychology,* 49 (1955): 287-92.

Sacks, James M. "Drama Therapy with the Acting-Out Patient," in Courtney and Schattner, *op. cit.:* II: 35-45.

Sarbin, Theodore R., in Gardner Lindzey. *Handbook of Social Psychology,* I. Cambridge, Mass.: Addison-Wesley, 1954.

Schaefer, C. A., and A. Anastasi. "A Biographical Inventory for Identifying Creative Talent in Adolescent Boys," *Journal of Applied Psychology,* 52 (1968): 42-48.

Schechner, Richard. *Environmental Theater.* New York: Hawthorne, 1973.

———. *Essays on Performance Theory 1970-1976.* New York: Drama Book Specialists, 1977.

Schultz, R. W. "Problem Solving Behavior and Transfer," *Harvard Educational Review,* 30 (1960): 61-77.

Schurr, E. *Movement Experiences for Children.* New York: Appleton-

Century-Crofts, 1967.
Schutz, Alfred. "The Stranger," *American Journal of Sociology*, 49 (1944): 499-507.
——. *The Phenomenology of the Social World.* Evanston, Ill.: Northwestern University Press, 1967a.
——. *Collected Papers*, 3 vols. Evanston, Ill.: Northwestern University Press, 1967b.
Schwab, Joseph J. "The Practical: A Language for Curriculum," "The Practical: Arts of the Eclectic," and "The Practical 3: Translation into Curriculum," *The School Review:* 78, 1 (Nov. 1969): 1-31; 79, 4 (Aug. 1971): 493-542; 81, 4 (Aug. 1973): 501-22.
Sears, R. R. "Symposium on Genetic Psychology, 3: Effects of Frustration and Anxiety on Fantasy Aggression," *American Journal of Orthopsychiat.*, 21 (1951): 498-505.
—— et al. *Identification and Child Rearing.* Stanford: Stanford University Press, 1965.
Seely, John. *In Context.* London: Oxford University Press, 1976.
Segal, Hannah. *Introduction to the Work of Melanie Klein.* London: Heinemann, 1946.
Severin, B. "Dramatic Education and the Theory of Psychological Health." M. A. thesis, University of Toronto, 1980.
Shaw, Ann M. "A Taxonomical Study of the Nature and Behavioral Objectives for Creative Dramatics," *Educational Theatre Journal* (Winter 1971): 361-72.
——. "Co-Respondents: The Child and Drama," in Nellie McCaslin, ed. *Children and Drama.* New York: David McKay, 1975.
Sherrington, Charles. *Man and his Nature.* Cambridge: Cambridge University Press, 1951.
Shinn, R., ed. *Culture and School.* Scranton, Penn.: International Textbook, 1972.
Siks, Geraldine Brain. *Drama with Children.* New York: Harper and Row, 1977.
Singer, R. N. *Coaching, Athletics, and Psychology.* New York: McGraw-Hill, 1972.
——. "To Err or Not to Err: A Question for the Instruction of Psychomotor Skills," *Review of Educational Research*, 47 (1977): 479-95.
—— and W. Dick. *Teaching Physical Education: A Systems Approach.* Boston: Houghton Mifflin, 1974.
—— and D. Pease. "The Effect of Different Instructional Strategies on Learning, Retention, and Transfer of a Serial Motor Task," *Research Quarterly*, 47: 788-96.
Skinner, B. F. *Science and Human Behavior.* New York: Macmillan, 1953.
——. *The Technology of Teaching.* New York: Appleton-Century-Crofts, 1968.
Slade, Peter. *Child Drama.* London: University of London Press, 1954.
Smilansky, Sara. *The Effects of Sociodramatic Play on Culturally Deprived Children.* New York: Wiley, 1974.
Smith, Frank. *Understanding Reading.* New York: Holt, Rinehart and Winston, 1971.
Solloman, R. W., and R. G. Wahler. "Peer Reinforcement Control of Classroom Problem Behaviors," *Journal of Applied Behavior Analysis*, 6 (1973): 49-56.
Sorokin, P. A., et al. *Forms and Techniques of Altruistic and Spiritual Growth.* New York: Harper and Row, 1954.

Southern, Richard. *The Seven Ages of Theatre*. London: Faber and Faber, 1962.

Spence, K. W. "Anxiety (Drive) Level and Performance in Eyelid Conditioning," *Psychology Bulletin* (1964): 129-39.

Spindler, George D., ed. *Education and Culture*. New York: Holt, Rinehart and Winston, 1963.

Spitz, Rene A. "Hospitalism," *Psychoanalytic Studies of the Child*, 1 (1945): 53-74.

Spolin, Viola. *Improvisation for the Theater*. Evanston, Ill.: Northwestern University Press, 1963.

Stake, Robert. *Evaluating the Arts in Education*. Columbus, Ohio: Charles E. Merrill, 1974.

Stephenson, Norman, and Denis Vincent, eds. *Teaching and Understanding Drama*. Windsor, England: NFER Publishing Co., 1975.

Stevenson, Paul. "A Conceptual Basis for Drama in Education," paper privately circulated, 1978.

Stewig, John W. *Spontaneous Drama: A Language Art*. Columbus, Ohio: Charles E. Merrill, 1973.

Strehlow, T. G. H. *Aranada Traditions*. Melbourne: 1947.

Sturtevant, W. C. "Studies in Ethnoscience," *American Anthropologist*, 66 (2), 1 (1964): 99-131.

Suchman, J. R. "Motivation Inherent in the Pursuit of Meaning; or The Desire to Inquire," in H. I. Day et al., eds. *Intrinsic Motivation: A New Direction in Education*. Toronto: Holt, Rinehart and Winston, 1971.

Sutton-Smith, Brian. *Child Psychology*. New York: Appleton-Century-Crofts, 1973.

────── and Gil Lazier. "Psychology and Drama," *Empirical Research in Theater*, 1, 1 (Summer 1971): 38-46.

Taylor, C. W., W. R. Smith, B. Ghiselin and R. Ellison. "Explorations in the Measurement and Prediction of Contributions of One Sample of Scientists," Report ASD-TR-61-96, Aeronautical Systems Divisions, Personnel Laboratory, Lackland Air Force Base, Texas, April 1961.

Taylor, D. "The Influence of Training Procedure on Multiple Choice Learning," *Ergonomics*, 13 (1970): 193-200.

Terrance, H. "Discrimination Learning With and Without 'Errors'," *Journal of Experimental Analytical Behavior*, 6 (1963a): 1-27.

────── . "Errorless Transfer of a Discrimination Across Two Continua," *Journal of Experimental Analytical Behavior*, 6 (1963b): 223-32.

Terrell, C. and H. W. Stevenson. "The Effectiveness of Normal and Retarded Peers as Reinforcing Agents," *American Journal of Mental Deficiency*, 70 (1965): 373-81.

Thorndike, E. L. *Animal Intelligence*. New York: Macmillan, 1911.

────── and R. S. Woodworth. "The Influence of Improvement in One Mental Function Upon the Efficiency of Other Functions," *Psychology Review*, 8 (1901): 247-61, 384-95, 553-64.

Tillich, Paul. *Theology of Culture*. London: Oxford University Press, 1959.

Tinbergen, N. *The Study of Instinct*. Oxford: Oxford University Press, 1951.

Titiev, Mischa. "A Fresh Approach to the Problem of Magic and Religion," *Southwestern Journal*

of Anthropology, 16 (1960): 292-98.
Torrance, E. P. Torrance Tests of Creative Thinking. Princeton, N.J.: Personnel Press, 1966.
——. "Predictive Validity of the Torrance Test of Creative Thinking," Journal of Creative Behavior, 6, 4 (1972): 236-52.
Troland, L. T. The Principles of Psychopathology. New York: Van Nostrand, 1932.
Turkewych, C. and N. DiVito. "Creative Dramatics and Second Language Learning," TESL Talk, 9, 3 (Summer 1978): 63-70.
Turner, Victor W. Dramas, Fields and Metaphors. Ithaca: Cornell University Press, 1974.
Valenstein, E. S., and T. Valenstein. "Interaction of Positive and Negative Reinforcing Neural Systems," Science, 45 (1964): 1456-58.
Vandenberg, Donald. Being and Education. Englewood Cliffs, N.J.: Prentice-Hall, 1971.
Vanderplas, J. M., W. A. Sanderson and J. N. Vanderplas. "Some Task-Related Determinants of Transfer in Perceptual Learning," Perceptual Motivational Skills, 18 (1964): 71-80.
Van Gennep, Arnold. Rites of Passage. Chicago: University of Chicago Press, 1960.
Von Bertalanffy, Ludwig. Problems of Life. New York: Harper and Row, 1960.
Vygotsky, L. S. Thought and Language. New York: Wiley, 1962.
——. "Play and Its Role in the Mental Development of the Child." Soviet Psychology, 12, 6 (1966): 62-76.
Wallach, M. A., and N. Kogan. Modes of Thinking in Young Children. New York: Holt, 1965.
——, and C. W. Wing, Jr. The Talented Student: A Validation of the Creative-Intelligence Distinction. New York: Holt, 1969.
Ward, Winifred. Playmaking with Children, 2nd ed. New York: Appleton-Century-Crofts, 1957.
Warden, C. J., and M. Aylesworth. "The Relative Value of Reward and Punishment in the Formation of a Visual Discrimination Habit in the White Rat," J. Comp. Psychol., 7 (1927): 117-27.
Way, Brian. Development Through Drama. London: Longman, 1968.
Werner, O. H. "The Influence of the Study of Modern Foreign Language on the Development of Desirable Abilities in English," Studies in Modern Language Teaching, 17 (1930): 97-145.
White, R. W. "Motivation Reconsidered: The Concept of Competence," Psychological Review, 66 (1959): 297-333.
Whiting, J. W. M., and I. L. Child. Child Training and Personality. New Haven: Yale University Press, 1953.
—— and B. B. Whiting. Children of Six Cultures. Cambridge, Mass.: Harvard University Press, 1975.
Williams, F. E. The Vailala Madness and the Destruction of Native Ceremonies in the Gulf Division of Papua. Papuan Anthropological Reports, 4, 1923.
Winnicott, D. W. Playing and Reality. Harmondsworth: Penguin, 1974.
Winterbottom, M. R. "The Relation of Need for Achievement in Independence and Mastery," in J. W. Atkinson, ed. Motives in Fantasy, Action and Society. New Jersey: Van Nostrand, 1958.

Witkin, Robert W. *The Intelligence of Feeling*. London: Heinemann, 1974.

Wittgenstein, Ludwig. *Philosophical Investigations*. Oxford: Blackwell, 1953.

Woodworth, R. S. *Dynamic Psychology*. New York: Columbia University Press, 1918.

———. *Dynamics of Behavior*. New York: Holt, 1958.

——— and H. Schlosberg. *Experimental Psychology*, rev. ed. New York: Holt, 1954.

Worthen, B. R. "Discovery and Expository Task Presentation in Elementary Mathematics," *Journal of Educational Psychology, Monograph Supplement*, 59 (1968): 1-13.

Young, P. T. "Food Seeking Drive, Affective Processes, and Learning," *Psychological Review*, 56 (1949): 98-121.

———. "The Role of Hedonic Processes in Motivation," in M. R. Jones, ed. *Nebraska Symposium on Motivation*. Lincoln, Neb.: University of Nebraska Press, 1955: 193-238.

———. "The Role of Affective Processes in Learning and Motivation," *Psychological Review*, 66 (1959): 104-25.

Zhdanov, A. A. *Essays on Literature, Philosophy and Music*. New York: International Publishers, 1950.

Selected Index

Acculturation, 19, **30—31**, 33, 35, 41
Acknowledgement, 140, 141—42, 147, 151, 159, 160
Acting, 36; area, 37, 39; style, 39
Aesthetic/s, 64, 66, 67, 71, 95, 96, 106, 145, 150, 158, 159, 163, 164, 165, 166, 178, 183
Affective, **13**, 50, 55, 56, 60, 64, 66, 67, 95, 96, 111, 112, 114, 124, 148, 150, 153, 160, 164, 166; *see also* Emotion
agape, 147, 153
Agriculture, agricultural societies, 23—4, 25, 26, 36, 37, 38, 39, 41
Aims, 176, 185, 186
Art/s, 3, 139, 148, 149, **154—65**, 170
Assessment, 130, **132—33**, 136, 168, 176, 178, 185, 186, 190
Awareness, 7, 8, 74, 76, 78, 95, 96, 110, 118, 157, 158, 160, 161

Be, Being, 8, 10, 11, 50, **52—55**, 56, 57, 59, 61, 62, 63, 110, 111, 144, 150, 151, 167, 169, 178

catharsis, 68, 133
cause, causal, 17, 52, 60, 67, 135, 136, 176, 182, 183, 186, 190, 194
Ceremonialism, 173—74
Child-rearing, *see* Mother
Cognitive, 3, 6, 9, **13**, 17, 50, 51, 55, 59, 60, 65, 66, 72, 92, 93, 96, 111, 124, 148, 150, 157, 158, 162, 166, 171, 188
Commitment, 146, 147
Community, 139—42, 147, 165
Competence, 44, 47—48, 49, 51, 57, 59
Concentration, 7, 8, 16, 70, 95, 96, 110, 128
Concept, 9, 14, 16, 61, 63, 64, 73, 94, 121, 122, 153, 160, 164, 177, 195

Confidence, 95, 96, 130, 157
Content, 176, 185, 186
Contrary recognition, 60
Costume, 6, **37—38**, 39
Costumed player, 6, 10, 59, 85, 127
Creativity, 4, **98—107**, 163
Criteria in contexts, 179—86, 190, 191
Cultural: anthropology, 171—74, 190; drama, 36—40; dynamics, **33—36**, 40, 41, 138, 139, 174; meaning, 147; phenomenology, 172, 174; residues, 32; transmission, 160; worlds, 139, 148—49, 152; *see also* Developmental stages
Culture, **135—53**, 154
Curriculum, 3, 4, **62—68**, 69, 71, 81, **135—53**, 155, 156, **166—91**; discourse, 175; event, 168—69; moment, 174, 175, 189, 190, 191

Dance, *see* Movement
Decor, 38, 39
Definitions, **186—89**, 190, 191
Design, 2, 168, 174, 190
Developmental drama, 5—42
Developmental stages, 12—18, **36—41**
Dialogue, 117—18, 119, 120
Double, 56, 59, 64, 158; double mirror, 127; *see also* Meaning
Dramatic: act/ion, *passim*; metaphor, 4, 126, 127, 131, 136, 166, 167, 189
Dramatism, 173, 174
Dreaming, 53—54
Dynamic/s, dynamism, 7-11, **33—36**, 142, 143, 144, 147, 149, 150, 151, 152, 158, 166, 168, 173, 183; cultural, 138, 139, 152, 161, 167, 174, 190, 196; human, 43-68

Emotion/al, 7, 9, 10, 14, 16, 17, 26, 53, 54, 55, 58, 59, 60, 61, 62, 63,

65, 68, 79, 83, 89, 94, 106, 108, 111, 128, 131, 132, 150, 151, 155, 158, 162, 168, 171, 181, 183; *see also* Affective
Empathy, 12, 15, 26, 32, 48, 94, 113, 114, 124, 139, 140, 151, 153
Empirical, 150, 181, 182, 183, 187, 194, 195
Energy, 51, 52, 54, 56, 64, 113, 122; *see also* Synergy
Errors, 88—90
Ethnomethodology, 171—72, 174
Ethnoscience, 171, 174
Evaluation, *see* Assessment
Evidence, 180—81, 182, 190
Existentialism, 50, 57
Expression, 11, 95, 96, 105, 108—25, 131, 132, 138, 140, 155, 157, 158, 160, 161, 162, 181

Fantasy, 53, 54, 106, 147
Feeling, *see* Affective; Emotion
Form, 142

Gestalt, 50, 52, 60, 75, 77, 127 158, 163
Gifted, 4, 98—107, 163, 164
Group drama, 13, 15—17, 41

Holism, holistic, 44, 48—50, 52, 59, 67, 69, 76, 108, 111, 112, 116, 117, 119, 124, 162, 171
Hypothesis, 17, 121, 181, 195

Icon/ic, 59—61, 62, 63, 64, 65, 66, 68, 85, 114, 115
Identification, 3, 8, 9, 12, 13, 14, 16, 26, 41, 46, 47, 49, 51, 62, 63, 64, 83, 92, 124, 127, 129, 139, 140, 141, 143, 150, 151, 153, 157; identification/impersonation complex, 8, 9, 55—56, 75, 131, 140
Identity, 138, 140, 147, 157, 165
Image, 7, 8, 26, 53, 109, 110, 112; *see also* Imagination; Imagining
Imagination, imagina/tive, imaginary, 2, 9, 15, 44, 47, 52, 54, 56, 59, 64, 66, 68, 71, 74, 78, 81, 94, 99, 104, 109, 113, 114, 115, 118, 120, 122, 124, 125, 128, 138, 141, 147, 157, 158, 160, 161, 164, 165, 167, 172, 186; theory of, 7—9
Imagining/s, 7, 8, 10, 53, 54—55, 73, 75, 104, 105, 109, 110, 112, 131, 146, 159
Imitation, 8, 9, 12, 14, 15, 19, 20, 21, 23, 25, 35, 36, 113, 117
Impersonation, 3, 9, 13, 26, 27, 28, 41, 47, 62, 63, 75, 76, 77, 78, 94, 113, 127, 128, 129, 139, 141, 143, 151, 153, 157
Implementation, 2, 168, 171, 177
Improvisation, *passim*
Industrial societies, 23, 26, 28, 32, 38, 39, 41, 66, 136, 149, 155
Inference, 16, 181
Initiation, 26, 27—28, 29
Insight, 73, 74, 79, 81, 84, 94
Instruction, 4, 40, 86—97, 102, 112, 150, 174, 175
Intention/ality, 93—97, 113, 125, 142, 173
Intuition, 111, 124, 150, 158, 163

Knowing, knowledge, 6, 7, 15, 51, 62, 144, 145, 150, 158, 159, 178, 180, 183, 187—89, 190, 191

Language, 4, 10, 11, 15, 17, 58, 60, 66, 71, 72, 74, 77, 81, 85, 94, 108—25, 132, 138, 162, 171, 179, 185
Learning, 158—59, *passim;* direct, 4; dramatic, 6; indirect, 4; language, 4, 108—25; learning to learn, 73—74, 81, 84; original degree of, 79; reciprocal, 115; theory of, 9—10; *see also* Transfer
Listening, 3, 116
Living, 53, 63
Logic/al, 17, 26, 58, 60, 101, 104, 150, 158, 160, 176, 178, 193; of curriculum, 179—86, 190
Love, 139, 140, 141, 147, 151, 153

Marriage, 140, 165

Mask, 6, 27, 28, 34, 35, 37, 38, 39, 109, 110, 111, 112, 113, 123, 125, 141, 167
Meaning, *passim*; aesthetic, 64; cultural, 147; double, 59, 60, 64, 158
Media, medium, 6, 9, 11, 16, 18, 25, 41, 42, 59, 61, 62, 65, 67, 76, 79, 81, 85, 94, 105, 109, 110, 111, 113, 125, 130, 131, 132, 133, 145, 146, 149, 156, 160, 185, 192; theory of, 10
Mediate object, 12, 55, 56
Mediation, 5—7, 8, 9, 41, 46, 52, 127, 142, 146, 169, 171, 172
Memory, 55, 79, 88—90, 159; *see also* Remembering
Method, drama as, 3, 77, , 81—84, 95, 124, 131
Mirror, 141; double mirror, 127; *see also* Double
Model/ling, 3, 15, 19, 20, 21, 22, 23, 24, 25, 29, 46, 56, 59, 63, 85, 92, 95, 109, 113, 128—29, 130, 139, 150, 151, 158, 166, 172, 178
Moral, 16, 17, 142, 147, 148, 149, 153; *see also* Reason
Mother/ing, 22, 33, 34, 35, 56
Motivation, 4, 16, 40, **43—68**, 70, 80, 81, 84, 89, 90, 95, 97, 99, 113, 114, 116, 122, 123, 152, 157, 161, 164, 177
Movement, 6, 8, 10, 11, 12, 15, 51, 59, 76, 79, 83, 84, 85, 87, 94, 110, 111, 112, 120, 121, 133, 138, 158, 167, 181
Multi-disciplinary, 66, 153
Music, *see* Sound; Therapy
Myth, **19—23**, 24, 26, 27, 29, 33, 34, 35, 39

Organism/ic, **50—52**, 61, 68

Participation, 143, 146, 151
Pedagogy, 63, 149
Peers, 91—93
Perception, 7, 8, 9, **10**, 15, 49, 55, 74, 75, 76, 77, 95, 96, 104, 105, 110, 112, 116, 143, 150, 156, 158, 160, 162, 163, 164, 172, 187, 188
Performance theory, 170, 171, 190
Personality, 110, 114, 125, **157—58**, 161, 162, 163, 164, 165; profiles, 99—104, 105, 106
Phenomenology, 172, 174, 196
Play, *passim*
Politics, 139, 148, 149
Possibility, 2, 9, 17, 54, 66, 146, 147, 150, 157, 160, 161, 162, 163
Praxis, 175, 177, 190
Priest, 24, **28—29**, 30, 39; *see also* Shaman
Primal act, 9, 11, **12—14**, 55, 59, 67, 105, 110, 111, 113, 114, 115
Programs, drama, 169, 185, 190; implementation of, 2, 171, 178, 188; planning and design, 62, 171, 174—76, 178, 188
Psychology, 131, 173; ego, 44, **46—47**, 49; experimental, **44—46**, 47, 48, 56, 74, 76; general, 47

Rational, 50, 58, 63, 111, 112, 158, 162, 176, 186
Reading, 3, 109, 116, **121—23**, 132, 159
Reality, **143—47**, 166, 169; and illusion, 2
Reason/ing, 72, 147, 148, 149, 150, 153, 179—86, 190, 191, 193; *see also* Rational
Reciprocity, 141, 151
Re-creation, 24, 25, 26, 27, 42, 54, 55
Religion, 139, 148, 149
Remembering, 53; *see also* Memory
Re-play, 3, 41, 53, 54, 55, 59, 63, 64, 65, 66, 67
Representation, 6, 10, 29, 64, 70, 75, 94, 105, 109, 111, 118, 121, 123, 124, 139, 173; re-presentation, 59, 106
Research, 4, 94—97, 100, **192—97**
Resurrection, 15, 20, 21, 24, 27, 28, 29, 32

Revitalization, 31—32
Rites of: intensification, 19—26, 33, 35, 41; modernization, 32—33; passage, 19, 26—30, 33, 35, 41
Ritual, 15, 19, 20, 23—26, 27, 28, 29, 33, 34, 35, 36, 39, 83, 173, 174; *see also* Rites
Role, *passim*

Science, 139, 148, 149, 170, 178, 181, 182
Secret societies, 27, 28, 29, 30
Self-worth, 95, 96, 114
Shaman, 27, 28, 29, 36, 39; *see also* Priest
Shape, 37, 121
Signs, 59—61, 63, 65, 85, 121, 159
Social, 139; environment, 5—7, 9, 11, 14, 17, 18, 91—93; growth, 159—60
Society, 142—43
Sound/ing, 6, 8, 10, 11, 12, 59, 85, 110, 111, 112, 116, 120, 121, 133, 138, 158, 162
Space, spatial, 17, 18, 21, 30, 38, 53, 58, 65, 94, 111, 118, 120, 138, 142, 143, 149, 158, 170
Speaking, speech, voice, 3, 76, 85, 87, 94, 109, 112, 114, 115, 116—20, 123, 167; *see also* Sound
Spontaneous, *passim*
Stimulus predifferentiation, 78—79, 81
Strategies, of instruction, 90—91
Subject, drama as, 3, 131
Substantiation, 181, 182
Substitution, 10, 11, 25, 105, 110, 132
Symbol/ic, 3, 4, 6, 10, 15, 17, 22, 27, 28, 32, 39, 54, 55, 58, 59—62, 63, 64, 65, 66, 67, 70, 73, 85, 109, 111, 113, 114, 115, 121, 125, 131, 148, 152, 158, 159, 164, 167, 173, 190, 196
Synergy, 57, 64, 66, 68

Task: complexity, 89; performance, 90; similarity, 75—78, 81; time interval between, *see* Time; variety of previous, 79
Theatre, 3, 11, 17, 25, 29, 33, 34, 36, 37, 39, 42, 43, 86, 108, 118, 124, 127, 131, 133—34, 138, 139, 141, 152, 156, 166, 167, 169, 170, 173, 174, 196
Theatrical metaphor, 167
Therapy, 3, 65, 126—34, 148, 149
Time, temporal, 21, 23, 24, 25, 53, 65, 94, 111, 120, 138, 142, 143, 146, 149, 152, 158, 160, 168, 170, 171, 172, 173; interval between tasks, 79
Transfer, 4, 40, 69—85, 87, 89, 90, 91, 95, 159, 177
Transformation, 8, 9, 28, 41, 64, 74, 75, 84, 109, 110, 141, 172
Tribal societies, 19, 20, 22, 23, 26, 27, 36, 37, 38, 39, 40, 41, 148
Truth, 135, 136, 137, 145, 146, 147, 148, 149, 150
Types, 140, 142, 143, 150, 173

Warm-up, 73, 74, 81
Writing, 3, 109, 112, 116, 123—24, 132